HERE TODAY...

Louise Tanner

 A Delta Book · 1963

To L. L.

A Delta Book
Published by
Dell Publishing Co., Inc.
750 Third Avenue
New York 17, New York
All rights reserved

Library of Congress Catalog Card Number 59–12498

Manufactured in the United States of America

First Printing

Contents

1
The Shifting Archetypes

A modern Columbus returns from his travels to explain that the world is really flat. A popular young writer is transformed in a few short years from *dernier cri* to back number to modern classic. A rebel of the twenties—expelled from college for writing an atheistic play—is reincarnated as a masculine Mary Magdalene. An heiress who has been adored, envied, spat upon, and pitied, trades the wreckage of her dream castles for the impersonal ministrations of Room Service. A lonely, bitter Negro escapes from a Devil's Island in Alabama to discover that nothing is staler than a warmed-over *cause célèbre*.

Different as they were, all had been stamped with the imprint of history before they were thirty. They belonged to a century of shifting values where the Jekylls of one decade were the Hydes of the next.

Their lives were affected by five great turning points of the twentieth century: the betrayal of Wilsonian idealism in 1919; the stock market crash of 1929; the bombing of Pearl Harbor in 1941; the dropping of the A-bomb in 1945; the launching of the Soviet satellite in 1957. To the class of 1963, graduating in blue serge and virginal white, many of them probably seem as archaic as creatures from the Stone Age.

Ideas have a short life expectancy in the twentieth century. Before the telephone and the video, a common intellectual heritage could be handed down from father to son for half a millennium. Today the beliefs of a period as close as the Depression seem as remote as the great auk.

After the Treaty of Versailles a world safe—briefly—for democracy gave way to a world with "all gods dead, all wars fought, all faiths in man shaken."

When the big bull market broke in 1929, the *Zeitgeist* of the Jazz Age vanished as abruptly as Wilsonian idealism. Gone was the brash, bumptious optimism which, for all the noisy "disillusionment," had gone with ever expanding horizons and ever rising stocks.

In the decade of the Depression and F.D.R. the spiritual center of youth's revolt moved from Montparnasse to Moscow. Where college students of the twenties had railed against monogamy and God, students of the thirties thought it urgent to abolish the breadline before going to work on the marriage ceremony. Between 1934 and 1941, the flowers-that-bloom-in-the-spring-tra-la were accompanied by the annual spring peace strikes. Campus dramatists turned from such familiar themes as the young man in search of his soul, to subject matter of a more sinewy nature: a longshoremen's strike, a criminal syndicalism trial, the blowing up of a textile mill. Students echoed the sentiments of one earnest young thing who had learned to "identify her malaise" with that of the rest of the world.

The identification stopped short of going to war. Depression radicals and conservatives alike were overwhelmingly isolationist. The Jazz Age had passed on the idea that Wilson was the world's greatest dupe, that the First World War had been humanity's supreme folly. Young people were exposed to a horror show of mangled bodies and handless Belgian babies.

All were presented as victims of scheming foreign diplomats and wicked munitions makers who were depicted in contemporary cartoons with top hats, morning coats, striped pants, and bloated bellies, licking their chops over a dragon's harvest of crosses in Flanders Field.

The years immediately preceding Pearl Harbor were marked by a bitter debate between the overwhelmingly pacifist young and the older generation, which had done its best to instill in them a loathing for war. The older generation, after all its warnings against "pulling Britain's chestnuts out of the fire," now rebuked its sons for their reluctance to shoulder arms.

The debate might have gone on forever, had not isolationism and pacifism died on the night of December 7, 1941. Pearl Harbor rang down the curtain on the anti-Wilson morality play: on the evil British propaganda machine, the downtrodden Teuton, victim of a "Carthaginian peace," on little Finland, the only one of those European nations to pay its war debt. Ten years later there were few who remembered ever seeing the drama, though they had spent two decades hissing the villains and cheering the heroes.

Hitler's invasion of Russia brought an upsurge of brotherly love for what Alistair Cooke has called "the vast progressive school on the steppes." This too was soon gone with the Bomb. The honeymoon was over shortly after the war, when America traveled down the sad road from San Francisco to Korea. In 1944 it had been unfashionable to cast the tiniest brickbat at Russia. By 1947, it was the bouquets which were in bad odor.

The world which emerged from the Second World War was infinitely less pleasant than the one which sent the "lost generation" on its tours of the Paris boulevards and bouts with Prohibition gin. The returning G.I. was quick to adjust to such atomic-age commonplaces as high taxes, hydrogen bombs, atomic fallout, "megadeaths," the un-American Activities Committee, the housing shortage, postwar building that looked like overgrown public washrooms, landlords who advertised "rooms for rent that cannot be confused with closets."

Politically and sexually, the G.I. had lost his taste for youthful revolt. Dwight D. Eisenhower, who became President in

1952, was an ideal standard-bearer for his cause. Eisenhower subscribed to a mellow conservatism in which the *laissez faire* of Adam Smith was tempered by tacit acceptance of the New Deal social reforms which once had caused near apoplexy in the reading rooms of the Union League Club.

Political conservatism was accompanied immediately after the war by a growing mistrust of the intellect. The Hiss perjury trial in 1949, the explosion of the Soviet atomic bomb, the Rosenberg espionage trial, the loss of China to the Communists, and the Korean War, caused a sudden preoccupation with "loyalty" and "security."

This preoccupation launched Senator Joseph McCarthy on his meteoric career and caused a number of liberal educators to lose their jobs because of associations nebulously defined as "left-wing." A movie about Longfellow was canceled because the Communist "peace offensive" might gain momentum from Hiawatha's attempts to end war among the Indian tribes. An attendant suspected of Communist activities was dismissed from a "sensitive" position in a New York men's room.

The wave of anti-intellectualism which swept the country was tied up with very real security problems caused by the rise of Russia. The fall of Germany caused a simultaneous postwar interest in the fate of minorities. Americans were guiltily aware of the inconsistency of fighting the Superman myth on the battlefield and perpetuating it in the Jim Crow railroad cars.

On May 17, 1954, the Supreme Court handed down its historic decision declaring racial segregation unconstitutional in the "separate but equal" schools of the South. The eyes of the nation were focused on Governor Faubus of Arkansas, who mobilized the local constabulary to keep Negroes out of Central High School in Little Rock—on Autherine Lucy and James Meredith, testing their constitutional right to a higher education at "Bama" and "Ole Miss." The fate of American democracy was hardly assured in the hands of such future political thinkers as the schoolgirl who said piously, "If God had wanted us to go to school together, he wouldn't have made them black and us white."

In the twenties and thirties the vast possibilities of science had dazzled the average man. The old-time religion was con-

sidered, along with most time-honored traditions, to be a
stumbling block in the path of progress. Those who joined
atheistic clubs in the twenties, many who subscribed to the
Depression belief in social justice, considered God hopelessly
unscientific.

Science for them was a secular religion. It had put Darwin
in the place of the family Bible. Its experimental techniques
were employed by adolescents in the back seat of the family
car. One branch of the religion—psychiatry—had unhorsed
the Victorian mother in the battle for sexual freedom. The
temple of modern science was the laboratory. Its patron saint
was Freud. Its Satan was the bogey of repression. Material
progress had replaced the Way of the Cross; and Heaven was
the coming mechanized millennium.

With the Frankenstein monsters that came out of the laboratory in the atomic age, a reshuffling of values took place.
The realization spread that science had more sinister by-
products than Electroluxes and frozen chicken potpies. As
man came face to face with his own frailty, religion became
once again intellectually respectable. The "futuristic" rebellion
of the twenties and the thirties bred in the fifties a counter
movement back to respectabilities of the past. In the ancient
war between psychiatry and religion there were signs of an
uneasy peace.

Ministers were urged to learn pastoral counseling, an
advisory service combining the insights of psychiatry and
religion. The burden of hearing about the sex drives and inferiority complexes of their flocks, added to an already crushing load of ecclesiastical duties, caused a record number of
clergymen in 1956 to succumb to nervous breakdowns. The
disciples of Carl Jung went so far as to suggest that neurosis
might result from a crisis of faith as easily as from some
Freudian crisis in toilet training.

Whatever its causes, neurosis was everywhere. Freud had
been on the side of the flapper in her battle against her corsets
and stays; but as the century progressed there was nothing
left for anyone to revolt against.

Psychiatrists struggled with knotty problems which woman's
emancipation had left in its wake: men who were motherly,
women who were fatherly, and the fruit of their unhappy

coupling, the disturbed child. Psychiatry even began to look more favorably upon that former bogey, the Victorian father. At least, according to one psychiatrist, the hateful paterfamilias made his children neurotic in ways that science could treat.

As waves of the totally unrepressed hit the nation's high schools, mid-century psychologists faced a baffling new set of problems: how to help a fifteen-year-old boy kick the dope habit, how to dissuade the ninth grade from wrecking the chem lab; what to do with two teen-age lovers who killed the girl's mother and cheerily gave beer parties after plastering the body up in a tub.

A strange malaise permeated the postwar world: people worrying about flying saucers, foreign relations, and tomorrow. It gave Eisenhower prosperity a different complexion from Coolidge prosperity, with its promise of a magical social order built on science and Westinghouse Common. As one inspirational book after another hit the best-seller list, the average man searched in ancient orthodoxies and new schools of psychiatry, in the orgone box and prenatal reminiscence, in blackstrap molasses and transmigration of souls for something he had lost with the theme of the 1939 World's Fair—when the much-touted World of Tomorrow blew up in his face.

On October 4, 1957, the American people got a glimpse of what it was that they feared. At that time the Soviet satellite Sputnik I began whirling about the earth, blasting sky-high the myth of America's built-in superiority in things scientific. America got a satellite off the ground only after several embarrassing snafus. Other satellites followed. The uncommitted world cynically kept score in this battle of prestige between East and West.

The satellites had repercussions on every phase of American life. First, they underscored the fact that the United States had lost the first lap of the Buck Rogers race for outer space. Secondly, they raised alarming visions of Soviet ballistic missiles, even now, the pessimists said, "zeroed in on New York." The horrors of atomic war increased the neutralism of America's allies. At home, Long Island and Westchester highways swarmed with peace marchers, bearing demands to the U.N. for a ban on nuclear tests; the marchers displayed more rucksacks, blankets, box lunches, and inflammatory placards, than had been seen since the great Depression.

Educators had long pondered why Johnny couldn't read. Sputnik underscored the fact that Ivan could. The "egghead" was once more respectable. There was talk of raising professors' salaries instead of ostracizing them from civilized society. There was a revulsion against Deweyism in the schools. The most progressive parents were seriously questioning whether Johnny would ever catch up with Ivan by taking courses in driving and co-ed cooking, by bringing "the community" into the schoolroom, or by extracurricular activities which contributed to his "horizontal enrichment."

President Eisenhower, though accused of Couéism, delivered reassuring little talks—one illustrated with a nose cone from a guided missile. The American Way of Life, he said, was better than ever. It seemed increasingly difficult to get this point across to anyone else. Eisenhower's Vice-President, Richard Nixon, returned in 1958 from South America after a "good will" tour spent dodging rotten eggs and tomatoes.

Americans accustomed to the father-image were jarred by the election of boyish John F. Kennedy to the Presidency in 1960. If Eisenhower had been referred to as the "nation's Miltown," JFK, like FDR, was for many a counter-irritant. It had, somehow, never seemed *nice* to make fun of Ike. Now political satirists came out of hibernation. The fabulously successful spoof on the Kennedy's home life—the long playing record of "The First Family"—solved the Christmas gift problem for 1962. Millions of delighted Americans heard a facsimile of the president's voice "appropriating" Yogi Bear beach balls for "tub use." They listened to the First Lady's breathy accents as a football crashed into a White House window. Once again, people seemed to care about politics. For the first time since the war the fiery campus insurgent came into his own. Ten years before, the college bell-ringer and petition-signer had resembled a middle-aged community leader in a civic-minded suburb.

With the Kennedy administration, the New Frontier and the Peace Corps, an attempt was made to brighten up America's image abroad. In 1962 President Kennedy brought off a successful adventure in what Adlai Stevenson used to call "brinkmanship" when it was practiced by John Foster Dulles. The discovery of missile bases in Cuba led Kennedy into a history-making decision to blockade the island and to search Russian ships for arms. The nation held its breath, and the ships turned back. World opinion was, for once, on America's side.

Downing Street cocked a quizzical eyebrow. In the witty English revue, *Beyond the Fringe,* a representative of John Bull wryly congratulates Uncle Sam on having taken a cue from British policy in Suez.

Never had the challenge to democracy been so tremendous. Never had it been more difficult to prepare for it. Values had been in a constant state of flux. A vast social leveling had taken place. A moral revolution had run its course. Science had released a Pandora's box full of horrors. The weather vanes pointed in the direction of religious and intellectual orthodoxy. The years between Versailles and the Bay of Pigs had seen the death of isolationism and the Victorian idea of Progress with a capital *P.*

In the shifts of public opinion which took place some young people achieved precarious eminence. They were children of the moment. The ideas and social conditions with which they were associated were often dated before anybody knew what hit them.

Each of these young people represents a state of mind which was briefly either popular or notorious.

For Fitzgerald it was the "disillusionment" of the Jazz Age with its underlay of hick-town hope.

For Millay it was the belief in a fun kind of revolution, and in the Lost Generation's answers to the problems of the Lost Sex.

For Whittaker Chambers it was the belief that Communism would eliminate the dry rot of the past.

For Lindbergh it was faith in the promises of science, in the isolationism that became obsolete in the world he helped to shrink.

For Haywood Patterson, it was a Depression kid's belief that Big Brother really cared.

For Barbara Hutton it was the notion that the world of Horatio Alger was here to stay.

For Brenda and Cobina it was a similar faith in continuity

—in the Sunday rotogravure society that had seemed so safe before 1929 and the advent of Tax Form 1040.

For Harold Russell it was a father's promise on Armistice Night that there would never be another war.

For Shirley Temple it was a director's promise that baby-hood could be prolonged forever.

John Aldridge, James Dean, William Buckley, Jr., and Claude Batchelor came along in the backwash of the Jazz Age. James Dean carried the protests of the twenties to a logical conclusion in a thrill-packed moment behind a splintering windshield.

John Aldridge wished for a nostalgic year or two for the simplicities of an age when it was enough to be against what everyone else was for.

William Buckley rode briefly to glory on the counterrevolutionary coattails of the junior senator from Wisconsin.

Claude Batchelor had a moment of need for Victorian strength to rebut the arguments of slick-talking Chinese.

The turning points came in different places for each one. No two people react in quite the same way to a stock market crash, the dropping of a bomb, a tax law, or a declaration of war. Yet the lives of these young people were changed by the crises of history—Fitzgerald's by the crash, Patterson's by the Depression hobo jungles, Russell's by Pearl Harbor; Buckley's by the postwar emergence of the Red Menace, Batchelor's by the Korean War.

The crises of history dated the novels of Fitzgerald, the poetry of Millay, the college literary idols of John Aldridge. The same trend had different effects on different people. Fitzgerald, no less than Barbara Hutton, reacted to a dying social order. Harold Russell, because of the war, belatedly learned the lesson of Scottsboro. Some led one revolution and the counterrevolution against it—the scientism of Lindbergh's youth, the antiscientism of his middle age. Whittaker Chambers, who espoused the popular radicalism of the twenties, and the equally fashionable reaction of the fifties, ended up in roughly the same camp as William Buckley, Jr.

Some of these young people changed the world. Others were changed by it. Few of them were privileged to live in the world they were promised on graduation day. One thing stands out in most of these biographies—how little intelligent guidance there was in the years that set the pattern for the future. It was perhaps because the guides themselves had lost their way.

Many of them played roles in dramas they only half understood. They fought battles for which their parents could never have prepared them without the aid of a crystal ball. Between the generations there was an almost total lack of communication. The Victorian railed ineffectually at a bored flapper for smoking and showing her knees. The Jazz Age cynic warned the child of the Depression against the perils of patriotic jingoism—and then discovered that he could not continue indefinitely to turn an ostrich eye on a globe designed by Charles A. Lindbergh. Today the Depression radical tries to justify his membership in the Abraham Lincoln Brigade to an uncomprehending young Ikeman in a gray flannel suit. Who knows what bitter battles will take place between youth and crabbed age when the gray flannel suit goes into mothballs along with the coonskin coat?

Each of these young people contributed some feature to the face of the typical American youth: Lindbergh's boyish smile, that inspired a generation of aspiring young barnstormers, the frosty gaze with which he faced the cameras at meetings of America First; Millay's bemused eye, mocking Victoria and Anthony Comstock; the hands of Harold Russell, symbolic of a whole civilization forced to cultivate the art of making do; the grim jawline of William Buckley, selling the world on his alien brand of "Americanism"; the shifting gaze of Claude Batchelor—one Korean War veteran whose picture was never used on defense bond posters.

The class of 1963 is heir to their hopes, dreams, frustrations, fears, and failures. Deep in the collective unconscious of those diploma holders who are scheduled to inherit the earth next June is the race memory of their forefathers' fall from grace.

1963 is affected by the struggles of these fourteen archetypal figures, buffeted by vast social forces set in motion when the doomed children of the Jazz Age were cast out of Mr. Wilson's Eden.

I THE UNEASY UTOPIA

"From the confusion of 1920 I remember riding on top of
a taxicab along deserted Fifth Avenue on a hot Sunday
night, and a luncheon in the cool Japanese gardens at the
Ritz . . . and paying too much for minute apartments, and
buying magnificent but broken-down cars . . . and lastly
from that period I remember riding in a taxi one afternoon
between very tall buildings under a mauve and rosy sky; I
began to bawl because I had everything I wanted and
knew I would never be so happy again." *The Crackup,*
by F. Scott Fitzgerald

"When he died of a heart attack age 44, hardly
anybody went to the funeral home. One who did was
his old friend Dorothy Parker. Taking the epitaph line
from *The Great Gatsby* she said, 'The poor son of a
bitch.'" *Time,* January 29, 1951

2

Babylon Revisited

F. SCOTT FITZGERALD

F. Scott Fitzgerald has long been fair game for the literary
archaeologists. He has had his footnoted biography, his posthumous revival. Everyone who has ever picked up a literary
quarterly is aware of his ambivalant attitude toward wealth,
his depleted emotional "bank balance"; of Malcolm Cowley's
image of Fitzgerald, A (the kid from St. Paul), nose pressed
against the glass, watching Fitzgerald, B (sophisticate-by-
transplantation), going through his urbane peregrinations on
the ballroom floor. The Hollywood columnist Sheilah Graham
described, in a lengthy memoir, his role in "the education of
a woman."

More than most of his generation Fitzgerald was buffeted
by the tides of change, by a moral revolution which he helped
to bring about, by a social revolution which he was powerless

to prevent. He viewed the big bull market with the double vision of a materialist with the heart of a child.

The story of his life is as familiar as his impetuous dives into public fountains. There was his boyhood in St. Paul, his extra-curricular triumphs and undistinguished academic career at Princeton. There was his military service as the "worst aide-de-camp in the army," and his meeting with a fiery Southern beauty named Zelda Sayre at an officers' club dance.

Zelda entertained dreams of fame and fortune which seemed unlikely to be realized on the ninety dollars a month which Fitzgerald made after the war as a copywriter for the Barron Collier advertising agency.

Following a rebuff from her, Fitzgerald threw up his job, got drunk, went back to St. Paul and finished his best-selling novel *This Side of Paradise*. In the fall of 1919 it was accepted by Scribner's, and from then on, as Glenway Westcott said, it "haunted the decade like a song, popular but perfect." Fitzgerald was twenty-three years old. The spurned copy-writer returned hat in hand to present his credentials as a great author. On March 20, 1920, Scott and Zelda were married and returned to New York.

Zelda's passionate approach to life was displayed by an incident which occurred shortly after their marriage. She put in a call to the fire department, and when questioned as to the whereabouts of the fire, she struck her breast and cried dramatically "here."[1]

Together the Fitzgeralds set a fashion for Jazz Age archness which must have been the bane of a hostess' life.

> They were as likely to be two or three hours late to a dinner party as on time, and even more likely not to come at all [wrote Arthur Mizener in *The Far Side of Paradise*]. They went to people's houses and then sat down quietly in a corner and like two children, went fast asleep. They rode down Fifth Avenue on the tops of taxis . . . or dove into the fountain at Union Square or tried to undress at the

[1] All footnotes are at the end of the book.

Scandals, or in sheer delight at the splendor of New York, jumped dead sober into the Pulitzer Fountain in front of the Plaza.[2]

Throughout subsequent years in New York, Westport, and Great Neck, the mood of whimsy persisted. There was Zelda's arrest as the "Bob-haired Bandit"; Fitzgerald's driving Max Perkins off a road and into a pond "because it seemed more fun"; there were the notices that "invitations to stay over Monday, issued by the host and hostess during the small hours of Sunday morning must not be taken seriously."[3]

With the publication of his second novel, *The Beautiful and Damned*, in 1921, Fitzgerald hit upon the *Zeitgeist* of the decade. In the words of his friend Edmund Wilson, he had discovered the "meaninglessness of life."

It was inevitable that this discovery should be followed by a period of European exile. Between 1924 and 1931, the Fitzgeralds wandered about Europe with brief trips back to America in 1927 and 1929. Early in these "seven years of waste and tragedy," in 1925, he published his finest novel, *The Great Gatsby*. He also perpetrated innumerable pranks in the company of various kittenish drinking companions. On a brief trip back to Hollywood, for example, Fitzgerald attended a party where he made a bouillabaisse out of the other guests' watches and jewelry. On leaving town the Fitzgeralds stacked the furniture in their hotel room with the unpaid bills on top, and crawled through the aisles of the train on their hands and knees to evade possible pursuers.

Shortly after the stock market crash, following an unsuccessful attempt to become a ballet dancer, Zelda had her first nervous breakdown. In 1931 they rented a house at La Paix outside Baltimore, where they remained until 1937, when Fitzgerald went to Hollywood with M-G-M. During this time Zelda had two more breakdowns. The mounting horror of these years is mirrored in *Tender Is the Night* (1934). Life outdid art years later when Zelda was burned to death in a nursing home fire—a finis to a saga of disintegration that even Fitzgerald did not foresee.

During the thirties Fitzgerald was faced with a growing alcoholic problem and a declining market for his work; for with hard times he went suddenly out of fashion. There was the episode of his befogged collaboration with Budd Schulberg on the movie *Winter Carnival*, which inspired Schulberg's best-seller *The Disenchanted*. There was *The New York Evening Post* "interview" with him which employed a tone "usually reserved by tabloid writers for broken down fighters."[4] So low did his stock fall that a movie star whom Schulberg met thought Fitzgerald was a character in a Katherine Brush novel.

For all of this he pulled himself together sufficiently to write several screen plays and to begin work on his final novel, *The Last Tycoon*. He was never to finish it. On December 21, 1940, he died of a heart attack. His literary reputation thenceforth became a property for re-evaluation.

Fitzgerald's obituaries reflected the contempt which every age feels for its immediate predecessor. Westbrook Pegler attacked the deceased with a relish generally reserved for subjects still in the land of the living. His death recalled to Pegler

> memories of a queer bunch of undisciplined and self-indulgent brats who were determined not to pull their weight in the boat and wanted the world to drop everything and sit down and bawl with them. A kick in the pants and a clout over the scalp were more like their needing.[5]

Dorothy Parker limited herself to a more succinct tribute: "The poor son of a bitch."[6]

Stephen Vincent Benét saw beyond the puritanism of a world on the brink of war:

> You can take off your hats, now, gentlemen, and I think perhaps you had better. This is not a legend, this is a reputation—and, seen in perspective, it may well be one of the most secure reputations of our time.[7]

Fitzgerald's wild fluctuations in popularity were closely related to the business cycle. For there were elements in his work that were palatable enough in good times, but were

guaranteed to irritate the apple seller or the derelict on a park
bench. Born as he was in 1896, he accepted as proper and
right the nineteenth-century ideas of the divine right of the
upper class. When he was young the world was still divided
between lowly born worker-bees and the elegantly Edwardian
drones.

Amory Blaine, the hero of *This Side of Paradise,* went on
trips attended by two maids, and frequently a physician. It
took "four disgusted specialists" to pull him through whooping
cough. When he had scarlet fever, fourteen doctors, nurses,
and assorted handmaidens danced attendance. A truly critical
ailment called for an even more impressive production. En
route to Europe his appendix burst "probably from too many
meals in bed, and after a series of frantic telegrams to Europe
and America, to the amazement of the passengers the great
ship slowly wheeled around and returned to New York to
deposit Amory at the pier. You will admit that if it was not life
it was magnificent."[8]

To later products of the Century of the Common Man it
would seem as though Fitzgerald were indulging in poetic
license. It must be remembered that a scant nine years before
This Side of Paradise was written, the *Titanic* went down with
dramatic differences in the survival rates of the steerage
passengers and the gilded globetrotters on A deck. Through
Fitzgerald's work there runs an unpleasant vein of inherited
snobbery. It is evident in casual references to the worship of
the prep school man at Princeton; in his allusions to "a nigger
scrap," to "the plebeian drunks," or to such high-spirited
college pranks as filling "the Jewish youth's bed with lemon
pie."

Fitzgerald's heroes shared a common respect for the "right"
club, the Ivy League college, and the New England prep
school. A character in *Tender Is the Night* remarks that "Mac
thinks a Marxian is somebody who went to St. Mark's school."
When Dick Diver learns of Abe North's death, he hears that,
like the salmon going upstream, North "just managed to crawl
home to the Racquet Club to die." The melancholy event
provokes a spirited debate as to whether the corpse had been
a member of the Racquet Club or the Harvard Club.

In Fitzgerald's day the figure of the "gentleman" still commanded envy and respect. In *This Side of Paradise* the description of Dick Humbird gave a handy guide to the identification of the species:

> He differed from the healthy type that was essentially middle-class—he never seemed to perspire. Some people couldn't be familiar with a chauffeur without having it returned; Humbird could have lunched at Sherry's with a colored man, yet people would have somehow known that it was all right.[9]

The shocking truth about this compendium of aristocratic virtues, revealed in a later paragraph, was that "his father was a grocery clerk who made a fortune in Tacoma real estate." Even a gentleman could not always guarantee a complete absence of perspiration a generation back.

A heroic death on the battlefield was one of a gentleman's manly prerogatives; and the upper-income groups rushed for the trenches with the gusto of turkeys being fatted up for Thanksgiving. Not only did a declaration of war precipitate a mass dash to Brooks Brothers; but Fitzgerald could write to his mother, "I just *went* and purely for *social* reasons."[10]

Anthony and Maury, in *The Beautiful and Damned*, looked upon war as the "one excuse for and justification of the aristocrat, and conjured up an impossible caste of officers to be composed, it appeared, chiefly of the more attractive alumni of three or four Eastern colleges." It was perhaps fortunate that in the sweatier engagements which followed the Jazz Age, these were not the standards used in enlisting recruits.

Girls of loose morals were not the castless tramps or floozies of later literature. Maury goes home to the back-street caress of a "girl of another class whose whole life he was." When Anthony Patch takes up with a mistress he is relieved at his unfamiliarity with the Southern idiom because "he could not have determined the social status of a Southerner from her talk. In New York a girl of a lower class would have been raucous, unendurable except through the rosy spectacles of intoxication." Even virtue itself was the special heritage of the gently born.

The lady did not spin. The gentleman frequently did not toil. Fitzgerald's characters had an irritating inability to perform life's most commonplace chores for themselves. Rosalind in *This Side of Paradise* would not marry Amory, because, among other things, she would have to learn to set her own hair. Gloria in *The Beautiful and Damned* was incapable of sending out the laundry. It would be difficult to imagine a mid-century novel like *The Beautiful and Damned*, whose central conflict was whether or not the protagonist should go to work.

As the big bull market catapulted bootleggers and bartenders to fame and fortune, the gentlemanly ideal began to disappear. The Great Gatsby, for example, came of highly suspect origins; yet society tolerated his peccadillos. His friends were content to drink his liquor while discussing his faults. They would flock to anyone who could offer them parties around the swimming pool and obsequious figures who materialized in response to a finger on a bell.

Few writers have portrayed with more power the corrosive spiritual effects of the national spending spree. The carefree parties which evolved into nightmare binges are described with a vividness born of Fitzgerald's own awakenings to many terrible dawns. There is the scene in *The Beautiful and Damned* when Anthony and Gloria realize that they have signed, without remembering it, a lease on a summer house they hate and can ill afford.

> But because of another wild revel, enduring through four days and participated in . . . by more than a dozen people, they did sign the lease; to their utter horror they signed it and sent it, and immediately it seemed as though they heard the gray house, drably malevolent at last, licking its white chops and waiting to devour them.[11]

There were the pukka sahibs who disappeared into "the dark maw of violence."

> A classmate killed his wife and himself on Long Island, another tumbled "accidentally" from a sky-

scraper in Philadelphia, another purposely from a skyscraper in New York. One was killed in a speak-easy in Chicago; another was beaten to death in a speak-easy in New York and [shades of Abe North!] crawled home to the Princeton Club to die; still another had his skull crushed by a maniac's axe in an insane asylum where he was confined. These are not catastrophes that I went out of my way to look for—these were my friends; moreover, these things happened not during the depression but during the boom.[12]

On the other hand, Fitzgerald was a master at capturing the charm of the life that money can buy. An article he wrote with his wife "Show Mr. and Mrs. F. to Number —" describes the pleasant vantage point from which the expatriate berated American materialism.

1924—The Deux Mondes in Paris ended about a blue abysmal court outside our window. We bathed the daughter in the *bidet* by mistake and she drank the gin fizz thinking it was lemonade and ruined the luncheon table next day. . . .

1926— . . . they were serving blue twilights at the cafés along the Promenade des Anglais for the price of a porto, and we danced their tangos and watched girls shiver in the appropriate clothes for the Côte d'Azur. We went to the Perroquet with friends, one of us wearing a blue hyacinth and the other an ill temper which made him buy a wagon full of roasted chestnuts and immediately scatter their warm burnt odor like largesse over the cold spring night. . . .

1929—In Paris we economized again in a not-yet-dried cement hotel, the name of which we've forgotten. It cost us a good deal, for we ate out every night to avoid starchy table d'hôtes.[13]

These were the palmy days when Fitzgerald's barber retired on half a million dollars; when even budgeting had its charms and when young married people lived like gypsies without worrying about who was going to feed the baby. It was a life that disappeared forever as "leisurely men played checkers in the restaurant of the Hotel de la Paix in Lausanne. The depression had become frank in the American papers so we wanted to get back home."

Other exiled esthetes were headed in the same direction; home to the Federal Theater, to the W.P.A. Writers' Project, to practice their craft under the wing of the Blue Eagle. When Fitzgerald came back to America in 1931, New York had changed and so, as the decade wore on, did some of his friends.

> With bowed head and hat in hand [he wrote in *The Crackup*] I walked reverently through the echoing tomb. . . .
>
> My barber was back at work in his shop; again the headwaiters bowed people to their tables, if there were people to be bowed. . . .
>
> And Bunny [Edmund Wilson] . . . frets about the wrongs of Southern mill workers and Western farmers whose voices fifteen years ago, would not have penetrated his study walls.[14]

The work which Fitzgerald did in the thirties was completely out of step with the times. Though *Tender Is the Night* was completed in 1934, most of it takes place in the twenties and the Divers are still suffering the *crises de nerfs* of the very rich. *The Last Tycoon* represents Fitzgerald's only attempt to deal with the economic man.

Various references in this work bear out the fact that, apart from personal hardships, Fitzgerald was aware that a Depression was taking place. "Since 1933," he wrote, "the rich could only be happy together." There were the stenographers who had "seen their bosses jittery" and lost the "dumb admiration" for them that they had in 1929. There was the actress riding in an airplane who feared an uprising of the masses:

> "I know what mother and I are going to do," she confided to the stewardess. "We're coming out to

the Yellowstone and we're just going to live simply
till it all blows over. Then we'll come back. They
don't kill artists—you know?"[15]

When Fitzgerald wrote *The Last Tycoon*, Hollywood technicians were currently being unionized. Using the resulting
conflict as a background, Fitzgerald intended to construct a
highly melodramatic plot. Monroe Stahr, the last tycoon, was
to be crushed between the minions of Wall Street and the
minions of Moscow.

The figure of the tycoon had undergone a dramatic meta-
morphosis as a result of the crash. In *The Beautiful and
Damned* (1921) old Adam Patch is almost a caricature of the
robber baron.

> Anthony surveyed his grandfather with that tacit
> amazement which always attended the sight. That
> this feeble, unintelligent old man was possessed of
> such power that . . . the men in the republic whose
> souls he could not have bought . . . would scarcely
> have populated White Plains, seemed as impossible
> to believe as that he had once been a pink-and-
> white baby.
>   . . . the first quarter-century had blown him full
> with life, and the last had sucked it all back. It
> had sucked in the cheeks and the chest and the
> girth of arm and leg. It had tyrannously demanded
> his teeth, one by one, suspended his small eyes in
> dark-bluish sacks, tweaked out his hairs, changed
> him from gray to white in some places, from pink
> to yellow in others. . . . Then through his body and
> his soul it had attacked his brain. It had sent him
> night-sweats and tears and unfounded dreads. It
> had split his intense normality into credulity and
> suspicion. . . . His energy was shrunk to the bad
> temper of a spoiled child, and for his will to power
> was substituted a fatuous, puerile desire for a land
> of harps and canticles on earth.[16]

In the course of a discussion with his ne'er-do-well grandson, old "Cross Patch" had dilated on the after life and the

need for settling down to some worthy pursuit. " 'Why, when I was just two years older than you,' he rasped with a cunning chuckle, 'I sent three members of the firm of Wrenn and Hunt to the poorhouse.' "

Had this anachronistic old gentleman been the villain of *The Last Tycoon,* it might have had more of a popular success. Instead, Fitzgerald made the fatal mistake of painting his industrialist as a sympathetic figure. Monroe Stahr comes over as an intelligent, humane, individualistic, and creative movie maker. He is anti-union because the unions complicate his life. They try to organize overpaid writers. They espouse the cause of directors who sabotage honest films by attempting to slip homosexual innuendoes past the wary eye of the Legion of Decency.

Stahr was impressed by the Russian films of the era but would have none of the Party Line.

In a scene with Brimmer, the Communist organizer, he displays a comic ineptitude which would have appalled old Adam Patch. The organizer is welcomed to his office as an interesting curiosity—with all the fanfare that would accompany the arrival of a visitor from Mars. As homework for the meeting Stahr has had films of the Russian revolution run off as well as *Doctor Caligari* and Dali's *Le Chien Andalou,* "possibly suspecting that they had a bearing on the matter."

When Brimmer arrives, they fence verbally for a while. Stahr is nervous and has one too many drinks. The two get into a fist fight. Brimmer hits Stahr, who disappears "out of sight below the level of the table." Tycoons were no longer all-powerful in the literature of the Proletarian Preach.

The Last Tycoon, in addition to being unfinished, had the wrong line-up of the good guys and the bad guys. The fact that its hero was an employer, and a paternalistic one at that, did not recommend it to the Party faithful. Depression writers presented social problems through the idealized figures of sandhogs and migratory workers. Fitzgerald was unique in keeping the perspective of the aristocrat awaiting the tumbrils.

Critics of the thirties with a sneaking fondness for Fitzgerald felt it necessary to apologize and explain. In a review of *Tender Is the Night,* G. Hartley Grattan compared the Divers to the ailing social organism. Dick stood in relationship

to Nicole "as the reformer to the sick society which he wishes
to cure because he cannot bring himself to abandon it."
Grattan points defiantly to the "feverish bloom" and "grace of
the Divers' way of life, which was lost on those austere individuals who see in the bourgeois world nothing but filth and
corruption."[17] The tone of the review was that of a man who
hears a strident offstage voice accusing him of Menshevik
deviationism.

Fitzgerald was never at home with social issues, and his
most moving views of the aftermath of the crash were concerned with its human wreckage. The short story *Babylon
Revisited* takes us to Paris the morning after the ten-year
binge. "The Ritz Bar was not an American bar any more."
The hero "felt polite in it and not as if he owned it." He remembers when Americans were a sort of franc-tossing royalty.
A letter from a superannuated madcap provides an unwelcome
reminder of an escapade on the Etoile with a stolen tricycle.
Fitzgerald combines social criticism with a bit of aristocratic
nose wrinkling.

> Again the memory of those days swept over him
> like a nightmare—the people they had met travel-
> ing, the people who couldn't add up a row of fig-
> ures or speak a coherent sentence . . . the women
> and girls carried screaming with drink or drugs out
> of public places.[18]

Yet along with the nightmare there was always the nostalgia, as in a piece on the Jazz Age which he wrote in 1931:

> It ended two years ago because the utter con-
> fidence which was its essential prop received an
> enormous jolt, and it didn't take long for the flimsy
> structure to settle earthward. And after two years
> the Jazz Age seems as far away as the days before
> the war. . . . Now, once more the belt is tight and
> we summon the proper expression of horror as
> we look back on our wasted youth—Sometimes,
> though, there is a ghostly rumble among the drums,

an asthmatic whisper in the trombones that swing
us back into the early twenties, when we drank
wood alcohol and every day in every way grew
better and better, and there was a first abortive
shortening of the skirts, and girls all looked alike in
sweater dresses, and people you didn't want to
know said, "Yes, we have no bananas," and it
seemed only a question of a few years before the
older people would step aside and let the world be
run by those who saw things as they were—and it
all seems rosy and romantic to us who were young
then, because we will never feel quite so intensely
about our surroundings any more.[19]

Fitzgerald never quite adapted to a society where the lunch
pail had taken the place of the old school tie. If Fitzgerald
came through the social revolution as a downgraded aristocrat, he came through the moral revolution as a wised-up
innocent. One cannot read the early Fitzgerald without being
impressed by his naïveté. It was fitting that the revolution of
the twenties should catch its mood from the *Weltschmerz* of
a very young man. For there was an adolescent quality to the
twenties. The most passionate rhetoric of the decade had the
violence of an argument between a daughter insisting on
siren's black and a mother still plumping for pink tulle.

Fitzgerald's interests were essentially touching and boyish.
As an older man he still numbered among his most crushing
defeats his disqualification for the presidency of the Princeton Triangle Club, his failure to get overseas in the First
World War, and his lone unmemorable performance on the
football field. His attitude toward sports had the Walter Mitty
quality of the perennial bench warmer. His attitude toward
war was like that of a seventeen-year-old caught lying about
his age to his draft board.

His romantic attitude toward war crops up now and then
in his novels. There was, in *This Side of Paradise*, the moment
war hit the Ivy Club:

Everyone bantered in public and told themselves
privately that their deaths at least would be heroic.

> The literary students read Rupert Brooke passion-
> ately; the lounge lizards worried over whether the
> government would permit the English-cut uniform
> for officers; a few of the hopelessly lazy wrote to
> the obscure branches of the War Department, seek-
> ing an easy commission and a soft berth.[20]

In *The Beautiful and Damned* he describes how the falter-
ing conversationalist seized upon war as a bored beach club
gossip seizes on sexual activity in the dunes.

> At last everyone had something to talk about—
> and almost everyone enjoyed it, as though they had
> been cast for parts in a sombre and romantic play.

The heroine of the same novel notes that war imparts a
new glamour even to her own husband. The "huge red light"
cast its flattering glow over every Harvey, Charlie, and Bill.
When Fitzgerald finished *This Side of Paradise,* he sent the
manuscript to Dean Gauss of Princeton, asking him to recommend it for publication because he thought he was going to
fall in battle. When caught in the beam of the "huge red light,"
Fitzgerald was not above turning his best profile.

Fitzgerald in the thirties wavered between the prevailing
mood of pacifism and the boyish regret of the hero manqué.
Once in *Tender Is the Night* he sounded the pacifist note.
Dick Diver takes Rosemary out to the "tragic hill of Thiepval."
He shows her the place where one empire walked very slowly
forward while "another empire walked very slowly backward
a few inches a day, leaving the dead like a million bloody
rugs. . . . No European," Fitzgerald wrote, five years before
the invasion of Poland, "will ever do that again in this
generation."

But the romantic was always rearing his head between the
lines of the tract. Diver goes on to explain that "they could
fight the first Marne again but not this" (the Western front).

> "You had to remember Christmas, and postcards
> of the Crown Prince and his fiancée, and little cafés
> in Valence and beer gardens in Unter den Linden

and weddings at the mairie, and going to the Derby, and your grandfather's whiskers. . . ."

"Why, this was a love battle—there was a century of middle-class love spent here. . . ."

"You want to hand over this battle to D. H. Lawrence," said Abe [who was in a position to practice gamesmanship].

Like Fitzgerald, Dick Diver suffered from inadequacies because "actually Abe North had seen battle service and he had not."[21] The postwar disillusionment which followed his orgy of romanticism had much of the callow cynicism of the college bull session. There is an aura of second-year philosophy in the way Fitzgerald's characters wrestle with life's great themes. In *The Beautiful and Damned* they dissect Art:

> DICK (*pompously*) Art isn't meaningless.
> MAURY It is in itself. It isn't in that it tries to make life less so.
> ANTHONY In other words, Dick, you're playing before a grand stand peopled with ghosts.
> MAURY Give a good show anyhow.
> ANTHONY (*To Maury*) On the contrary, I'd feel that it being a meaningless world, why write? The very attempt to give it purpose is purposeless.
> DICK Well, even admitting all that, be a decent pragmatist and grant a poor man the instinct to live.[22]

Like Eleanor in *This Side of Paradise*, his characters frequently repudiate God.

> Well—I'm not afraid of the dark, so I put on my slicker and rubber boots and came out. You see I was always afraid, before, to say I didn't believe in God—because the lightning might strike me— but here I am and it hasn't, of course, but the main point is that this time I wasn't any more afraid of it than I had been when I was a Christian Scientist, like I was last year.[23]

Eleanor also shocked the reading public with her daring opinions on the illusion of love.

> "Listen," she leaned close again, "I like clever men and good-looking men, and, of course, no one cares more for personality than I do. Oh, just one person in fifty has any glimmer of what sex is. I'm hipped on Freud and all that, but it's rotten that every bit of *real* love in the world is ninety-nine per cent passion and one little soupçon of jealousy."[24]

The meaninglessness of life is the inspiration for many nocturnal discussions like the one which takes place between Maury Noble, Dick Caramel, and the beautiful and damned Patches.

> [Maury says] "So I wrapped myself in what I thought was my invulnerable scepticism and decided that my education was complete. But it was too late. Protect myself as I might by making no new ties with tragic and predestined humanity, I was lost with the rest. I had traded the fight against love for the fight against loneliness, the fight against life for the fight against death." . . .
> "There's only one lesson to be learned from life, anyway," interrupted Gloria, not in contradiction but in a sort of melancholy agreement.
> "What's that?" demanded Maury sharply.
> "That there's no lesson to be learned from life."[25]

For all its loudly professed despair, the "lost generation" was essentially optimistic. At the end of the First World War the average American had never had it so good. He had "suffered enough for poignancy but not for bitterness." The bitterness which came later had a slightly ersatz quality, like the pleasant melancholy of a Puccini finale or a sad-eyed gypsy strumming a violin. It brought in its wake torch songs and protest novels, and a boredom which in Fitzgerald's own words "is another name and a frequent disguise for vitality."

No one sings a sad song when his heart is really breaking. The disillusionment of the "lost generation" became considerably less appealing in the atomic age. Sociologists might do well to ponder the exact date when the bored and disillusioned worldling ceased to be the heroine of popular music. The prospect of one's own extermination inspires many emotions, but ennui is not among them. The hypochondriac ceases to bemoan his imminent death when he narrowly squeaks through his first critical operation.

The romantic view of life upon which Fitzgerald put his trademark was nowhere more evident than in his attitude toward sex. He was well aware that the subject was a source of fascination to his contemporaries. As he wrote in *The Crackup:*

> We begin with the suggestion that Don Juan leads an interesting life (*Jurgen*, 1919); then we learn that there's a lot of sex around if we only knew it (*Winesburg, Ohio*, 1920), that adolescents lead very amorous lives (*This Side of Paradise*, 1920), that there are a lot of neglected Anglo-Saxon words (*Ulysses*, 1921), that older people don't always resist sudden temptations (*Cytherea*, 1922), that girls are sometimes seduced without being ruined (*Flaming Youth*, 1922), that glamorous English ladies are often promiscuous (*The Green Hat*, 1924), that in fact they devote most of their time to it (*The Vortex*, 1926), that it's a damn good thing too (*Lady Chatterley's Lover*, 1928), and finally that there are abnormal variations (*The Well of Loneliness*, 1928, and *Sodom and Gomorrah*, 1929).[26]

The fact that Fitzgerald included *This Side of Paradise* in this literary catalogue suggests that he considered it the last word in daring naturalism. For example, he described with horror the free and easy ways of the "P.D." or popular daughter. A mother attuned to mid-century mating habits would rest far more easily if she could be certain that *that* was all her daughter did on a date.

Amory saw girls doing things that even in his memory would have been impossible: eating three-o'clock, after-dance suppers in impossible cafés, talking of every side of life with an air half of earnestness, half of mockery, yet with a furtive excitement that Amory considered stood for a real moral letdown. . . .

Afternoon at the Plaza, with winter twilight hovering outside and faint drums down-stairs. . . . The theatre comes afterward; then a table at the Midnight Frolic—of course, Mother will be along there. . . . But the P.D. is in love again . . . it was odd, wasn't it?—that though there was so much room left in the taxi the P.D. and the boy from Williams were somehow crowded out and had to go in a separate car. Odd! Didn't you notice how flushed the P.D. was when she arrived just seven minutes late?[27]

One could only feel that the P.D.'s escort must have worked very nimbly indeed if he accomplished her ruin in seven minutes in a moving taxicab.

Fitzgerald betrays his innocence whenever he attempts what he considers to be a racy love scene. Take for example the bit of dialogue between Amory and Rosalind in *This Side of Paradise:*

Rosalind: Listen! They're playing "Kiss Me Again."
   (*He looks at her.*)
Amory: Well?
Rosalind: Well?
Amory: (*Softly—the battle lost*) I love you.
Rosalind: I love you—now.
   (*They kiss.*)
Amory: Oh God, what have I done?[28]

The scarlet "pasts" of Fitzgerald's heroines seem as horrifying as a round of Spin the Bottle. Isabelle in *This Side of Paradise* is chided by a censorious girl friend:

"He knows you're—you're considered beautiful
and all that"—she paused—"and I guess he knows
you've been kissed."

At this Isabelle's little fist had clenched suddenly
under the fur robe. She was accustomed to be thus
followed by her desperate past, and it never failed
to rouse in her the same feeling of resentment; yet
—in a strange town it was an advantageous reputation. She was a "Speed," was she? Well—let them
find out.[29]

This Side of Paradise was admittedly a tale of adolescents,
but even Fitzgerald's grown-up heroines subscribe unconsciously to the double standard:

"Women soil easily [said Gloria in *The Beautiful
and Damned*] far more easily than men. Unless a
girl's very young and very brave it's almost impossible for her to go down-hill without a certain
hysterical animality, the cunning, dirty sort of
animality. A man's different—and I suppose that's
why one of the commonest characters of romance
is a man going gallantly to the devil."[30]

Fitzgerald may have considered himself a revolutionary.
Behind ever daring manifesto of his heroines one could feel
the massive presence of the Victorian mother—the mother
who said "*servant*-girls are that way, they are kissed first and
proposed to afterward"; the mother who told the P.D. that no
man would respect a girl who allowed him to take liberties;
and that if a woman went wrong it would show in her face.

When Fitzgerald advanced as a writer, his characters advanced in sophistication. Nick Carraway in *The Great Gatsby*
is oppressed by the carnage beside the swimming pool. By
the time the novel ends the victims of an afternoon of motor-
ing-cum-adultery were piled as high as the casualties on
Desdemona's couch. The narrator regards such happenings
with "provincial squeamishness"; for he, like Gatsby and the
Buchanans, is an apostate Westerner. Tom Buchanan, despite
his provincial origins, has acquired the Eastern patina. He

keeps an urbane calm when his wife runs over his mistress.
He tells his mistress's husband that the accident was the fault
of an innocent bystander, and he regards with suavity the
death toll of two which results from this little white lie. For
a man from the provinces, Buchanan has clearly mastered the
technique of the Gallic shrug.

Fitzgerald's writing struck a responsive chord in a society
which was learning to shrug Gallically at everything from
companionate marriage to Peaches Browning. Yet in those
days you could still scratch a sophisticate and find a hard-
shell Baptist, a lace-curtain Irishman or even, God forbid, one
of Mencken's "boobs."

> In trouble such as yours (of the reality of which
> I am by no means convinced) [Fitzgerald wrote to
> a friend] the proper tradition is that the mouth is
> kept shut, the eyes are lowered; the personality
> tries to say to itself "I will adjust and adapt, I can
> beat change. . . ." Anything short of that would be
> dishonor to the past and whatever you believe in.

The stern voices of Fitzgerald's childhood were dictating
the cosmic phraseology of this pep talk—addressed to a small
boy who was suffering a bout of homesickness at summer
camp. Faced by the lukewarm reception of *Tender Is the
Night,* and his wife's periodic departures to a nearby sanitarium, Fitzgerald had a chance to put into practice his
Victorian preachings on the stiff upper lip.

The unhappy camper, Andrew Turnbull, whose parents
rented to Fitzgerald during the La Paix period, grew up to
write a charming portrait of the author as he looked at this
trying time. [Later, Turnbull was to write a Fitzgerald biography adding his voice to the chorus of posthumous praise.]
Turnbull recalls his tenant's performance on the tennis court:

> I can see him now—a little paunchy in his white
> flannels swaggering up to his alley and crouching
> professionally to await the return of service. (His
> walk was a self-important strut with a slight hunch
> of the shoulders—the stagy, dramatic walk of a

man of action come suddenly on the scene to set
things straight.) . . .

He recalls that Fitzgerald performed the most transparent
card tricks with a dash that made the deck seem bewitched.

He applied the same conviction in helping us to
build an igloo once when a blizzard was followed
by a heavy freeze. Joining us in his hat and
galoshes, with his overcoat collar turned up, he
showed us how to cut the blocks of crusted snow
and fit them together. When the structure was completed, we could all get inside. Fitzgerald couldn't
make it last forever—he wasn't quite enough of a
magician for that—but I do remember that when
the thaw set in, the igloo was the last patch of
snow to disappear from the lawn.[31]

The tragicomic figure in white flannels was a magician in
more ways than one. From the most improbable materials
he conjured up the beauty of an age—from its sticky highball
glasses, and its ravaged playgrounds; from the noisy table at
the country club and the erotic byplay in the kitchenette.

Few could touch Fitzgerald when it came to crystallizing
the fleeting second—the brilliant half-hour at the party before
repartee degenerated into repetition—the carefree time in history "when the fulfilled future and the wistful past were
mingled in a single gorgeous moment." It is thanks to his
peculiar genius that we remember the snow sculpture as well
as the slush underfoot.

Turnbull also recalls another Fitzgerald—the man with a
sense that time was running out, working late with his light
blazing into the small hours of the morning, "a point of desperate and mysterious energy in the surrounding dark." He
remembers Fitzgerald in the wreckage after his wife had set
the second floor on fire, toiling on amid "the water-stained
walls and woodwork, in that hulk of a house whose bleakness
matched the color of his soul."[32] He had need of the "mouth
kept shut," "the eyes lowered," to shut out the image of the
world which ended in October 1929.

One wondered if the iron which kept him returning to the typewriter would be vouchsafed to those whose childhood memories were of a gentler nature; whether his unexpected intestinal fortitude would have been nurtured by classes in clay modeling and finger painting, by soft-voiced nursery school teachers with questions about elimination habits, and tactful ways of "distracting" the young from murdering their playmates.

Fitzgerald to the end was a child of simpler society, guided by the ethics of yesteryear. The Left Bank and the North Shore may have left their mark on him; but when his daughter Scottie was born, he and his wife preferred to go home to St. Paul. His puritanism never quite deserted him. When he tries to horrify us with tales of tricycling around the Etoile or stripping at the Scandals he confuses the sinister with the silly. He comes off as a highly improbable Dorian Gray.

His was the story of the disinheritance of a whole generation, born, as one writer put it, "in the quiet afterglow of the nineteenth century." Like Gatsby, their eyes were on "the green light, the orgiastic future that year by year recedes before us."[33]

The educative process was not to end with Fitzgerald. In his daughter's day, young people kissed without horrified exclamations of "What have we done?" After World War II they barely batted an eye when a less fortunate sister showed evidence of pregnancy in French class. But the excitement of revolt decreased as the P.D. became more compliant—as the "necker" extended the range of her favors from "first base" to second and to third.

"His modest smile has done more for the reputation and standing of the United States than all the diplomatic notes written through many years." *Literary Digest,* June 25, 1927

"I don't think many people care." *Newsweek,* December 26, 1949

3

The Apostle of Speed

CHARLES A. LINDBERGH

If Fitzgerald represented the citified provincial, Charles A. Lindbergh showed what happened when the hick went global. Fitzgerald believed in his heart of hearts in a turn-of-the-century ethic. Lindbergh believed more disastrously in turn-of-the-century geography. Both of them helped to destroy the world of their childhood. Neither could quite throw off the influence of a boyhood in the Western Marches.

Lindbergh was born in Detroit in 1902, the son of a Minnesota congressman and a Detroit chemistry teacher. His father had actually been raised in a log cabin, where his days were enlivened by folk tales of Indians building fires on men's stomachs, by the occasional materialization of flesh-and-blood Sioux. Lindbergh absorbed prejudices with his daily breakfast egg, unfortunate in one fated to hasten the advent of the jet age. The training of the boy produced a man with a chronic intellectual myopia which kept him from ever seeing the big picture.

In 1906 his father was elected to Congress, where he remained for eight years. Congressman Lindbergh was one of the founders of Minnesota's Farmer-Labor Party, an organization with a deep-dyed mistrust of everything east of the Alleghenies. He was the author of such political tracts as *Why Is Your Country at War?* and *The Economic Pinch*. As he and his son fished for bass in the headwaters of the Mississippi, he regaled the boy with the iniquities of the Atlantic seaboard. Tariffs, monopolies, the "money trust," big business, high interest rates, European loans, and "foreign entanglements" were lumped together in the Lindbergh lexicon as evil machinations of the city slicker. Young Charles was brought up with a fear of the Lorelei lure of European propaganda designed to arouse the bellicose instincts of impressionable young Midwesterners.

On one point the elder Lindbergh proved to be a clear-eyed prophet. "Charles, you're young," the senior Lindbergh was wont to remark. "You'll live to see great changes. They may not come in my lifetime, but they will in yours."[1]

At the age of twenty Lindbergh left the University of Wisconsin to enroll as a flying student in Nebraska. The airplane was still a Sunday fairground attraction. Lindbergh's tales of his early days as an aviator make romantic reading. As a "wing walker," he learned the secret of standing on the wing of a looping plane or hanging by his teeth from the landing gear. On barnstorming tours he often went for weeks without touching an airport, bringing his plane down in cornfields, spending nights in haystacks. Once he landed before the eyes of an astonished citizenry in the middle of a public square.

In 1925 he was commissioned as an army air mail pilot with the rank of captain. By the time he took off for Paris, he had made four emergency parachute jumps from disabled planes.

When Raymond Orteig offered a $25,000 prize for the first New York–Paris flight, Lindbergh interested a group of St. Louis businessmen in financing the venture. The experiences of his competitors were discouraging. One plane crashed before the take-off, another on a test flight. Two of the world's greatest flyers took off from Paris and were lost.

Nonetheless, on May 20, 1927, Lindbergh took off across the Atlantic at the controls of the *Spirit of St. Louis*. He was equipped with five sandwiches, a quart canteen of water, and charts with all the unnecessary areas cut out of them.

So precarious was the equilibrium of the plane that Lindbergh dispensed with such excess baggage as toothbrush and parachute. On the evening of May 21, Lindbergh landed at Le Bourget airfield. He had covered a distance of nearly 3,600 miles in the record time of 33 hours and 29 minutes.

He had naïvely looked forward to taking "a day or two off to walk through the streets and buildings of Paris."[2] He was hard put to find time for so much as a tour of the Louvre. He was met by tens of thousands of men and women breaking down fences, pushing past guards. A cheering crowd lifted the flyer to its shoulders. A swarm of souvenir hunters swooped down on the plane, cracking the wood and ripping the fabric. A French newspaper reporter was carried by mistake, kicking and protesting, to the official reception committee.

In Europe Lindbergh was showered with honors and greeted with a pomp and circumstance hitherto reserved for royalty. His modesty in the face of all this led the *New York Times* to suspect the intervention of cosmic forces. "He could not have been improved on if made to order by an omnipotent and discerning fate."[3]

He came home to face the long ordeal of deification. When Lindbergh returned to New York his triumph outdid the wildest dreams of the Caesars. Four million people turned out to welcome him; 1,800 tons of paper fell on the city in the Big Blizzard of '27. He was decorated with more medals, commissioned as a colonel by the President, commemorated in a popular song, "Lucky Lindy," and deluged with 500,000 letters, 75,000 telegrams, and two freight-car loads of press clippings.

His mailbag was crammed with mash notes, proposals of marriage, offers of movie contracts, plans for flights to the moon and communication with Mars. Would-be Lindberghs popped up all over the country with requests for financial assistance. Inventors plagued him with ideas for "sure-fire" inventions, samples of which included perpetual-motion machines; recipes for making gold from sea water; a device for preventing horses from running away, with a strategically placed boat davit to hoist the renegade animal off the ground. An owner of a small-town garage, soliciting advice on leaky valves, threw in some uncomplimentary asides on the trials of living with one's mother-in-law. "Better write me direct to the shop and don't mention the mother-in-law," he concluded cautiously.

Nearly one letter in twenty contained a poem. The flight awakened in the American public a long-dormant lyric gift. "Fair haired Apollo, your meteoric traverse of the sea, your transcendent victory over boundless space shall thunder down the avenues of time," enthused one correspondent.[4]

"The Flying Fool," by H. I. Phillips, struck a eulogistic note which was echoed in thousands of poems dedicated variously to "Slim," "the White Knight," the "Lone Eagle," or the hero's mother.

> "The Flying Fool," a youth with nerves of steel;
>   Devoid of any boastfulness and bluff,
> A modest lad whose manner makes you feel
> That, come what may, the kid will do his stuff. . . .[5]

It was an evil day for the harried newspaper editors who presided over columns of unsolicited verse. The *New York Times* noted waspishly the recurrence of the words "east and west," "dare and do," "red and blue," in the rhyme schemes. The *New York World* was more tolerant, admitting "the occasion is not for syllogization but for rhapsody" and urging the poets to "sharpen their pencils and do their best; if they have a turn for music let them write tunes to their lyrics and sing them to ukulele accompaniment. Only don't send them to us."[6]

Besides offering a stimulus to the arts, Lindbergh accelerated the pulse of industry. Manufacturers of airplane parts took full pages in the papers to express their gratitude for his services as a press agent. Vacuum Oil stock went up the day after a newspaper advertisement acknowledged his debt to Gargoyle.

President Coolidge dug up a résumé of Lindbergh's character from the War Department files, which sounded less like a description of a human being than a model for the ideal

Eagle Scout. Newspaper reporters turned from the Hall-Mills murder and the Pig Woman to the temperate, modest youth who embodied all the better qualities of the American boy-man. "Women," said the *Washington Post,* "sought to take this man and embrace him. The men in turn, experienced quick pulses of the heart and thought wistfully of things they might have done, things they would like to do, things they wished they had the nerve to do."[7]

Quizzed by the *Literary Digest* in February 1928, 363 out of 682 boys of Belleville, New Jersey, voted for Lindbergh as the person they would most like to be if they were not themselves. President Coolidge, the runner-up, polled only 110 votes. Bringing up the rear with two votes apiece were Benito Mussolini and "my Dad."

Lindbergh's admirers developed the odd habit of sending gifts to him. By 1929 there were enough to fill a special section of the Jefferson Memorial Building in St. Louis. The trophies included such memorabilia as an airplane cut from a single diamond; a reminder from the Woman's Christian Temperance Union of Cuba that "success and glory are trophies of pure living and abstinence from alcohol"; a plaque representing the flyer as a triumphant Icarus, nude except for a nimbus formation around his loins. There were hundreds of medallions, portraits, etchings, lithographs, and busts of the flyer. "If these varied works share anything in common," said the *Literary Digest,* "it is an idealized vacuity of expression."[8]

It was Lindbergh's fate to inspire idealized vacuity in every branch of the arts. Kurt Weill and Bert Brecht commemorated the flight in a cantata in 1931. A review in the *Boston Transcript* described its heavy overload of symbolism:

> The chorus bids Lindbergh into his plane and off on his job. He (solo tenor) describes himself, the machine, the equipment
>
> The flight begins. A solo-voice cries for news. A chorus answers as if it were telegraphing from a ship that has heard Lindbergh's motor. Then ensues the first imaginative interlude . . . the aviator's dialogue with fog; (male chorus), snow (soprano voices); sleet (bass voice)

The narrative is resumed. Baritone and chorus, as American newspapers, proclaim Lindbergh's luck. He himself, less optimistic, hears them saying "He's coming." Therefore he must come—the second imaginative interlude. The third, after a pessimistic chorus from the Parisian press, is a solicitous and affectionate monologue to his motor.

In addition, the cantata suffered from problems with the language barrier:

Brecht's text runs in everyday German, or in what he rightly or wrongly believes to be everyday American (Mr. Stokowski uses an English version, not too well made, by George Antheil, another and less fortunate experimenter.).[9]

Similar difficulties beset a Sacha Guitry version of the event which flopped after a brilliant premiere in 1929. It was notable for a badly trained ballet and some Parisian gamins with Cockney accents who assured a policeman, "We weren't doing any 'arm, sir." It had the inevitable galaxy of tempests, winds, and fogs, and the *New York Sun* described it as "peopled among other things with supernatural beings who concoct wicked plots against the knight in shining armor whenever the scene shifters have a particularly troublesome set to arrange."[10]

These two creative efforts were evidence of Lindbergh's enormous following among foreigners. The French hailed his achievement as marking the end of an era of selfish nationalism. The Lindbergh smile still magically erased all memories of the grubbier aspects of American foreign policy. Early in 1928, he went on a good-will tour of Latin America, and an observer from *El Diario* of San Salvador commented in plain language, "Whoever chose Lindbergh to bear the olive branch to Latin America is to be congratulated on his foresight and tact. This is why we strongly doubt that the thought originated in the mind of Mr. Coolidge or of his faithful Secretary of State."[11]

It was a British journalist, P. W. Wilson, who analyzed Lindbergh's hypnotic appeal for people of all nations.

> Every era has its allotted evangel. The Middle
> Ages built churches. Reformers read the Bible. Our
> faith is locomotion. We believe with all our hearts in
> the happiness of going somewhere else . . . To fly
> is thus a supreme mysticism. . . . Charles A. Lindbergh is our Elijah.[12]

Only a few Cassandras foresaw that the conquest of space could be a mixed blessing. One was an unknown editorial writer for the *Binghamton Press and Leader:* "The United States is no longer invulnerable, because Lindbergh has destroyed the fiction that the distance factor of the oceans protects us."[13]

This still, small voice was drowned out in the swelling chorus of self-praise. Heywood Broun spoke for the vast majority of his countrymen in one of the many cocky editorials variously addressed to posterity or the Diety. He wrote in the *New York World:*

> A common foe of all mankind has been defeated
> . . . Nature can't bully us indefinitely with wind
> and wave and peril of vast oceans. One of our boys
> has put the angry sea in its place. The big pond,
> hey? Why, after this, it is a puddle, and we may
> step across as neatly as Elizabeth upon the cloak of
> Walter Raleigh.[14]

The job of eliminating war and hatred had been hopefully expected of every new form of transportation since the opening of the New York subway system. Contemporary cartoons showed doves of peace flying along the transatlantic air lanes. It took a decade for the public to realize what a hopeless burden they were putting on their evangel, or what a lot they were expecting of the T.W.A. noon plane to Paris.

The Lindbergh fever was a symptom of many things. He satisfied the spiritual cravings of a materialistic people who

found the old God passé. He was the last late flower of a dying
Victorian optimism. He was the idol of an age which was confident of its power to cross the final frontiers of knowledge,
whose high school textbooks had proclaimed a few years before that "there are eight riddles of the universe and seven of
them have already been solved."[15]

Lindbergh was the first to tire of his honeymoon with the
public. He said a flat "No" to all attempts to commercialize
his achievement, except for a few of the more respectable
offers—airline stock, writing payments from the *New York
Times*, a $25,000 prize for his Latin American flight; royalties
from his book *We*. He chafed at the concern of oversolicitous
admirers who tried to "ground" him. People pawed at him, and
he angrily pulled away. The fetishism of the public revolted
him—the women in St. Louis, who, after he had eaten at an
outdoor table, fought over the damp corncobs he had chewed
and left beside his plate.

Lindbergh's marriage was a crucial defeat in his long, bitter
battle for privacy. While in Mexico he met Anne Morrow, the
daughter of the ambassador Dwight Morrow. On May 27, 1929,
the two were married in a secret ceremony at the Morrow
home in Englewood, New Jersey. Ten days later, aboard the
yacht *Mouette*, a tabloid reporter ran "the world's most elusive
newlyweds" to earth. Later Lindbergh whitened with rage
when a reporter inquired if his wife were pregnant yet. This
desire for seclusion was taken as a betrayal of trust by a country which believed that fame conferred upon its victims the
responsibility of providing bulletins on everything from their
sex patterns to their favorite breakfast foods.

In the early years of their marriage, the Lindberghs flew
as a team. In Tokyo an unmanageable mob threatened to over-
run their car. When they visted the Kurile Islands, hairy
Ainus crawled out of caves and burrows to see them. The press
chronicled their doings under such headlines as "Two Chutes
Instead of One," "We Three Win Another Record," "Banzai
for the Eagle Man and His Mate." One of the minor prices
the Lindberghs paid for fame was having their every move
described in ornithological terms.

Then on March 1, 1932, came the story which pushed everything else off the front page—news of the kidnapping of the

Lindberghs' first child, Charles Augustus Lindbergh, Jr. The Lindberghs received 100,000 letters of advice and an army of reporters converged on their home to cover "the greatest human interest story of the decade." On May 12, 1932, the search came to a tragic end with the discovery of the child's body in a shallow grave near the Lindbergh home.

On September 19, 1934, a Bronx carpenter, Bruno Richard Hauptmann, was discovered to have a large amount of the ransom money in his possession. Early in 1935 he went on trial for his life in Flemington, New Jersey.

Later in the thirties, Lindbergh was to display an arrogant contempt for his countrymen. It must be said that the Lindbergh kidnapping trial afforded an unparalleled view of them at their worst. The *Literary Digest* reported that "more correspondents, sob sisters, sports writers, psychiatrists" crowded into Flemington than had represented American papers in France during the First World War. Restaurants advertised "Lindbergh steaks" and "Hauptmann beans." On Sundays thousands of visitors flocked into the courtroom to pose on the judge's bench, and "a locust plague of cheap vendors traffic with the mob as at a country fair."[16]

As the court awaited the verdict, a holiday crowd screamed at the jurors, "Kill him! Send him to the chair!" Defense lawyer Reilly joined Adela Rogers St. John in a rendition of "When Irish Eyes Are Smiling." At eleven o'clock the jurors returned a verdict of guilty, and Hauptmann was sentenced to die in March in the Trenton death house. The jurors celebrated until 3 A.M. and were said by *Newsweek* to be considering a "dignified stage appearance."[17]

Hauptmann's execution was actually delayed until April 3, 1936. The Lindberghs were not around for the event. A reporter tried to sideswipe their car on a New Jersey road in an effort to get a picture of their second son Jon. There was a second kidnap alarm when a canvas-covered truck was seen in front of the Morrow home in Englewood, which proved to contain movie photographers. The Lindberghs sailed secretly for England on December 22, 1935. They had seen enough of the show to decide that they didn't want to stick around for the last act.

When Lindbergh next returned to American shores, he

seemed to be talking an alien tongue. In 1936 and 1938 Lindbergh visted Germany, and was much impressed by what he saw of the German Air Force. On his second trip he was decorated in the name of the Führer, with a Nazi Eagle, which he later removed from his collection of trophies. He was such an enthusiastic salesman for the Luftwaffe that he was even accused of engineering the capitulation at Munich.

When war broke out in 1939, he became the leading advocate of a neutrality that strongly favored Germany. In speeches between 1939 and 1942 he advanced the opinion that America should abandon the British, retire behind her natural barriers, and root enthusiastically as the Nazis conveniently destroyed the Russians.

Other articles which Lindbergh wrote at the time extolled not only German culture but German political ideas and racial theories. "As revolutions go," he was quoted by Roger Butterfield in *Life*, "this one has been pretty orderly."[18] In an article written for the November 1939 *Reader's Digest*, he called upon the Western nations to create a wall of "arms and race" against the invasion of inferior blood.[19] This strange tract described aviation as "one of those priceless possessions which permit the white race to live at all in a pressing sea of yellow, black and brown."[20]

England was said by Lindbergh to be doomed. The future was to belong to the supermen of the Wehrmacht instead of to the decadent democracies, for "no system of representation can succeed when the voice of weakness is equal to the voice of strength."[21] The parliamentary process was to join the old Southern mansion as the nostalgic relic of a charming but moribund society.

At the height of the isolationist-interventionist debate, Lindbergh was periodically boomed for President. He became the most important spokesman for the isolationist America First— an organization which numbered in its membership many sincere devotees of the anti-war cause, as well as such native Fascists as Gerald L. K. Smith, Joe McWilliams, and Lawrence Dennis. At one big rally in Madison Square Garden, *Life's* reporter detected a strong Teutonic inflection to the choruses of "The Star-Spangled Banner."

In September 1941, Lindbergh killed himself politically. At
a rally in Des Moines, he followed the German propaganda
line almost to the letter, in deploring Jewish infiltration of
American life, and naming the Jews as one of the "three most
important groups who have been pressing this country toward
war." The second was the British; the third, the Roosevelt
administration.[22] This outburst cost Lindbergh the support of
even the isolationist Hearst papers. The final blow came when
Pearl Harbor was bombed by Orientals who were unaware of
the airplane's Aryan patent.

Lindbergh resigned his army commission after a brush with
President Roosevelt. When he offered his services to the War
Department, it was hinted that he might serve his country
better in some civilian capacity unless he repudiated his views.
He refused, and in the spring of 1942 he went to Willow Run
as an adviser to Henry Ford.

Years later, with the rise of Russia, the old Lindbergh credo
was wistfully revived. "If only we had made a deal with
Germany instead of fighting the war," the argument ran. The
problems of coexistence with a Prussianized Europe were
frequently glossed over when the wisdom of hindsight combined with the wisdom of the third Martini.

Before Pearl Harbor, Major Alexander de Seversky had put
his finger on the flaw in the Lindbergh logic. "Colonel Lindbergh apparently bases his judgment on existing aeronautical
equipment, and on an immediate strategic picture, which may
well prove to be ephemeral. I think he has failed to grasp the
full potentialities of air power; he has failed to understand
the revolution in warfare that it is forcing relentlessly on the
world, the United States included."[23] It was not until the
mid-forties that the Lone Eagle fully appreciated the effects
of his victory over the Big Pond.

In 1948, Lindbergh felt the sudden compulsion to "communicate belief" which, at various times, had punctuated long
periods of silence. The result of this compulsion was a spiritual
travelogue entitled *Of Flight and Life*. Three episodes during
the war had made a profound impression upon the author. He
had had a narrow escape during an altitude test at Willow
Run. A close call with a Japanese plane in the Pacific had

brought him face to face with the specter of "Oriental capture." A view of the ruined German cities had clouded his
earlier roseate view of a Teutonic Valhalla. These three events
had brought Lindbergh to a recognition of man's increased
capacity for destruction—a home truth which he had failed to
grasp when he tried to fit the isolationism of Washington's era
into a world which had long since outgrown it. "In the past,"
he wrote, "time and space and man's own weakness localized
his destructive power. . . . The oceans protected us as the
Channel protected England in a seaborne age. They can no
longer do so in a rocket atomic era."[24]

Lindbergh's answer was a sermon against the materialism
which had brought the world to this state. He appealed for
a return to God, and to the much-neglected things of the
spirit.

This was a new development in his thinking, yet the outlines of the old Lindbergh cosmos were still recognizable.
Lindbergh shrugged off the U.N. as "Utopian" because of the
power it gave to the masses of Asia. As usual, his awareness
of the rest of the world lagged one continent behind the times.
Asia was still consigned to exterior darkness, though Europe,
pitted at last against the Soviet Union, was belatedly permitted
inside the *cordon sanitaire.*

The atom bomb was to be the exclusive property of the
American people. America was to lead the world in the harmony of "body, mind and spirit," which was the new Lindbergh prescription for psychic health. The doctrine of universal
equality remained a "doctrine of death." The earth was still to
be ruled by supermen. The only difference was that Americans
were to take over where the Luftwaffe and the Wehrmacht
had failed. Whatever Lindbergh's debt to Nietszche and
Wotan, whatever one might think of the devious route by
which he reached his conclusions, it was difficult to deny the
existence of the problem as he presented it—the problem of a
world in which "time has become disjointed . . . where man
still ages with the seasons, while science brings more changes
to his life in a single generation than it underwent in the
previous thousand years."[25]

Others were alarmed by the descendants of the *Spirit of St.*

Louis—the intercontinental jet bomber and the missile with the nuclear warhead. Others were appalled by what had happened when the scientists "reached into the future and took the problem of long range rockets and atomic explosives from our great grandchildren's hands, and placed it like a burning coal in our own."[26] Since the landing at Le Bourget, both Lindbergh and his public had lost their first careless rapture over "the supreme happiness of going somewhere else."

In 1949, *Newsweek* published an article on the hero's doings. He was at last enjoying his long-sought anonymity as a consultant on a secret project for the United States Air Force. *Newsweek's* mildly laudatory tone brought forth a revealing cross section of reader opinion. "It's a relief to read something about him that isn't derogatory," wrote one correspondent. "You are to be congratulated," said another. "Now how about a eulogy on Grover Cleveland Bergdoll or Tokyo Rose?" From a third, "Your article . . . amused and annoyed me. I don't think many people care."[27]

By the fifties, the Lindberghs' tempestuous past was largely forgotten. Lindbergh was quietly recommissioned as a brigadier general on April 7, 1954. His wife continued to pursue her literary career. In the early thirties she had chronicled their adventures together in the air, in *North to the Orient* and *Listen, the Wind.* In the early forties, with *The Wave of the Future,* she had followed her husband at least part of the way on a more dangerous journey of the intellect. Now, matching her husband's contemplative mood, she produced a best-seller entitled *Gift from the Sea,* which introduced the housewife to the rewards of reflection, with the apparently startling news that it is good to get off by oneself every now and then.

Dearly Beloved, in 1962, gave what was for many an equally revealing insight into the truths behind familiar things. In this novel the guests at a wedding are moved to reflect upon their own marriages. They are also mouthpieces for Anne Lindbergh's own matrimonial philosophy—involving the interdependence of marital partners, the vital role of children—the fact that marriage may be a gamble but is still an honorable estate.

"No writer speaks to everyone," said Orville Prescott of this

work, "and few indeed speak to as many as Mrs. Lindbergh."
Her "quivering sensibility and her quintessentially feminine
turn of mind" are, in his opinion, responsible for her success.
Prescott also suspects that millions of women "flatter themselves that they share some of Mrs. Lindbergh's delicate per-
ceptions."[28]

The later years of the Lindberghs' own marriage have been
uneventful. They are now the owners of a house in Vevey,
Switzerland. In June 1961, their daughter Anne was presented
to society with several other debutantes at a "glittering ball"
held in the Empire Salons of the Versailles Palace.[29] Another
milestone was the birth of a baby girl to son Jon in December
of the same year.[30] In simpler ages, such homely happenings
might have been recorded in the back of a family Bible. In the
Golden Era of Publicity, they were relegated to obscure squibs
in the *New York Times*.

Flashbacks to high points of the Lindbergh career occasionally create a ripple of excitement. Publication of George Wal-
lers' *Kidnap* in 1961, and a subsequent paperback edition,
subjected the Lindberghs to the fate of all, whose past can
brighten up a Sunday supplement. It is a pity for the Lindberghs that the kidnapping has taken its place in history along
with the Hal-Mills Case, Lizzie Borden's ax and the amours of
Evelyn Nesbitt.

In 1953, Lindbergh also hit the best-seller list when he re-
told the story of his flight in the Pulitzer Prize winning book,
The Spirit of St. Louis. In 1957, a screen version of the story
was released by Warner Brothers. A poll was taken at a sneak
preview, and the painful discovery was made that no one
under forty knew or cared about Lindbergh. A big publicity
campaign was accordingly planned to drum up business for the
picture. Tab Hunter, a matinee idol of missile-vintage, was
sent around the country on a speaking tour to revitalize the
Lindbergh legend.

In making *The Spirit of St. Louis*, Warner Brothers faced
the problems which had defeated Lindbergh's earlier eulogists.
James Stewart in the lead was a diffident and appealing hero;
but writers were confronted with the specter of ending up with
a two-hour monologue; and there were difficulties of creating

suspense in a situation which could not avoid telegraphing its ending.

The producers shied away from anthropomorphic elements and chats between man and machine. Excitement was created quite effectively by the onset of bad weather, motor trouble, and sleep. A replica of a housefly was constructed at a cost of $100,000—to whom James Stewart addressed various ripostes. The housefly, though inarticulate, buzzed about in the cockpit, creating a mild illusion of conversational give-and-take.

The long interludes over the ocean were broken up by flash-backs to the barnstorming days of Lucky Slim. There were fine shots of Lindbergh landing a disreputable Jenny on an army flying field; Lindbergh changing planes in mid-air at a flying circus; Lindbergh bantering with simple folk who said the durn thing wouldn't fly—the suspender salesman whose approach to the problem of ascent and descent was embodied in the slogan "We hold up the pants of the Middle West."

An age of innocence was brought to life in the camaraderie of air-borne nomads; in the faded overalls of the fairground crowds; in the figure of an Atlantic fisherman staring open-mouthed at the big gull. Innocence was lost in the final sequences with searchlights sweeping the sky at Le Bourget —with the jerky rerun of a 1927 newsreel of the great paper parade. One left the theater disturbed by the knowledge of what lay beyond the happy ending—as one often feels for the boy and girl whose troubles are just beginning with the final fade-out.

Lindbergh and Scott Fitzgerald were denizens of the same Eden. In an age of hope, in their different ways they both pursued Gatsby's green light. For Fitzgerald in the early years in New York, for Lindbergh approaching Le Bourget, "the dream must have seemed so close that he could hardly fail to grasp it." Like Gatsby, neither of them knew that it was already behind them, "somewhere in that vast obscurity be-yond the city, where the dark fields of the republic rolled on under the night."

Once Lindbergh had had a rare flash of intuition. He re-called that, as he approached the European continent, he felt like a "Western pioneer when he saw barbed-wire fence lines encroaching on his open plains. The success of his venture brought the end of the life he loved."[31]

It was perhaps the only inkling he had of the world he was helping to create. The hopes and illusions of the age of flight had died with Lindbergh's slow decanonization . . . the isolationist who abolished boundaries . . . the hermit who put an end to privacy . . . the smiling boy, the frozen-faced man who winced at the sight of a flash bulb . . . the youth for whom "science alone was tangible and clear,[32] who became the Machine Age Savonarola.

"How do I like New York? O, inexpressibly! Yes, the
Public Library is! No, the subway *isn't*. O, the St.
Patrick Cathedral!—Quite too sweet, I assure you! And
the view—charming! charming! So many roofs and
things, you know; warships, and chimneys, and brewery
signs—so inspiring! Yes, to the Madison Avenue
Presbyterian! Dr. Coffin is *wonderful*, O, my dear,—
tremendous!" A letter from Edna St. Vincent Millay to
her mother, February 9, 1913 (*Letters of Edna St.
Vincent Millay*)

" 'I'll go out and get my child,' he said. I did not
realize at first that this meant Edna." "Edna St. Vincent
Millay—A Memoir," by Edmund Wilson, *The Nation*,
April 19, 1952

4

Our Own Latchkeys

EDNA ST. VINCENT MILLAY

To a whole generation, Edna St. Vincent Millay represented
Bohemianism, the single standard, the Greenwich Village odd-
ball, feminism on the march. Her literary contributions were
credited with having sold free love to the women's clubs. Born
in the 1890's, this stormy petrel grew up in Rockport, Maine,
in a world as placid as a millpond.

In Edna's youth wars were considered the romantic prerog-
ative of less civilized times. A hundred-mile journey was a
momentous undertaking. There were middy blouses, gaslights,
corsets, *St. Nicholas Magazine, Dolly Dimples* and *Rollo on
the Atlantic.* Later the poet was to recall the minor crosses of
a Victorian girlhood: "the beautiful afternoons dissipated in
sitting on the porch taking out long stitches and trying to put
in short ones . . . evening after evening embittered by op-

timistic juvenile literature—as if it were not bad enough to
have to be good without having to read about being good."[1]

Negro lynchings and Asiatic famines barely caused a ripple
in the millpond. School children learned that Kipling and
James Whitcomb Riley were the greatest of living poets. The
bars of a nearby insane asylum walled off a totally alien race of
people. The Millay girls never saw their own conflicts mirrored in the faces of the inmates. They never reflected with a
later generation, "There, but for the grace of God, go I."

Edna's mother was something out of the ordinary among
Victorian parents. Edna, or "Vincent" as her family called her,
was the oldest of three sisters. Norma was to become an
actress, Kathleen a writer. Edna's mother had divorced the
girls' father, a school superintendent with a fatal love for
games of chance. Mrs. Millay, a registered nurse, brought the
girls up in "gay and courageous poverty."

The Millays were an unusually happy family. "Some parents
of children that are 'different' have so much to reproach themselves with," Edna wrote to her mother, "but not you Great
Spirit."[2] Mrs. Millay anticipated the Bohemianism of her
daughters. She taught Edna to write poetry at the age of four,
to play the piano at the age of seven, to respect the conventions of art rather than the conventions of behavior. Edna contributed to *St. Nicholas* until she was disqualified by the
eighteen-year age limit. In her teens, through the columns of
The Lyric Year, she burst on the adult literary world.

She submitted her poem *Renascence* to a *Lyric Year* competition under the name "E. St. Vincent Millay." The editor
wrote back to "E. St. Vincent Millay, Esq." saying that he expected *Renascence* to win a $500 prize. *Renascence* finished
fourth with no award. It appeared, nonetheless, in *The Lyric
Year* in 1912. Orrick Johns' *Second Avenue* won first prize, an
error which even the author immediately recognized.

Miss Caroline B. Dow, executive director of a Y.W.C.A. in
New York City, heard Miss Millay reciting *Renascence* at some
local function in Maine. She was so carried away that she ar-
ranged to provide funds for Edna's education at Vassar. Arthur
Davison Ficke and Witter Bynner, two young Iowa poets, read
Renascence and wrote to the author, "This is Thanksgiving

Day and we thank you." Arthur Ficke compounded the error
of thinking that the poet was a man. "No sweet young thing
of twenty ever ended a poem precisely where this one ends;
it takes a brawny male of forty-five to do that."[3]

On December 5, 1912, Edna wrote back: "Gentlemen: I
must convince you of your error; my reputation is at stake.
I simply will not be a 'brawny male.' Not that I have an
aversion to brawny males; *au contraire, au contraire*. But I
cling to my femininity!"[4] As the years wore on, both Mr. Ficke
and Mr. Bynner were to become acutely aware of her sex.

Edna Millay graduated from Camden High School in 1909.
She did not enter Vassar until 1914. Soon after she was unleashed on Poughkeepsie, she began to complain. She complained about the ashcans on the Vassar sidewalks; about the
faculty's furtive snooping into the students' love lives; about
the college policy of balancing this spiritual saltpeter with
bribes of Sunday ice cream.

She got a lot out of Vassar in spite of herself. She contributed to *Forum, Century*, and *Poetry*. She won a prize for
her poem *Interim* and a cup for her poem *Suicide*. She went
in for amateur dramatics, played Marchbanks in Shaw's *Can-
dida*, wrote and played the lead in a verse play, *The Princess
Marries the Page. The Lamp and the Bell*, another verse play,
written just after she graduated, was performed at Vassar in
1921. She composed the marching song for the class of 1917.

She almost lost her part in the commencement exercises
because of a technicality about overnight leaves. A wave of
petitions from her classmates melted the faculty into reinstat-
ing her. Even rebellion was tempered by her Down East practicality. "She was true," according to one biographer, Elizabeth
Atkins, "to the Shelleyan tradition . . . she felt that bullying
a well-meaning college into expelling her was a necessary part
of testing her poetic nature. But her instinct for thrift showed
itself here, and she did not seriously court expulsion until her
four-year course was complete and she had only the formalities
of graduation to forfeit."[5]

The poetic dramas of her Vassar period are studded with
schoolgirlisms. The mythical kingdom of Fiori, setting for *The
Lamp and the Bell*, sounds a lot like Poughkeepsie. The theme

of *The Lamp and the Bell* is, according to Elizabeth Atkins, "one of burning concern to students at any girls' school"— whether a feminine friendship can be healthy and lasting. The heroine is a princess whose stepmother takes a dim view of her attachment to a young lady of the court. The princess proves the constancy of her friendship by giving up her lover to her friend, by submitting to the importunities of a foul seducer who demands her virtue as a price for letting her go to the friend's deathbed. Happily the foul seducer is killed before he can execute his master plan. In viewing the extraordinary lengths to which the princess was willing to go on behalf of the young lady of the court, one wonders if the prurient stepmother was not right to be mildly alarmed.

Both *The Princess Marries the Page* and *The Lamp and the Bell* were written in Shakespearean English. Arthur Ficke sparked the young poet's interest in the Elizabethans. It is questionable whether he did her much of a service. It took Greenwich Village to purge her vocabulary of "towers" and "scullions" and the "prithees," the "thous," and the "harks."

After graduation in 1917, she went to live in a tiny room on Waverly Place. To keep the wolf from the door Edna wrote for *Vanity Fair* and *Ainslee's Magazine* under the pseudonym Nancy Boyd. She acted without pay with the Provincetown Players, and took part in a Theatre Guild production. Her family joined her, and Mother Millay took to garret life like a duck to water.

In 1921 *Second April* came out. *A Few Figs from Thistles* was kicked off in the same year by the four lines which were to become the watchword of Flaming Youth.

> My candle burns at both ends;
> It will not last the night;
> But ah, my foes, and oh, my friends—
> It gives a lovely light![6]

Like Fitzgerald, Millay enjoyed almost instantaneous recognition. In 1923, *The Harp Weaver and Other Poems* won a Pulitzer Prize. *The Buck in the Snow* was less well received in 1928. A poetic drama, *Aria da Capo,* written in 1920, was put on by the Provincetown Players. *The King's Henchman,* written in 1927, became the libretto for an opera, with music by Deems Taylor. In 1931, *Fatal Interview* marked the end of her Zeitgeist success.

Sometime after Miss Millay hit Greenwich Village, the war drew to a close. She, with Floyd Dell and John Reed, celebrated the false armistice by riding back and forth all night between New York and Staten Island.

> We were very tired; we were very merry—
> We had gone back and forth all night on the ferry.[7]

When she was in college, boys and girls had roared around in Model T's, shouting, "The past is a bucket of ashes." Now Flaming Youth was joyously obliterating the last of its parents' hypocrisies. "The aim of art," according to Elizabeth Atkins, was "to pierce through callous cuticle and jaded areas to a nerve that could still jump." The world was paraphrasing the lines of Keats: truth was sex; sex truth; that was all one needed to know. The behaviorists were earnestly discussing "thought as a laryngeal process." Dadaism swept the continent. Amy Lowell advised the folks back home: "Don't reason. . . . Don't experience emotion. Simply drink in the nowness of now. Smell it. Taste it. Touch it. Listen to it. Look at it." Truth, according to the more succinct Jean Cocteau, points to her sex.[8]

As Millay the poet made her first success, her alter ego Nancy Boyd, the social satirist, found "everybody sitting around looking frank, and spading about in one another's ill-smelling unconsciousnesses."[9] Nothing was as simple as it had been in the days of simple Nervous Prostration. When in *Second April* Miss Millay composed elegies to a dead school chum, scholars invested her sorrow with philosophical implications. According to Elizabeth Atkins grief provided her with a "bulwark against the doubt of her own existence suggested by an utterly skeptical age." As *The Harp Weaver* appeared, John Barrymore was exposing the Freudian neuroses of Hamlet and a wave of biographies revealed the geniuses of the past as victims of unsavory complexes. Miss Millay chose this timely

moment to put her psyche under the microscope. In the poem
Scrub she gives us a view of her hard childhood:

> Is it that a wind too strong
> Bent my back when I was young,
> Is it that I fear the rain
> Lest it blister me again.[10]

Wry and bitter as this poem is, it is refreshingly free of the
insistent whine of a later generation. *The Harp Weaver* itself
is a tribute to her mother. Never is Mrs. Millay forced to take
the rap for her daughter's numerous neuroses. This somewhat
Spartan view places *The Harp Weaver* in the Early Snake Pit
period of twentieth-century letters.

Edna Millay attempted to echo the Greek chorus of doom
whose keynote had been sounded by Ezra Pound. The war had
been fought, Pound said,

> For an old bitch gone in the teeth,
> For a botched civilization.

Try as she might, Millay could never quite go along with
this mood. In *The Buck in the Snow,* she was betrayed by her
lust for living into an expression of unfashionable hope.

> Not that it matters, not that my heart's cry
> Is potent to deflect our common doom,
> Or bind to truce in this ambiguous room
> The planets of the atom as they ply;
> But only to record that you and I,
> Like thieves that scratch the jewels from a tomb,
> Have gathered delicate love in hardy bloom
> Close under chaos,—I rise to testify.[11]

For the most part, however, Miss Millay had a talent for
capturing a popular mood, exceeded only by her love of unpopular causes. Her poetry often suffered from her pamphle-
teering activities. She was an ardent feminist. She was schooled
in a college where girls, born to the Republican fold, spent a
tempestuous four years on the barricades before settling down

to a life of community service with the P.T.A. and the League of Women Voters.

A few years before, the Vassar campus had been rocked by the activities of Inez Milholland, a militant champion of women's rights, who held clandestine feminist meetings in a graveyard abutting on the dormitories. Suspended from Vassar, she had finally died in 1917. *The Buck in the Snow* includes a tribute to Inez's "adventurous will," read at the unveiling of a statue of three pioneers in the cause of women's rights.

Miss Millay, champion of the oppressed, rushed also to the defense of Sacco and Vanzetti. She marched on Boston to protest the execution of these two anarchists accused of murdering a shoe factory paymaster. When one of her strong letters failed to produce a stay of execution she unleashed a few thunderbolts in the direction of Governor Fuller of Massachusetts. Five poems in *The Buck in the Snow* take him to task for his unsatisfactory response to hers of August 22, 1927:

> Cruel of heart, lay down my song.
> Your reading eyes have done me wrong.
> Not for you was the pen bitten,
> And the mind wrung, and the song written.[12]

It was suggested that the righteously wrathful Edna might really have gone to town on the theme of Governor Fuller in Hell.

The propagandist sank her teeth into the evils of nationalism in the drama *Aria da Capo*. One part of the action involved a pair of primitive shepherds who offered each other poisoned drinks and choked each other with necklaces of pearls in an orgy of symbolic manslaughter. Back at the ranch, bearing up the forces of civilized decadence, are the actors in a play-within-a-play about a shallow New York Pierrot and Columbine, overwhelmed with the futility of existence. The play reaches a tragicomic end with the final futility of the First World War.

Aria da Capo was a box-office flop, since the unsophisticated were never certain whether they were watching a tragedy or a comedy. It did, however, cause a renaissance of the stock literary figure—the tragic clown. The intelligentsia tried to goad Charlie Chaplin into playing Hamlet on the screen. Eliot was advised to use the style of the music-hall comedian as a medium for tragic utterance, while Cocteau fiddled around with adaptations of Shakespeare's tragedies to be played by chalk-faced pantaloons.[13]

The avant-garde was also impressed by *The King's Hench-man,* one of Miss Millay's less fortunate forays back through English history. The diction was that of Beowulf's day:

> Ywis, lad, let us thither, and give her
> the gift I bought
> 'Tis a wee thing, but belike 'twill gladden
> her eye[14]

The plot involved an act of early Anglo-Saxon hara-kiri—incomprehensible by contemporary standards. It was suggested that twentieth-century skeptics were driven to the theater by admiration for a primitive moral code which they envied, if they could not share it. Thirty years later, reading *The King's Henchman,* it is almost impossible to imagine *what* could have driven people to the theater. The Millay which stands up best is Millay in the most modern of moods. The gamine with her thumb to her nose is as enchanting today as she was in 1922.

> The fabric of my faithful love
> No power shall dim or ravel
> Whilst I stay here,—but, oh, my dear,
> If I should ever travel![15]

We forget the connoisseur of early English vowel changes, and remember the Maine girl casting an approving eye at a comely Italian on Macdougal Street. This was the Edna of the legend, described by her ferryboat playmate Floyd Dell as the "frivolous young woman with a brand new pair of dancing slippers and a mouth like a Valentine."

Miss Millay, John Peale Bishop, and Edmund Wilson once amused themselves by writing self-portraits. Miss Millay was enjoined by her family to decline an offer to print hers:

Hair which she still devoutly trusts is red.
Colorless eyes, employing
A childish wonder
To which they have no statistic
Title.
A large mouth,
Lascivious,
Ascetized by blasphemies.
A long throat,
Which will some day
Be strangled.
Thin arms,
In the summer-time leopard
With freckles.
A small body,
Unexclamatory,
But which,
Were it the fashion to wear no clothes,
Would be as well-dressed
As any—.[16]

Miss Millay's early success was in part a *succès de scandale.*
In *The Singing-Woman from the Wood's Edge,* she asked her
readers: "What should I be but a harlot and a nun?"

The reaction, according to Elizabeth Atkins, was felt from
coast to coast. Rumor fathered two bastards on the "harlot"
by the time the horrified whisper hit Nebraska.

In his autobiography *Homecoming,* Floyd Dell gives a
fascinating picture of the Village, where Edna and her chums
proclaimed their fealty to the god of sexual *laissez-faire.* In
1913, the old Liberal Club moved down to Macdougal Street.
John Reed, the father of American Communism, was a war
correspondent with Pancho Villa. Dell's piece, *Jessica Screams,*
appeared in the *Smart Set,* and was reported by its proud
author to have caused more canceled subscriptions than any
other story the magazine ever published. John Sloan was il-
lustrating Dell's stories with pictures of girls being beaten
by reform school matrons. *The Masses* was loudly trumpeting
the approach of a new order based on fun, truth, beauty,

realism, freedom, peace, feminism, and world revolution.

The Liberal Club balls at Webster Hall were annual pagan routs. A young playwright called Eugene O'Neill was causing a stir with the Provincetown Players. Alice Duer Miller was writing suffragette poems. Dorothy Day, another militant suffragette, imprisoned in Washington, went on a successful hunger strike to be accorded the rights of a political prisoner.

There were nude swimming parties on Staten Island, which ended with everybody reading poetry around a bonfire. There were gay times at the favorite Village saloons, the Working Girls' Home and the Hell Hole. The daughters of clergymen damned Anthony Comstock, dabbled verbally or actually in premarital love, and assuaged their guilt feelings with quotations from Edward Carpenter and Havelock Ellis. The marriage ceremony was looked on, in advanced circles, as a bourgeois, reactionary institution. Floyd Dell, however, capitulated to Mrs. Grundy. He married one "B. Marie"—a veteran suffragette who was once arrested in a charge upon the Metropolitan Opera House. Dell finally got the reputation of a hopeless counterrevolutionary; for, when B. Marie finally produced a baby, he found himself suddenly reluctant to hand it over to the state.

Political radicalism was inseparable from Advanced Thought. Hippolyte Havel, of Polly Holliday's restaurant, was an anarchist who greeted unsympathetic patrons as "bourgeois pigs." The Russian Revolution had wild repercussions along Macdougal Alley. John Reed went to Russia as correspondent for *The Liberator*, and wrote *Ten Days That Shook the World*. The *Masses* editors were tried twice under the Espionage Act—John Reed was later to resign from *The Liberator* because he did not wish to be "responsible for a magazine . . . cautious enough or non-revolutionary enough to get through the mails."

Reed settled for a time in Croton's Mount Airy. In Croton, Reed welcomed Floyd Dell into what he described as the "Mount Airy Soviet." Later he abandoned this ersatz Soviet for the real thing. He went to Russia, where he became a member of the executive committee of the Third International. He died in Moscow in October 1920 and "was buried with honor under the walls of the Kremlin."

Reed, with Dell, was one of Edna's companions on the ferryboat. On the night of the Armistice he discoursed on his adventures as a war correspondent and Communist conspirator. Dell recalls Miss Millay's reaction. "She said, like Desdemona, 'I love you for the dangers you have passed.'"

Dell attempted to advance Edna's education along revolutionary lines. Discoursing at the drop of a hat on pacifism, revolution, Soviet Russia, and psychoanalysis, "Edna proved to be an apt pupil. She was very much a revolutionary in all her sympathies and an ardent feminist. Once," Dell recalls, "I idly gave to Edna Millay a bronze button which had been left in my room, one of those which were awarded to the women and girls who had suffered arrest and imprisonment during the militant suffrage campaign. Tears came into her eyes. 'I would rather have the right to wear this than anything I can think of,' she said."[17]

The firebrand happily had her lighter moments. Some of the potboilers which Miss Millay turned out under the pseudonym of Nancy Boyd reveal features of Village life which have endured to this day. In "Art and How to Fake It," she imparts some advice to the art-lorn. One of her mythical correspondents named "Artistic" wrote that freethinkers shunned her studio despite a ukulele made of a cigar box, a leaky gas jet, a back number of a Russian newspaper, Chinese backscratchers, an army of cockroaches, and ashtrays to encourage the minor vice of smoking.

> The trouble [Edna replied] is with the ash-trays. Remove them. Get into the habit when alone, of crushing out your cigarette against the wall-paper, or dropping it on the floor and carelessly grinding it into the rug, or tossing it in the general direction of the fire-place, if you have one, being very sure never to look anxiously after it to see where it lands. This easy manner on your part will do more than anything else to put your guests at ease.

To a mythical landlady troubled by artists who failed to pay their rent, Miss Boyd advised:

The only thing to do is this. Buy a tin bank and place it on the table in the hall. Above it tack the following placard:

"FREE THINKERS
FREE LOVERS!
and FREE BOOTERS!

"If you have any heathen Pity on your Hearts Drop a Nickel in the Slot for the Starving Baby—Anarchists of Russia WHO DOES NOT CONTRIBUTE TO THE CAUSE OF ANARCHY IS MID-VICTORIAN!!!"

I think you will have no further trouble.

The influence of the mysterious East on advanced décor was discussed in yet another letter.

Dear Miss Boyd:

I am Chinese girl, but attend American college, Vassar, and enjoy very much. My room-mate is very nice girl, blue eye, yellow hair, very pretty, but in one fact very peculiar. She insist on decorating room with old awful Chinese screen and picture and little ugly dog and Buddha which is not true god, also old piece of weaving made long time ago all by hand and most uneven by dirty peasant, all thing such as in my country no nice family permit be found in attic. In vain I exhort, O cherished room-mate, behold beautiful American golden-oak rocking chair, behold wonderful miraculous American victrola, behold incomparable American imitation lace, all, all made by machinery and without flaw!—In vain, in vain. She tack up on wall unspeakable object such as my baby-brother could do better. She offend my artistic eye with hideous Chinese teak-wood table-atrocity. She break up our friendship. Advise me, most honourable Boyd. I am in despairs.

Signed,
CHU CHIN CHOW[18]

In 1921 *Vanity Fair*, which had published many of these pieces, offered Miss Millay an opportunity to go abroad as a correspondent. Two *Vanity Fair* editors, Edmund Wilson and John Peale Bishop, were in love with her. Both had refrained from seeing her off for fear of the unknowns they might have to confront on the pier.[19] For the morale of the Condé Nast offices alone, it was well that she got out of the country.

Edna was a faithful and provocative correspondent. . . . She confided in her family to an unusual extent. Few daughters would have written home such explicit references to the opposite sex. She describes to her mother a galaxy of suitors, including John Carter, "the boy from the Embassy who was travelling with me." Less tolerant parents even twenty years later would have found in this news item sufficient provocation to board the next steamer.

There was a flurry of correspondence with her Thanksgiving pen pal Witter Bynner, in which Edna got the notion that he wished to marry her. One of her letters to Bynner alludes to Arthur Davison Ficke. "It is true that I love Arthur. But we have all known that for some time,—haven't we?"[20] At the same time she was writing to Ficke:

> You, best of all, know how I feel about you, and always shall. No one can ever take your place with me. We know each other in such a terrible, certain windless way. You and I have almost achieved that which is never achieved: We sit in each other's souls.
>
> But that's no reason why I couldn't marry Hal [Bynner], and be happy with him. I love him, too. In a different way.[21]

The situation was complicated when one of her letters to Ficke was opened by Bynner by mistake; and by the fact which emerged after Miss Millay had decided to accept Bynner's proposal—that marriage was the farthest thing from his mind.[22]

Miss Millay's wanderings took her to Rome, Montenegro, Albania, and Hungary. In Albania "the boy from the Embassy" was in attendance. When she reached Vienna she was broke, and Arthur Ficke helped bail her out. The Austrian diet gave her one of the severe digestive attacks which were to plague her for the rest of her life. Back in Paris she sent for her mother, who displayed her usual accommodating spirit— accompanying her daughter to the most raucous of Paris parties, whipping up wholesome puddings in a rustic hut in England to combat the devastating after effects of too much cabbage and Schlagsahne.

The poet came back to the United States in 1923, much the worse for wear. In July 1923 she was married to Eugen Jan Boissevain, a prosperous Dutch coffee importer. While playing charades at Mount Airy, she and Boissevain had had the roles of lovers in a farcical invention both Rabelaisian and romantic. Floyd Dell quickly sensed that the partners in fantasy yearned to be partners in life. Boissevain was one of the few men who were temperamentally suited to life with Edna—having been broken in through a previous marriage with Edna's old idol Inez Milholland. The militant feminist went all soft and bridal at the last moment, and a ring was borrowed for the occasion from Boissevain's cook. Boissevain nursed his bride back to health with the care of a mother. From 1923 on he devoted his life to tending the flame of genius.

The Boissevains moved briefly to Bedford Street in the Village. After a round-the-world tour they finally bought a place called Steepletop, in Austerlitz, New York.

There they presided over a sort of rustic Algonquin Round Table surrounded by such visting luminaries as Deems Taylor, Elinor Wylie, the Benéts, "Bunny" Wilson, and Dorothy Thompson. The Boissevains soon had congenial neighbors —for they were joined by the omnipresent Arthur and Mrs. Ficke.

Boissevain hired the servants, farmed, and ran the house, so as not to distract "Vincent" from her work. Vincent talked a good cuisine, but was frequently hazy about such little details as the number of people who would be around to eat it. Her relations with the servants were stormy. "It will be some time before I get the house clean and in order after three months of that French slut," she expostulated to a correspondent in 1931. But times were good for them and there was always another "slut" arriving on the next train.

Fatal Interview, published in 1931, was the last work by what one might call the old Edna. It commemorated an extramarital love affair, on which the biographer Miss Atkins turns an urbane and civilized eye.

> I, all unwilling and unworthy, must be the first post-Victorian critic on record, to state in cold print, in a book designed to stand on a family bookshelf, that a still breathing married woman, name and dates given, has written a poem of extramarital passion, not as a literary exercise in purple penmanship, but as an honest record of immediate experience.[23]

This "honest record of immediate experience" was evidently considered by the patient Mr. Boissevain as another of the crosses to be borne by a self-appointed tender of the flame.

At the time *Fatal Interview* appeared it was found, like Fitzgerald's *Tender Is the Night*, to be lacking in social significance. Strange to say, the great tractarian seems to have had an aversion to proletarian poetry. In the thirties she wrote the editor of *Poetry*, saying that the magazine would have to look elsewhere for the "revolutionary element."

Wine from These Grapes, published in 1934, does, to be sure, have two propaganda sonnets on the old familiar theme of Sacco and Vanzetti. There is a poem in praise of a conscientious objector, and one called *Apostrophe to Man*, which railed against the wicked businessmen who were about to plunge the world into another war by commercializing "bacteria harmful to human tissue." Though this particular phase sounds straight out of the pages of *Hygeiea*, this volume contains some of her finest poetry. *Epitaph for the Race of Man* sounds a note of cosmic terror which had always been present to some degree in Miss Millay's work, but which became more pronounced in the thirties. It is almost as though the author had looked forward twenty-five years to the space age:

> Now for the void sets forth, and further still,
> The questioning mind of Man . . . that by and by
> From the void's rim returns with swooning eye,

Having seen himself into the maelstrom spill,
O race of Adam, blench not lest you find
In the sun's bubbling bowl anonymous death,
Or lost in whistling space without a mind
To monstrous Nothing yield your little breath:
You shall achieve destruction where you stand,
In intimate conflict, at your brother's hand.[24]

Conversation at Midnight, written in 1937, is a verse play in which speakers for various viewpoints express themselves in highly polished strophes. But the author does not allow any of them to get the final word in the discussion. There is Merton, a Republican exponent of the Protestant ethic, for whom Miss Millay clearly has no time. A Catholic priest comes off very well by contrast. There is a Communist, a cynic, a liberal agnostic, and an ad man. Miss Millay exhibits a new political sophistication which suggests she has come a long way since the days when she loved John Reed for the dangers he had passed.

The play is filled with shrewd political observations and prophetic insight, combined with a somewhat prosy delivery. It sounds occasionally as if the poetess were Marguerite Higgins or one of the Alsop brothers writing a column in verse for the *Trib.* The liberal agnostic, Ricardo, takes a tolerant view of the opiate of the people, remarking that modern man has taken the loss of God hard.

Not that he says much, but he laughs much louder
      than he used to,
And he can't bear to be left alone even for a min-
      ute, and he can't
Sit still.[25]

Another character, John, notes that the liberal belief in the natural goodness of man has failed him.

I believed in man, in his essential goodness; *I knew*
No nation would attack the undefended, the dis-
      armed,—
But now, having been defiled, I do not trust
So far.[26]

There is a flash of the old cosmic terror again in Ricardo's speech on science:

> The trick is this,—and it is a good trick, worthy a
>   divine
> Chicanery: in our impious determination
> To build this bean-stalk, Science; climb it, peep
> At Heaven through a key-hole; eaves-drop
> On the ultimate Mystery; spy on God; learn all;
> We have given eyes to one, and hands to another:
> No man can both climb, and see.
> We have specialized ourselves out of any possible
> Acquaintance with the whole.[27]

Proletarian poetry is described as

> . . . the love-song of the claustrophobiac who has
> espoused the crowd.[28]

The chilling speeches of Carl the Communist present Miss Millay's revised views on the proletarian paradise.

> *We* are MAN, emerging again out of the dark past;
> this is the second coming
> Upon the earth of MAN.[29]

> It doesn't matter what we're thinking; we don't
>   have to think at all; we don't even have to act;
> The dictatorship of the proletariat, though not yet
>   present and in this room, is a fact!
> It's present in its causes, like a bomb, that has just
>   been dropped
> From an air-plane, and hasn't hit the ground yet,
>   but can't be stopped.[30]

> Before you see it, with eyes turned so resolutely
>   toward the west
> We must allow another hundred years, at best . . .
> Except that long before then your shadow before
>   you, black on the dazzling ground,
> Will force you to look over your shoulder,—if not
>   indeed to turn around.[31]

Pygmalion, a cynic, echoes Ezra Pound's dirge for "a botched civilization"—

> Democrat or Republican at the bedside, the patient
>   will die.
> Give the poor old girl two minutes of silence, say
>   I.[32]

Conversation at Midnight is a fascinating as well as a beautifully written document; for it shows a dedicated member of the avant-garde watching the rise of the totalitarian state knock down every one of the ideological props of advanced thought.

As the thirties wore on, Miss Millay became more and more exercised over Hitler, referred to in *Conversation at Midnight* as the "soda fountain Siegfried."

Huntsman, What Quarry?, published in 1939, was her last work of pure poetry until the end of the war. From the late thirties on she resigned herself to writing poems which would aid the Allied cause.

Make Bright the Arrows, in 1940; *There Are No Islands, Any More* in 1940; *The Murder of Lidice*, 1942; *Poem and Prayer for an Invading Army*, which was read over N.B.C. by Ronald Colman in 1944, were a form of war work on a par with rolling bandages and saving bacon fat.

Miss Millay was well aware that she was not at her best in such stanzas as

> Joan, Joan can you be
> Tending sheep in Domrémy?
> Have no voices spoken plain:
> France has need of you again?[33]

or

> You, young man out of a job, but eating hearty
> Still, somehow at the State's (L'état c'est moi's) ex-
>   pense,
> Would you join the army for a year—for the state's
>   defense?[34]

One could only respond to a poem like this as to a poster saying that Uncle Sam Needs You.

The war between the poet and the propagandist finally caused her to have a nervous collapse.

In the late thirties the Boissevains' luck ran out. Eugen's family in Holland had had hairbreadth escapes from the Nazis, and one of them had been tortured and killed. Edna no longer gave readings, and Boissevain's income from Java had ceased at the time of the war. The housing arrangements at Steepletop became progressively more primitive. Automobiles gave way to horse and buggy "for the duration." Later the removal of electric lights and telephone plunged them further into the handicraft age. Miss Millay suffered from chronic ill health. There were incidental, annoying disasters. In 1936, the manuscript of *Conversation at Midnight* was destroyed in a fire, so that it had to be painstakingly reconstructed. Later the door of a station wagon flew open and the poet fell out. She wrenched her right arm and injured her back. Gravitational pull, not a push from the driver was responsible, as she wryly informed a correspondent. She was in and out of hospitals for years thereafter.

Edmund Wilson, who had not visited them since 1929, came to Steepletop in 1948. He recalls the visit in a memoir written after the poet's death. The startling décor which had confronted him on his first visit was still there—now dingy and faded—the black human head, the bronze bust of Sappho, the immense marble pedestal, the hangings from India showing golden birds on a green tree of life.

His host and hostess seemed as weatherbeaten as their surroundings. Boissevain in moccasins was graying and stooped. Edna in slacks and shirt seemed old and dumpy. When Boissevain said, "I'll go get my child," Wilson recalls his shock. "I did not realize at first that this meant Edna." She seemed constantly on the brink of tears. Her hands shook and there was a look of fright in her eyes. Boissevain was now doing all the housework without benefit of French sluts. "It disturbed me," Wilson recalls, "to find Edna and Eugen haunting like deteriorated ghosts their own comfortable house in the country."

Latterday weekends with the Boissevains were something
of an ordeal. Vincent Sheean visited them at "Ragged"—
an island they owned in Casco Bay, Maine. Sheean approached the poetess with something of the awed deference
one might show to Mahatma Gandhi. He recalls that she had
a tendency toward alarming withdrawal symptoms; sudden
shrinkings into some private hell and cryptic utterances. "Did
you remember the thingumabob?" "I hope you didn't forget
the tiddlywinks?" She referred to Sheean as "the buffalo," a
reference to a previous incarnation.

The Boissevains' house had become a "hotel for birds."
Guests spent long hours identifying feathered friends—when
they were not discussing Gerard Manley Hopkins, Hindu beliefs, the rebirth of souls, the inviolability of life, or whether
Keats was more miserable than Shelley. Conversation was
likely to be a bit trying for those uninterested in ornithology.

"That is the . . ." the poet would say, indicating a bird. "He
lives in Maryland, usually on the Eastern Shore. He is on his
way North. Perhaps he is going to Nova Scotia. He says that
this is a nice place, that the evening is calm, and that he believes he will rest here for the night before going on."[35]

She was wont to look out to sea, reciting verses and ad-
ministering first aid to crippled seagulls. Conversations about
birds alternated with conversations *to* birds.

In this unearthly atmosphere there were occasional throw-
backs to the good old days. On the Maine island bathing suits
were forbidden. "It is a rule of the island," said the poetess.
"I think bathing dress of any sort is indecent, and so do the
waves and so do the seagulls, and so does the wind."[36]

Sheean self-consciously dropped his trunks in deference to
the local wildlife.

Miss Millay's warmest admirers found her an exhausting
companion. Her old friend Edmund Wilson never saw her relaxed. She had several nervous breakdowns, was given to un-
motivated fits of weeping, and was afraid to cross a street
alone. At the height of her popularity in the twenties she burst
out to Wilson, "I'm *not* a pathetic character." Vincent Sheean
remembers that her terror of meeting people was so acute that
he once had to switch cards at a public dinner so that she

could sit next to her husband. Anticipating her mercurial moods was a strain on him. "Miss Millay was, to put it bluntly, a frightening apparition to many of us."[37]

Her imposing personality had a humbling effect on her admirers, inspiring even Floyd Dell to unaccustomed doubts about his own genius.

> To this girl poet, as to one to whom it rightly belonged, I yielded in my mind the right to the heroic egotism of genius, and for myself I decisively staked out a claim in the field of more ordinary and happier humanity.[38]

Miss Millay was never to regain the popularity she had enjoyed in the twenties. The figures of the great days were dying off. Edna's mother had died in 1931, John Peale Bishop in 1946, Arthur Davison Ficke in 1945; her own husband on August 30, 1949. So low had she fallen that she sold a Thanksgiving Day poem to that organ of the petty bourgeoisie—the *Saturday Evening Post*. Yet a flash of the old Lucy Stoner came out in a letter written in 1950 chewing out the tax collector for referring to her as Mrs. Boissevain. To do so, Miss Millay implied, was to profane the memory of Eugen.

On the night of October 19, 1950, she was reading the galleys of Rolfe Humphries' translation of the *Aeneid*. Toward dawn she started up the stairs and evidently felt faint. She sat down on a step. The next afternoon she was found dead of a coronary occlusion. The poems she wrote after the war were published posthumously under the title of *Mine the Harvest*. With Fitzgerald she had suffered in her final years from the after effects of a flaming youth.

It was difficult, as Edmund Wilson remarked, for the romantics of the twenties to recapture the old excitement. Edna St. Vincent Millay remains to this day a poet of stature. Yet the sale of her books was certainly not harmed by the titillating details of her private life. Friends who picked up her poetry always thought they were mentioned in it. She had a highly charged correspondence with Arthur Davison Ficke in 1937, on the subject of Sonnet VIII in *Second April*.

> When you came to me like a prosecuting attor-
> ney the other night in the La Branches' gun-room
> asking me so casually—and I at least six cocktails
> off my guard—"To whom did you write that sonnet,
> Vince?" I glibly and immediately countered with
> the only name which in the circumstances it would
> not be indiscreet to mention: your own.—To keep
> my loosened tongue from folly.

The poetess also expressed irritation at Ficke's questioning
her about Llewellyn Powys.[39] ("Lulu" was another of Miss
Millay's illustrious admirers. In 1936, we find her sending him
$1,000 to cover expenses he had incurred in an attack on
repressive practices in a home for delinquent girls.)

Years later, in the fall of 1945, Miss Millay finally admitted
that the *Second April* poem *had* been dedicated to Ficke.
"Perhaps, also, I didn't want you to know, for sure, how terri-
bly, how sickeningly, in love with you I had been."[40]

Miss Millay's volumes occasionally contain love poems to
women.

> Love is not blind. I see with single eye
> Your ugliness and other women's grace.[41]

She has the capacity for evoking the most extravagant admiration from biographers. She can do little wrong in the eyes
of Elizabeth Atkins. Toby Shafter—another lady of letters—
remarked of Miss Millay's life: "Even in death, it cast a lovely
light."[42] One wonders if the poet would have recognized herself as presented by Miss Shafter, a biographer who was
forced to concentrate heavily on "Vincent's" Maine girlhood—
a wise solution to the difficulties she encountered in presenting "America's best-loved poet" to an audience of children.

To more adult readers some of the steamier passages of,
say, *Fatal Interview* offered possibilities for a fascinating
guessing game. Her publishers were well aware of the commercial possibilities of this erotic *Who's Who*. On May 10,
1948, we find Miss Millay dispatching a strongly worded note
to an editor at Harper's. She refused to bring out a volume of
love poems, with the circumstances of inspiration described

in a "Mellow Foreword in Retrospect." Miss Millay dashed the editor's hopes of mining the gold in the La Blanches' gun room.

"I did get a grin out of it, though," she wrote; "pretty hard put to it, weren't you, dearie, to say it with flowers, and yet say it?"[43]

Edna at the escritoire was a formidable figure. "Consider, old friend," she wrote to Arthur Davison Ficke, "that someday our letters may be published in print!"[44]

The suspicion that she was writing for posterity was also raised in a letter to her mother. "Do you suppose, when you & I are dead, dear, they will publish the *Love Letters of Edna St. Vincent Millay & Her Mother?*"[45]

Eventually her letters were collected: her girlish outpourings to her sisters "Wump" and "Hunk"; such tributes to friends as the "little pome" she wrote to Allan Ross Macdougall:

> Allin dear, li'l wisdom toot:
> Edna luvs you,—thet's the trut.[46]

At times she lapsed into an unfortunate cuteness. She was at her best when blasting the forces of reaction—the official of N.Y.U. who had excluded her from a public dinner because of her sex; The League of American Penwomen, which had dealt a snub to Elinor Wylie. All of them felt the impact of Millay's mighty line.

"Believe me," she wrote to the Penwomen, "if the eminent object of your pusillanimous attack has not directed her movements in conformity with your timid philosophies, no more have I mine. I too, am eligible for your disesteem. Strike me too from your lists, and permit me, I beg you, to share with Elinor Wylie a brilliant exile from your fusty province."[47]

One of her Nancy Boyd pieces set up rules for the Impolite Letter Writer. A sample was addressed to a "hostess with whom you have just been spending a fortnight in the country." "What a house! And what a crew of guests! Not a dance record newer than *Too Much Mustard*,"[48] wrote Miss Boyd in her model bread and butter letter.

A model letter for accepting a proposal of marriage con-

cluded with the thought that, after some consideration, the
idea did not strike the writer as being so "screamingly" funny
as it had at first.

Her actual social correspondence contained many words
of one syllable. When a friend threatened a visit she wrote,
"Can you arrange to come after lunch and leave before dinner? . . . No, my dear. Don't bring me any lobsters. And
don't bring me any sea-weed."[49]

Looking back, one is impressed with the freshness and sense
of adventure with which Flaming Youth made its assault on
life. A later generation ceased to care whether Sacco and
Vanzetti lived or died, or whether Elinor Wylie had a right
to lead her own life. Neurotic, misguided, and even ludicrous
she often was. Yet her successors could envy Edna Millay her
generous spirit, her lust for living, the dignity and taste with
which she conducted her raffish private life.

She inhabited a Bohemia of heroic simplicities. Floyd Dell
looked forward to the day when feminism would produce "a
band of capable females, knowing what they want and taking
it, asking no leave from anybody, doing things and enjoying
life—Freewomen!"[50]

By the midcentury the "band of capable females" held a
third of the jobs in the business world. Almost a third of
America's newsprint seemed to be devoted to their problems.
Psychiatrists wrung their hands over them and their emascu-
lated mates. Edna and her friends had fought to abolish guilt
feelings about enjoying sex, only to give rise to a generation
of women who had guilt feelings if they didn't enjoy it. Eman-
cipated as modern women were, their problem had not
changed much since Floyd Dell's day—"to be a person as well
as a mother."

In the 1950's society realized that mother needed every help
it could give her in the battle of mind vs. diaper pail. But
society no longer believed that woman's troubles could be
solved by abolishing marriage, by forbidding her to have
babies, or by leading a charge on the Met.

The aftereffects of the "ten days that shook the world"
eventually sent Max Eastman to writing diatribes against
Russia for the Reader's Digest, Dorothy Day to the arms of

the Catholic Church, and Louis Untermeyer to editing beloved poetry anthologies for school children. Ezra Pound's
successors ceased to lament the sickness of Western civilization in the hope that by some miracle "the old bitch gone in
the teeth" might manage to pull through.

The social solutions of Edna's youth seemed as quaint at
the time of her death as high button shoes. The Bohemian
pose had become a cliché. Jack Kerouac, the literary James
Dean who inherited the Millay-Dell-Reed mantle, had none
of their hopeful love of a program.

The "beat generation" who followed Kerouac's maxim,
"Avoid the authorities," still searched for the nerve that could
jump. The search generally ended up in a nightmare hunt
for an abortionist or in a frantic attempt to get rid of a monkey
on the back.

The Village that had housed the Liberal Club had lost its
bravado and intellectual distinction. It had become a refuge
for the lunatic fringe, for insurance men, bank clerks, and
tourists in search of long-haired men and short-haired women.

As mid-century bopsters smoked tea, shouted "Yes, yes, yes,"
and beat their feet to the records of Charlie Parker, the handwriting of the landlord was on the Village wall. The *New York
Daily News* sounded a "Requiem for Bohemia." Plans were
going through for a $75,000,000 slum-clearance project, which
would replace the studios of Miss Millay's day with glass-and-
glazed-back dormitory buildings at sixty dollars a room.
Goateed hipsters fought a stand against a 48-foot road which
would extend Fifth Avenue through Washington Square down
to Canal Street.

"We don't want no daddies from Squaresville barreling
through and scaring the pigeons," one such original said.

Bohemia was dying because the Bohemian could not, as he
had in Miss Millay's day, rally the sympathies of intelligent
people. America had outgrown Greenwich Village. In their
mid-century, middle-class, middlebrow housing, the "daddies
from Squaresville" had inherited the earth.

". . . his decision to become a Communist seems to
the man who makes it as a choice between a world that
is dying and a world that is coming to birth," *Witness,* by
Whittaker Chambers
"I have testified against him with remorse and pity,
but in a moment of history in which this nation now
stands, so help me God, I could not do otherwise."
Witness

5

The Campus Radical

WHITTAKER CHAMBERS

The time was the early twenties. Remy de Gourmont was the
latest intellectual fad. College magazines glorified the burner
of temples and the destroyer of idols. The young socialist had
given way to the young cynic. Professors worried as to how
they would excite the interest of classes too torpid even for
boob-baiting.

In the *New Republic* Mark Van Doren explored the psyches
of that infinitesimal segment of the college population still
capable of remaining awake in class. These rarefied beings
whiled away their hours debating the idea of perfection and
looked forward to a paradise that seemed just around the
corner. It was to be a paradise freed of religion, divorced from
considerations about the good of society, from incorrect, outmoded, or vulgar habits of taste, from the things "which men's
irrelevant loyalties have gummed together to no good."

The idea of Christianity was considered by many of these advanced spirits to be among the most irrelevant of loyalties. As an index of student trends, Van Doren quoted a play titled *Play for Puppets*, which appeared in the *Columbia Morningside*, by a pseudonymous author named John Kelley, who had freed himself from the dross of the past.

In it, Christ was portrayed as a sleepy Redeemer, who, inside the tomb, had no wish to respond to the angel's summons to "arise." Told that he is the Son of God, Christ answers, "Some thoughtless one has betrayed thee. My father is Joseph the Carpenter of Nazareth. Roll back the stone and go thy way." Only because the angel remained stubbornly unconvinced did Christ meekly go up to Heaven, muttering, "I am the Way, the Truth, and the Light."[1]

Shortly after the production of this work, the author found it expedient to leave college. Having created a ripple of scandal in a dull academic year, *Play for Puppets* gathered dust in the college library until some twenty-five years later when it saw the light of day once more in a courtroom on Foley Square.

The boy had also been briefly the editor of the *Morningside*. This publication was dedicated at the time to the philosophy of "profanism"—a system of thought reported to be as radical as progress itself. The editors lauded Henry Ford for having weakened the ties between Ford owners and the Church, and otherwise carried on the noble work of freeing mankind from "the lactic droolings of the late century." The *Morningside* published one more work by the author of *Play for Puppets* —a curious tale entitled "The Damn Fool," fascinating to read in the light of later events. The hero was a picaresque character named Everett Holmes, who was darkly suspected of being a Bolshevist. The author describes him as a puritan, a radical, and an extremist.

Holmes set off for Russia to fight Bolshevism around the end of World War I. He elected to do it the hard way. He declined offers to go by way of Antwerp or Bombay. Bombay was fraught with particular peril because of "what the English would do to him." At no point is it made clear what he had done to annoy the English. At last he shipped off to Constantinople, disappeared, rode for miles on a bicycle, following the stars. He ditched the bicycle, crept behind a bush, and stayed without food or water, munching on leaves. The natives marveled at his fortitude. "He couldn't have eaten more than a dog—and for a Westerner!"

At one point he pretended to be deaf and dumb, got himself up as a monk, and roamed the countryside much in the manner of a mad Czar. After shipping out on a dhow, he reached the Crimea, where his exploits were even more startling. Feats of fantastic bravery, a succession of suicidal charges, once again made the local populace gasp in admiration. While going over the top with him, the men, who adored him, had a mystical reaction to a wooden crucifix that had come along with the monk's costume.

Once, he killed a soldier and retreated back to a trench, carrying the corpse as a shield. Sometimes he went out carrying only the cross. He always avoided fighting, indulging in it only when he was carried away with the justice of a cause. Such a cause presented itself when a Cossack officer tried to have him held for trial. Holmes, followed by a cheering bunch of soldiers, charged once more. When the dust cleared the Cossack was dead.

"Not killed by the Reds, either," as the author explains. "When there is insurrection flaring everywhere you can't expect a troop of hungry wild men to be tame."[2] No one seemed to know why they were fighting. Confusion was everywhere, in the reader's mind above all. When we put "The Damn Fool" down, we are never certain just who we are supposed to have been rooting for.

The story reaches its grand climax with Holmes tied by his enemies to two birch trees. The trees are cut apart, tearing him in half. It is never made clear which faction of Russians he had offended. The author apparently feels that Holmes' weird crucifixion proved something. He leaves us in doubt as to what the something was.

"The Damn Fool" gives certain clues about its author's character. Fanaticism, puritanism, a Messianic complex are combined with the wildest romanticism. One imagines him looking over his shoulder during his peregrinations to see if

"they" are following him. Holmes' motives are lost in a fog
of ideological confusion. The martyr's cross is all that counts.
The cross for which Holmes yearned so desperately was to
materialize many years later, in the strange, guilt-haunted
world of Whittaker Chambers.

Whittaker Chambers was born in 1901, disastrously chris-
tened Jay Vivian. He was the son of a moderately successful
commercial artist. A rebel like Edna St. Vincent Millay, he
also came from a home cluttered with Victoriana. The two
had other things in common—the sense of belonging to a
generation that would make a clean break with the past—
the feeling that the wave of the future would break somewhere east of the Crimea. Though middle age would find
them worlds apart, both were prepared to devote their youth
to wiping up the "lactic droolings."

As Edna St. Vincent Millay had an off-beat Victorian
mother, so did Chambers, but in this case the influence was
not so fortunate. Over the Chambers home hung a pre-
Raphaelite miasma. Mrs. Chambers, whose name was Laha
(according to her parents, Malay for "Princess"), gave up a
stage career to live entirely for her children. There were the
determinedly whimsical touches: Taurus the bulldog, Claude
the cat (a mildly ribald play on the loss of Claude's man-
hood).

The house was full of the sort of dust catchers that epicene
young men would one day find "amusing." There was the
India print against which hung a round, flat Spanish wool
basket; the illustrations for "The Goblin Market," the framed
prints of Holbein, Velásquez, and Dürer. There was a plaster
cast of Venus de Milo, an Italian painting showing a hooded
skeleton beckoning to figures with bundles. During the tooth-
aches that plagued Chambers as a boy, he recalls staring for
hours at this picture titled "Death, the Comforter."

His father fell under the spell of the mysterious East, deck-
ing himself out in flowing robes, sketching views of the Bos-
porus, reading *The Arabian Nights* and Omar Khayyam, and
patronizing oriental restaurants. Rossetti, Beardsley, Wilde,
Pater, Whistler, William Morris, and Du Maurier's *Trilby* were
part of young Chambers' intellectual baggage. The brooding

boy lived out his wretched childhood amid bookplates, copies of *St. Nicholas,* and *Little Lord Fauntleroy;* coached by his mother in the "gentlemanly ideal," smarting under his given name of Vivian; dressed in V-necked sailor suits with a whistle on a braided cord. As Chambers points out in *Witness* there is a difference between the words "art" and "arty." Not till much later did Chambers appreciate the fact that his home was arty. Chambers grew up in the twilight of a tranquil age when everyone had the Waverly novels.

Chambers' family background was not guaranteed to provide him with much stability. "The voices around me in my early childhood were all gentle voices," he said; but in them was an undercurrent of hysteria. There was the mother, the frustrated actress, singing *"Au claire de la lune"* to her children—lowering her voice over the dramatic passages. There was the father with the inability to give or receive affection, who never, within Chambers' memory, played with his sons. There was the father's abandonment of the family and the moment when the mother moved a heavy bureau in front of the door, as if "father's departure might be a signal for marauders to swarm in. "Chambers himself soon fell into the habit of sleeping with a knife under his pillow.

Father returned to take his meals apart from the rest of the family. Chambers' grandmother, another cheerless addition to the household, was inexplicably brought home from the insane ward of the city hospital. This menacing figure drifted about the house, muttering, growling, rocking back and forth in her sealskin coat, a knife clutched in front of her. The days were enlivened by the grandmother's battles with Chambers' father, by her tirades against John D. Rockefeller, by her cooking up little messes in a tomato can.

There was also the brother, twice dissuaded from suicide, who finally ended up with his head in a gas oven.

There were the plans for doing over the house which never came to fruition. With its back torn out for two stories, rigged with scaffolding, with furniture piled in a Collyeresque rabbit warren, the Chambers house was "a peeling outpost" of culture, inhabited by people living in spiritual anarchy.

The summer Chambers graduated from high school, he ran

away. For a time, he lived like a character in one of his stories. Dressed in his graduation suit, he headed for Mexico. He first encountered "the wretched of the earth" when he joined a gang of workers who were laying the street railway tracks in Washington. He hitchhiked to New Orleans where his neighbors included a prostitute named One-Eyed Annie. During this period he took one of many pseudonyms, Charles Adams. At last, he threw in the towel and wired his father for money. He returned home and in 1920 entered Columbia, where he remained till the atheistic play cut short his college career.

In the summer of 1923 he went to Europe with two other students. Germany was then in the throes of inflation, and what he saw there made a deep impression on him. He re-entered college and worked nights at the public library. By now, the apocalyptic rumblings had shattered the calm of the pre-Raphaelite dusk. In 1925 Chambers became a Communist.[3] He felt that he had made the choice between a world that was dying and a world that was coming to birth.

He first went to work on the staff of the *Daily Worker*. He broke briefly with the party over problems of political strategy and became an "independent Communist oppositionist." He did occasional translations, among them *Bambi,* and Franz Werfel's *Class Reunion.* In 1932 he became editor of *The New Masses.*

His meeting with his wife was in the revolutionary tradition —a flowering of love on the barricades. He first saw Esther Shemitz when she "walked forward as the police closed in, swinging their clubs" during the Passaic textile workers' strike. They met later on, when Miss Shemitz was living in a tiny house on Eleventh Street, in New York, with Grace Lumpkin. Both girls were known for their implacable purity. Chambers' courtship followed a Montague-Capulet course, with intervention on all sides from the Party. The devout Miss Shemitz belabored Chambers for his "renegacy." Various comrades implored her to give up "the anti-party element." One day in 1931 Chambers resolved her doubts by entering her window at 5 A.M. and finally sweeping her off to City Hall. The first of their two children was born in 1933.

In 1932, Chambers went into the Communist underground.

In the eyes of the world, he had become a respectable bourgeois. Yet in the anonymity of a great city he was leading the
life of a spy—trysts with loitering figures; whispered conversations with mysterious people known simply as Ulrich or
Charlie or Keith.

It is at this time that his superior, Colonel Boris Bykov,
enters Chambers' narrative. Chambers was working for the
second of two spy apparatuses when he met Bykov. Beset by
linguistic difficulties and a fear of being liquidated, Bykov led
Chambers on mad plunges into B.M.T. kiosks, forced him to
take hasty leaps from cabs into the 6th Avenue traffic. In
Witness, Chambers tells of Bykov's mistaking the shoppers in
the Rockefeller Center arcade for agents of the secret police;
and of Bykov's conflicting instructions to a baffled cab driver,
"Drive on! Drive on! Stop! Stop!"[4]

As Chambers paints him, it is difficult to understand how his
superiors could have placed much confidence in such a mercurial conspirator.

During this period, Chambers adopted a number of aliases,
becoming variously "Cantwell" or "Breen." At the time of the
Hiss trial, he was unable to recall whether he had ever used
the pseudonym George Crosley, the name under which Hiss
claimed to have known him.

Chambers' second spy assignment was centered on Washington. He was a member of a Soviet espionage group dealing
in stolen government documents.

When Chambers broke with the party, he took with him a
sort of "life preserver." It consisted of copies of documents on
the Hiss Woodstock, penciled memos in Hiss's handwriting,
and microfilmed copies of stolen papers.

Part of the guilty evidence was deposited with his wife's
nephew, Nathan Levine, in Brooklyn. The custodians of this
bombshell were seemingly unaware of its explosive possibilities. The rest was hidden in a pumpkin on Chambers' Maryland farm. He fled to Daytona Beach, Florida. He obtained a
job translating a book for the Oxford University Press. He
rose in the world of letters to become a senior editor of *Time*
at $30,000 a year.

On September 2, 1939, Chambers went to see Adolf Berle
to divulge the Communist connections of various prominent

New Dealers, including Alger and Donald Hiss. His disclosures laid something of an egg. Berle did not turn the Chambers dossiers over to the F.B.I. until four years later. In 1948 Berle said that he had been unable, in 1939, to take seriously the "idea that the Hiss boys and Nat Witt were going to take over the government."[5]

Berle did pass on the information to President Roosevelt who was equally unimpressed. The President, according to Chambers, told Berle "in words which it is necessary to paraphrase to 'go jump in a lake.' "[6] Chambers bought a large farm in Maryland, became an Episcopalian and later a Quaker. It was not until well after the war that anyone took Chambers seriously. By then any lapsed Communist had a ready-made claque.

As the cold war progressed, renegade comrades were turning in spies, fellow-travelers, and leftist sympathizers by the dozen. When the one-time Communist Elizabeth Bentley testified before the House Committee on Un-American Activities, one of the people who turned up on her list was the author of *Play for Puppets*.

In a public session before the Committee, Chambers testified freely concerning his lurid past with the Communist underground. But the charge that galvanized the American people was his accusation against Alger Hiss, whom he named as one of his sources of state secrets. Hiss's career had been distinguished. He had graduated Phi Beta Kappa from Johns Hopkins in 1926, and in Harvard Law School had been nominated for the coveted post of secretary to Oliver Wendell Holmes. From 1933 to 1935 he had served with the Agricultural Adjustment Administration. He had been a member of the Nye Committee which was investigating the armaments industry. Later he entered the State Department. He participated in the Yalta Conference. At the San Francisco Conference he had taken over what *Time* called the "paper-clip and pencil chores of an international meeting."[7] When the U.N. charter was signed, it was Hiss who flew from San Francisco to Washington to get it ratified by the Senate. When Chambers accused him in 1948, he was president of the Carnegie Endowment for International Peace.

According to Chambers' testimony, Hiss had been a dues-

paying party member. He had belonged to the Harold Ware
unit of the Communist Party. Its other members had included
Nathan Witt, John Abt, Lee Pressman, and Harold Ware, a
son of Mother Bloor, the grand old woman of the Communist
movement. The party had put the finger on Hiss as one of the
bright young men who were "going places in the government."

On August 5, 1948, Hiss denied everything in a public session before the House Committee on Un-American Activities.
Both men then appeared separately before the committee in a
private session. Testifying as he did without knowledge of
Chambers' story, Hiss unwittingly confirmed some of its secret
details including the fact that he had, as a birdwatcher, sighted
a prothonotary warbler on the banks of the Potomac. As a
result, on August 17, Hiss and Chambers confronted each
other before a special subcommittee at the Hotel Commodore
in New York.

Hiss had originally denied ever having heard of Chambers.
Fred Cook, author of *The Unfinished Story of Alger Hiss,*
points out that Hiss made an unnecessarily "heavy weather
task" of recognizing Chambers. He questioned Chambers
about his dental work, commented on his increased jowliness,
and finally identified him as George Crosley, a writer whom
he had known in the early thirties.

On August 27, Chambers repeated his accusations on the
"Meet the Press" program. On September 27, Hiss brought a
$75,000 libel suit against him in Baltimore. On November 17,
following a lull in the proceedings, Chambers produced some
of the documents that had been moldering in Nathan Levine's
dumbwaiter shaft. The documents included four memos in
Hiss's handwriting, along with typed copies and summaries
of various State Department cables and coded reports. Chambers hinted at further dramatic disclosures. On December 2
the House Committee investigators visited Chambers' farm
bearing a subpoena. Chambers presented them with five rolls
of microfilm which he had removed from a hollowed-out
pumpkin. To the public, the press and posterity, these became
"the pumpkin papers."

On December 6, the Justice Department reconvened the
federal grand jury investigating espionage. On December 10,

Chambers resigned from *Time*. On December 13, Hiss offered to resign from the Carnegie Endowment. The offer was tabled and he was given three months leave with pay. On December 15, Hiss was indicted for perjury by a federal grand jury in New York. He was accused of having lied on two counts: in denying that he had transmitted copies of the documents to Chambers, and in claiming that he had not seen Chambers after January 1, 1937.

On May 31, 1949, Hiss's first trial began. It ended on July 8 with a hung jury. On November 17, 1949, he was tried for a second time; he was convicted on January 21, 1950. On January 25, 1950, Alger Hiss was sentenced to five years in prison.

"We proceed on the conclusion that if either one of you is telling the truth on the verifiable data, that you are telling the truth on all of it."[8] Such was the logic of the committee. The stories told by the two men were so different that it was assumed that one had to swallow either one or the other *in toto*. Hiss described their relationship as casual in the extreme. Chambers by contrast claimed friendship with Hiss from 1935 to mid-April 1938. They had been close both as friends and co-conspirators. Hiss had turned State Department papers over to Chambers in the first months of 1938. The last of the papers was dated early in April. Such was the Gospel according to Chambers.

During the period under discussion, the Hisses had lived in four different houses. The validity of Chambers' testimony hinged on his knowledge of the Hiss domestic appointments.

From June 9, 1934, to July 2, 1935, the Hisses lived at 2831 28th Street, N.W., in Washington. From April 19, 1935, to June 15, 1936, they lived at 2905 P Street, N.W. A duplicate phone connection between April 19 and July 2 established an overlapping in the 28th Street and the P Street leases, which was to assume paramount importance in the case. From July 1, 1936, to December 29, 1937, the Hisses lived at 1245 30th Street, N.W. From December 29, 1937, to November 1, 1943, they were at 3415 Volta Place N.W.

Both men agreed that Chambers, with his wife and child, had spent time in the 28th Street apartment during the period of the overlapping leases. Hiss claimed that he had sublet the place to Chambers, whom he had known as George Crosley. He had run into Crosley while he was working for the Nye Committee, and Chambers had represented himself as a freelance writer. Chambers invested his 28th Street stay with a sinister purpose. It was part of the Communist pattern. "There was no question of my renting or leasing the apartment, and if I offered to pay rent for it, as I must certainly have done, Alger refused it."[9]

In the Hiss version, Chambers turned out to be a dead beat who welshed on the rent. The apartment arrangement had not been conducive to further intimacy. "We had met and talked about a dozen times; in particular he had been in my P Street house for two nights, we had lunched together a couple of times, we had driven from Washington to New York, passing through my home town of Baltimore on the way."[10]

To Chambers, by contrast, the Hiss home had been "a sort of informal headquarters." He rattled off details of décor. He described the "little box" on 30th Street, where, to make sure that their voices did not carry, the conspirators took to forgathering downstairs. "But, at P Street, the dining room was at the front of the house and, at 30th Street, it was at the back; a small kitchen and closet storeroom were at the front."[11]

Chambers unfolded a tale of repeated meetings with Hiss at Volta Place. He described a tearful interlude in which he had returned to the Hisses' home to get them to break with the party. They had refused and he had wept.

On August 3, Chambers set this meeting in 1937. On August 25, for the first time, he put it at Volta Place. The date was altered to "toward the end of 1938."[12] At the trials Chambers had originally assigned April 15 as the date of his break with Communism. Discrepancies were later to develop in the Chambers timetable.

Chambers also depicted the two families as being involved in cheery country outings and homely baby-sitting chores. One such trip involved an excursion to Peterboro, New Hampshire, where, in August, 1937, Chambers and the Hisses supposedly set out for the home of Harry Dexter White. Chambers claimed that they had seen Goldsmith's *She Stoops to Conquer,* which indeed did play in Peterboro, on August 10, 1937, and never before or after.

On August 9, however, the morning they were said to have set off from Washington, Hiss brought out the fact that he was driving his brother-in-law to Wilmington to catch a train for New York. Hiss testified that he and his wife were vacationing on the Eastern Shore of Maryland at the time. Chambers, undaunted, claimed that they must have returned to Washington or Baltimore "on personal business or for the purpose of meeting me."[13] The defense located the guest book of the Peterboro inn where Chambers said they had stayed. But it showed no signature of any member of the group.

A 1935 expedition took place under a similar shroud of anonymity. In her testimony at the Baltimore pre-trial libel proceedings, Mrs. Chambers said that Mrs. Hiss had visited her for ten days at a summer cottage in Smithtown on the Delaware River. Mrs. Hiss had looked after the Chambers baby while Mrs. Chambers painted. The landlord denied ever having seen hide or hair of Mrs. Hiss.

In support of their conflicting stories, the two principals brought in character witnesses. Bearing up Chambers' end were Hede Massing and Edith Murray. Hede Massing, the former wife of Gerhard Eisler, came up with a tale of having met Hiss in 1935, when they had joked as two "apparatchiks" about which of them was to claim the service of Noël Field. Mrs. Massing recalls that one of them japed, "Whoever is going to win, we are working for the same boss."[14]

Mrs. Massing's testimony had been barred at the first trial by Judge Samuel H. Kaufman, bringing about demands for his impeachment. At the second trial, Judge Henry Goddard, who maintained a more charitable attitude toward the prosecution, allowed Mrs. Massing to testify. The defense countered by producing one Henrikas Rabinavicius, who had met Mrs. Massing at the Eugene Lyonses and from her had heard the story of her meeting with Hiss. Rabinavicius claimed that she had described her efforts to lure Field into an organization to fight fascism—not into the Communist underground. He had no recollection of the all-important phrase about the "same boss."

Edith Murray, a maid who had worked for the Chambers family from the fall of 1934 to the spring of 1936, testified that she had seen Mrs. Hiss in their home four times and Hiss once. Once, she claimed that Mrs. Hiss stayed with the Chambers

baby while Mrs. Chambers was in New York visiting her
doctor. This corroborated Chambers' picture of a cozy inter-
family relationship. Judge Goddard permitted her to appear in
rebuttal at the last minute in the second trial, instead of her
being introduced as a prosecution witness, whose credibility
could have been questioned. This brought from the Hiss forces
cries of "foul."

After the trial the defense forces attempted to shake Mrs.
Murray's story. They produced William Reed Fowler, husband
of the niece of the housekeeper at 903 St. Paul Street, Baltimore, where Chambers had lived during Mrs. Murray's tenure;
and Louis J. Leisman, custodian at 1619 Eutaw Place, Baltimore, next door to 1617, whence Chambers had moved after
leaving St. Paul Street. Both seemed positive that Chambers,
or Cantwell, as he was then calling himself, had never employed a colored maid. The prosecution introduced counter-
testimony depicting Leisman as a shifty, untrustworthy individual with inclinations toward criminality and the bottle.

There was conflicting testimony on the subject of the Ware
group. Lee Pressman, an admitted former member, testified
that while the group existed, Alger Hiss was not a member of
it. As with others who were at loggerheads with Chambers,
Pressman's testimony is dismissed in *Witness* as falling "far
short of the full facts."[15]

Nathaniel Weyl related in 1952 that Hiss had belonged to
the Harold Ware unit but described it as a kind of Marxist
study group. Fred Cook, however, points out that Hiss seemed
to grow redder in Weyl's opinion with the passage of time.
Weyl's 1952 testimony conflicted with a description of Hiss as
"a very moderate New Dealer with strongly conservative instincts," which Weyl quoted in a book called *Treason* in 1950.[16]

Two former Hiss maids emulated Edith Murray in backing
their employers to the hilt. Martha Pope and Claudia
("Cleide") Catlett cast doubts that Chambers had ever used
the Hiss home as an "informal headquarters." Cleide Catlett
admitted having seen Chambers on P Street but had no recollection of seeing either Mrs. Chambers or the Chambers baby
at P Street, at 30th Street, or at Volta Place.

Chambers was unable to recall the street number of the "informal headquarters." Cleide Catlett testified that Chambers

could not have stayed overnight with the Hisses on 30th Street. She had no recollection of making up extra beds for them. The "tiny box" had only two bedrooms, both of which were occupied.

The Chamberses do not sound like guests whom any maid would be likely to forget. At 30th Street they would have had to bed down with the Hisses. At Volta Place Mrs. Chambers testified that their baby had "wet the floor" and that Mrs. Hiss had given her as a diaper a beautiful linen towel which was subsequently lost. At P Street the whole Chambers ménage was alleged to have moved in bag and baggage with special foods for the baby. Almost any of these details would have been calculated in most noncommunistic households to inspire mutinous rumblings from the kitchen.

Faced by Cleide Catlett, Chambers began to backtrack. After the pre-trial deposition, his memories of the stay in 30th Street became successively vaguer. By the second trial he denied having "a clear recollection of spending the night there."[17]

In the parade of witnesses summoned by the defense one did tremendous damage to the Hiss cause. Dr. Carl Binger, a psychiatrist, testified to Chambers' mental instability. On the basis of Chambers' testimony and writings, he ventured rashly to diagnose Chambers' case. He and the psychologist Dr. Henry Murray described Chambers as a psychopathic personality with an abnormal emotionality and paranoid delusions. Extraordinary parallels were pointed out between the Hiss-Chambers case and the plot of Franz Werfel's *Class Reunion*—a tale translated by Chambers, dealing with forgery and false accusations.

The prosecutor, Thomas F. Murphy, ridiculed Binger's remote-control diagnosis. He played on the popular conception of the psychiatrist who is himself one jump ahead of the men in white. Whatever Binger's prowess as a diagnostician, he was unsuccessful as an expert witness. Alger Hiss might well exclaim, "God protect us from our friends."

There were a number of objects brought up in the trial that bore silent witness against Hiss. One was a Ford roadster, another a Bokhara rug.

The subject of the car was introduced by Chambers on

August 7. Chambers recalled that Hiss had had an archaic Ford roadster. Chambers claimed that Hiss, through the Communist owner of a car lot, had put the car at the disposal of the party.

Hess testified that Chambers had gotten the car as part of "the apartment deal." Yet motor vehicle records placed the sale on July 23, 1936, after Crosley, according to Hiss, had proved to be a dead beat, and after close contact between the two should have ceased. The records showed that title to the Hiss Ford was transferred to the Cherner Motor Company in Washington. The car did not go through the usual channels. The title had gone on the same day to one William Rosen who, when questioned as to his disposal of the Ford, pleaded the Fifth Amendment.

Hiss's vagueness about the disposal of the Ford had the odor of something rotten in Denmark. He had no clear memory of having given, sold, or loaned it to Crosley. Crosley had had the use of it and, according to Hiss, might have disposed of it.

"Whether I gave him the car outright, whether the car came back, I don't know."[18] As to the relationship with the apartment deal, "It could have been tied in toward the end, it could have been tied in toward the beginning. My best recollection is that there is a connection between the two transactions."[19]

> My act of signing the transfer in my office before the colleague who notarized it, is the one item I have never been able to recall. My colleague was equally unable to recall the incident. I can only assume that on July 23, 1936, someone came to my office in the Department of Justice, presented the assignment which the Cherner Company had accepted, and asked me to fill out the form and have it notarized.[20]

Mr. Marvin Smith, the "colleague in the Justice Department," having plunged into the stairwell of the Justice Department Building a few weeks later, was unable to contribute anything to the discussion.

Following testimony of this sort, Richard Nixon brought down the house with the question, "How many cars have you given away in your life, Mr. Hiss?"[21]

A second car also appeared to incriminate the luckless Hiss. Late in 1937 Chambers claimed that Hiss had loaned him $400 to buy a new car. On November 19, 1937, the Hiss bank account reflected a $400 withdrawal. On November 23, a Ford car was sold to Esther Chambers for a trade-in of a 1934 Ford sedan and $486.75 in cash. Hiss claimed that the $400 withdrawal financed new furniture for the Volta Place house. After the trial, Hiss brought to light the fact that Chambers mentioned the second car only *after* the F.B.I. had shown him the Hiss bank account. In the Baltimore libel deposition, moreover, Mrs. Chambers had remarked that she thought they had gotten the money from Chambers' mother. The second car could be shrugged off by the defense a good deal more easily than the first.

It was Hiss himself who introduced the fatal subject of a Bokhara rug. He claimed that Chambers had offered him the rug as a payment on account of the rent. Chambers' explanation of the rug was invested with the usual E. Phillips Oppenheim overtones. On the instructions of Colonel Bykov, he had personally given Hiss the rug on behalf of the grateful Soviet people. A Professor Meyer Schapiro had been commissioned by Chambers to purchase four rugs for four of Chambers' government contacts. One was clearly earmarked for Hiss, or as the shadowy Boris Bykov called him, "der Advokat."

The date on which "der Advokat" received the rug became a matter of paramount importance. A delivery receipt showed that the rugs had been delivered to Schapiro on December 29, 1936. Since the four rugs could not have been delivered in Washington until after January 1, 1937, Hiss would be automatically incriminated if it could be proved that one of the four rugs was his. He would be shown to have lied under oath when he said that he had not seen Chambers after January 1, 1937. The doughty Cleide Catlett remembered seeing the rug on the floor of the P Street house which the Hisses left in 1936. This jibed with Hiss's memory that he was living on P Street when Chambers gave him the rug. The effect of the

Bokhara was most damaging to Hiss. Neither the defense nor the prosecution subpoenaed the rug to see if it matched the three other tokens of Moscow's gratitude.

In December, 1950, an appeal was denied to Hiss. On March 22, 1951, he went to prison. He was not idle. In his dry, dispassionate, aloof fashion, Hiss went to work on the story that had put him behind bars. In 1957, Alfred A. Knopf brought out the results of Hiss's efforts—a book entitled *In the Court of Public Opinion.*

Hiss pointed out discrepancies in Chambers' story that had been widely overlooked at the time of the trial. Chambers had, for instance, given three different versions of the method by which the Hisses paid their party dues. There was the mysterious Colonel Bykov, wild-eyed participant in Chambers' cops-and-robbers chases through the New York subway system.

Julian Wadleigh, one of Chambers' self-confessed government contacts, met Chambers' underground boss. He recalled him as a one-armed man who used the pseudonym "Sasha." Chambers' Bykov had two arms and used the pseudonym "Peter"—this suggested to Hiss that Bykov was a figment of Chambers' imagination, whom he might have met once and later fabricated into his manic "superior." Chambers dismissed Sasha's handicap as an "error of recollection." (Wadleigh testified without Chambers' knowledge.) However, Chambers' co-conspirator "Keith" equipped Bykov with functioning arms and legs. It remains something of a mystery how Wadleigh's vision could have been so faulty as to deprive Chambers' superior of anything quite so fundamental as a limb.

Hiss showed up Chambers' vagueness on other subjects involving specific names and dates. Chambers was ignorant of such details of the Hiss family history as the occupation of Hiss's sister, the maiden name of his sister-in-law, the near-fatal accident of Hiss's stepson Timothy.

Possibly his contempt for material possessions made Chambers oblivious to such details of the Hiss décor as a spinet-sized piano, a beautiful Queen Anne mirror, and Hiss's prize possession, a facsimile of Justice Holmes's notebook. The outstanding Hiss bibelot as far as Chambers was concerned was a red cigarette box.

Chambers claimed that Hiss was a teetotaler. Hiss confessed to mild social drinking. Mrs. Chambers was off on the outside paint color and on the color of the living-room walls of the house on 30th Street. Mrs. Chambers' description of the Volta Place house tallied with a recent photograph. A contractor testified that a stone porch was built later; that the white brick had been unpainted in Hiss's time; that, in a remodeling, windows had been cut through which had not existed when the Hisses were there. Following the contractor's first trial testimony and his drawing of plans for the F.B.I., as Hiss caustically remarks, Mrs. Chambers' description of Volta Place came "closer to the realities of 1938." At both trials, however, she furnished the house with imaginary wallpaper, bedspread, and curtains. None of the furniture described by the Chamberses was, according to Hiss, "acquired after we had moved from P Street."[22]

Hiss is particularly acid on the subject of one festive evening described in several versions by Mr. and Mrs. Chambers.

At the Baltimore libel proceedings, Mrs. Chambers claimed to have visited Volta Place on the occasion of Hiss's wedding anniversary. The Hisses apparently lapsed from total abstinence this evening and served champagne. Chambers was said by his wife to have become ill on the way home. Hiss pointed out that his wedding anniversary was December 11, and that they did not move to Volta Place till December 29, 1937. And an anniversary party in December 1938 "wasn't within the bounds of any of Chambers' changing testimony." On June 10, 1949, Mrs. Chambers changed the occasion to New Year's Eve on January 1, 1937. The judge asked if she meant New Year's Eve 1936, and she said yes. She alluded once more to Chambers' digestive disturbance, though the offending beverage had changed from champagne to port. When informed that the Hisses had not moved till December 29, 1937, she postdated the occasion to New Year's Eve 1937. "Within a few minutes," wrote Mr. Hiss, "the wedding anniversary appeared a new version." It became a wedding anniversary celebrated at the Chambers' Baltimore house with the Hisses contributing a bottle of champagne.

Later the Hisses unearthed a letter that proved that on

December 30, 1936, Timothy Hiss was with his mother in Chappaqua with the chicken pox. Mrs. Hiss was therefore unavailable for a New Year's party on 30th Street, Mrs. Chambers' final locale for her story.

Chambers' story of close association with the Hisses seems less impressive than it did originally when one examines the inconsistencies involved in this movable feast.

However, the prosecution's testimony was all forgiven and forgotten in the shadow of the larger evidence—the documents and the typewriter. Alistair Cooke in *A Generation on Trial* pictured the defense as wishing that some conjurer could make these incriminating artifacts disappear. In Hiss's book what Prosecutor Murphy called the "immutable witnesses" come under the scrutiny of Hiss's analytical pince-nez.

Chambers had originally accused Hiss of stealing documents from the files of the Nye Committee. A Nye Committee employee upset this applecart by denying that the committee had any documents that were not intended for the eyes of any and every journalist.

The charge that stuck revolved around what loosely came to be referred to as the "pumpkin papers." Though not all of the documents were unearthed in Chambers' pumpkin, the press generally lumped them together with the cache in Nathan Levine's dumbwaiter shaft. There were four memos in Hiss's handwriting, brief notes on incoming State Department cables. Chambers claimed that these referred to documents that Hiss had been unable to copy *in toto*. Hiss claimed that they were memory joggers which he used in making oral reports to his superior, Francis Sayre. There were 65 pages, either copies or summaries of State Department cables, reports, and memos, allegedly typed on Hiss's old Woodstock by Priscilla Hiss.

The second batch consisted of 58 microfilmed pages drawn from the pumpkin—supposedly photographed from stolen papers brought home in Hiss's brief case. The typing had begun, Chambers said, after Bykov had demanded a step-up in the flow of documents. Fred Cook questions the fact that the flow could be increased by replacing the cumbersome and less accurate process of typing with the efficient one of microfilming.

Chambers testified most emphatically that he got all the documents from Hiss. "Chambers insists on all," says Fred Cook, "and because he does one stray black sheep taints the whole flock." Some of the sheep were strangely gray. Cook points out that one of the typed documents—a 22-page discussion of economic policy on Manchukuo—as intricate as a Wall Street balance sheet—would have been infinitely simpler to microfilm than to copy. Another, known as Exhibit No. 10, went only to the Far Eastern section of the State Department, not to Francis Sayre's office, where Hiss worked. Exhibit No. 10 was, furthermore, *not* typed on the Hiss Woodstock. Here was a document to which Hiss could *not* have had access, could *not* have been typed on the Hiss machine. Exhibit No. 13 also appeared to have gone only to the Far Eastern Division. Among the microfilmed papers were two which were photographed from carbons. Vagaries in the typing showed that they were not filmed from the originals that were sent to Sayre's office but that they might have been taken from carbons filed in the Trade Agreements Section, where Julian Wadleigh worked. On one of the typed documents the spy painstakingly copied all the irrelevant data, omitting the only part that was of any interest to the Soviets—word of a planned Japanese attack on Russia.

Claude Cross, Hiss's attorney at the second trial, pointed out that among the typewritten documents, at least five never went through Sayre's office. An information copy of the documents that formed the basis of the Baltimore typewritten papers went to the Trade Agreements Section, where Wadleigh worked, and to the Far Eastern Division, whence Exhibit No. 10 was stolen. Wadleigh's departure for Turkey on March 11, 1938, however, points to the impossibility of his being the source of all the documents, some of which go up to April 1.

Experts in document examination, employed by Hiss, discovered that the 65 typed pages could be divided into two sets, and one set gave evidence of having been cut down from a larger size. The paper on which the two sets of documents were typed exhibited markedly different degrees of aging. One expert believed that the two sets could not have been stored together for most of their existence. A typewriter analysis showed that at least four ribbons had been used and

that the variety of ribbons bore no relation to the time se-
quence of the documents, belying the idea of chronological
night-by-night espionage. The envelope which Levine extracted from the dumbwaiter shaft had been sealed with an
oblong white sticker. The grimy appearance of the envelope
was relieved by one striking detail. The bottom half of the
sealing sticker was startlingly white. Fred Cook suggested that
this might indicate the use of a solution that permitted a
sealing label to be lifted without breaking the seal.

The documents and the Woodstock typewriter convicted
Hiss. In his book Hiss came up with an extraordinary charge.
It was possible that Woodstock No. 230,099 was a forgery.
Hiss's final counsel, Chester T. Lane, set out to have a typewriter built that could duplicate the writing of the stolen papers. Martin Tytell, a New York typewriter expert, at the
behest of the Hiss forces, constructed a machine that was
capable of fooling an expert.

The Woodstock that convicted Hiss had been located after
a long search by the defense forces. The trail led through the
sons of the ubiquitous Cleide Catlett, who had received it
from the Hisses, to a truckman named Ira Lockey. Lane suggested that No. 230,099 might have been substituted for the
real Hiss machine—planted on the defense—at some time
during the search.

At one point in *Witness*, Chambers described how he had
obtained translating work immediately after his break with the
party. A book that he translated, *Dunant, The Story of the Red
Cross*, inspired Chambers to what he called "a ferocious little
parable."[23] In his days at the Luce publications, when editing
Life's History of Western Civilization, Chambers had been
tempted to moralize a bit. He described Dunant, in his white-
washed cell, with a Testament beside him, asking to be carried
to his grave "like a dog, without a single one of your ceremonies, which I do not recognize. I am a disciple of Christ
as in the first century, and nothing more." Chambers contrasted this spirit of abnegation with the excesses of the pleas-
ure-mad Edwardians. Here was the didactic Chambers turning
on the worldlings of the Machine Age with the wrath of the
reformed rake. The voice of the circulation department whis-

pered to him, however, following a rebuke from the managing editor and the ending was killed.

After the trial, Alger Hiss unearthed evidence which suggested that the "ferocious little parable" might have backfired on its author. In the files of the Oxford University Press, he discovered letters that showed that Chambers' employment as a translator began in the middle of March, 1938. A shipping tag in the Oxford offices showed that a final batch of the Dunant manuscript had been sent to Chambers at Mount Royal Terrace on March 18, 1938, at least a month and a half before the April 15 date he gave at the trials as his time of breaking with the party. Dr. Gumpert, the author of the book, remembers being told that he couldn't see his translator because he was in hiding from the G.P.U., and both he and Mr. Paul Willert of the Press have a clear recollection of Chambers' fugitive status.

The government shrugged off Hiss's discoveries, producing affidavits of payments for rent on Chambers' Terrace residence, correspondence with a gas and electric company, records of an automobile repair company, all of which indicated that *Mrs.* Chambers was in Baltimore in April. Only one of these communications, to their daughter's school, headed Mount Royal Terrace, bore Chambers' name as well.

Chambers had repeatedly testified that he had broken with the party in 1937. "I soon realized that the latter date was wrong and corrected it to April, 1938 before the Committee. Only gradually did I become aware of the necessity for absolutely exact statement."[24] Such ignorance seems strangely naïve, in anyone with even a passing exposure to courtroom thrillers. Both Chambers and the government overlooked the vital point about Chambers' lapse of memory. If Chambers was known by the Oxford staff to have been on the lam in March, Hiss could hardly have passed him the Baltimore documents in early April.

Fred Cook summarizes some of the inconsistencies in Chambers' tale: his conflicting statements about collecting Hiss's party dues; contradictions in Nathaniel Weyl's testimony; Lee Pressman's denial that Hiss was a party member; Chambers' failure to produce independent witnesses to the Hiss-Chambers friendship; Chambers' backtracking on his 30th Street sojourn.

The prosecution painted Hiss as a fairly slick article; yet this diabolically cunning fellow passed incriminating notes in his own handwriting, stuck his head in the noose by running the Woodstock typewriter to earth and edited from his reports to his Soviet bosses anything of any possible interest to them. In the annals of espionage his ineptitude has rarely been equaled since the days when Franz von Papen left a notebook bearing his master plan in the New York subway.

One is asked to believe in a relationship between four people, two of whom at one moment were the fanatical Communists "Carl" and "Lisa" and at the next enjoyed the Kaffee-klatsch domesticity of neighbors in the suburbs. The picture strains the credulity. As Fred Cook points out, one has to be more than Carl and Lisa to a maid.

On the other side of the ledger, credulity is also strained by Hiss's explanation of the apartment and the car. By admitting to only the most passing acquaintance with Chambers, Hiss cut the ground out from under himself. Chambers' motivations are obscure even to those who might be willing to buy the forged documents and the rigged typewriter. Why, as Alistair Cooke asked, did Chambers wait so long to spring the trap? Like Othello, the case raises the question, for anyone he knew so slightly why would Iago go to all that trouble?

Among the odder aspects of the case was the procession of mute witnesses. Hiss unsuccessfully attempted to produce three people who had known Chambers as Crosley. There was the death of Marvin Smith, who had notarized the Ford transfer. Laurence Duggan, named by Chambers as a contact of the "Massing apparatus," was killed by a fall from his New York office window several days after questioning by the F.B.I. There was the suicide of Congressman McDowell, who "gave credit" to the F.B.I. for finding the typewriter that typed the letters found in the pumpkin[25] (indicating possibly that the typewriter had been found by government agents *before* it was turned up by the defense). There were the harassments, the sudden clamming up on the part of witnesses, the disappearance of relevant data that beset the Hiss forces in their investigations after the second trial. Martin Tytell reported an inexplicable disappearance of type specimens. All in all, the whole affair was so fraught with penny-dreadful implications and seemingly coincidental "jumped or fells" that it might have emanated from the brain of Van Wyck Mason.

So violent were the passions aroused by the Hiss case that to their supporters Hiss had to be Dreyfus—Chambers, Magdalene. Few seem to have considered that the truth might be somewhere in between—that neither man was quite as he represented himself—that each may have been lying a little, that there was more meat hanging on both of them than ever came to light at the trials.

For a number of years Hiss's name was on a par with that of Benedict Arnold.

When the trial broke, the McCarthy era was in swing. For many Americans the Hiss case became tied up with such reversals in foreign policy as the loss of China, the Soviet explosion of the atom bomb, the outbreak of the Korean War. By one of those simple-minded misreadings of history, it was fashionable to blame this series of disasters on Roosevelt and Harry Truman and their "twenty years of treason" in the White House. When Joe McCarthy wanted to discredit Adlai Stevenson in a campaign speech, he made a purposeful *lapsus linguae* and called him Alger.

There was a widespread tendency to read philosophical implications into what Chambers portentously capitalizes as The Great Case. The experimental, relativistic, secular, intellectual ethic of the New Deal was embodied for many in the figure of Alger Hiss. When Hiss was on trial, there were those who saw behind him the shadow of Oliver Wendell Holmes, the Prince of Pragmatism.

Hiss was also credited with having engineered the "Yalta sellout," of all but starting Russian tanks rolling into satellite streets. Against him was pitted the massive figure of Chambers, the regenerate sinner, whose factual lapses slipped by unnoticed in his chorus of *mea culpas*. "We were close friends," says Chambers in his best more-in-sorrow-than-in-anger tone, "but we are caught in a tragedy of history. Mr. Hiss represents the concealed enemy against which we are all fighting."[28]

The testimony of Dr. Carl Binger contributed to the popular picture of Hiss. Here was the effete intellectual reclining on the analyst's couch vs. hoss-sense, the "plain people," the steak-and-potatoes man.

The apologias that Hiss and Chambers each wrote point up the differences between the two. Hiss has written a dispassionate, factual tale peppered with names and dates. Chambers' wandering 794-page revelation *Witness* has a *Dostoievskian* tone, though as a seller it proved somewhat less durable than *The Brothers Karamazov*.

A religious note permeates Chambers' work. In *Witness* he invests the rite of "informing" on former comrades with the solemnity of the rite of the confessional. Yet in all of Chambers' theological system there is no mercy for one kind of sinner, the man of good will who in the Depression years might have traveled in spirit with the comrades—the dilettante revolutionary who may have done nothing more than do freelance work for the *New Masses*.

A sampling of the *New Masses* under Chambers' editorship takes one back to an era of fashionable radicalism as obsolete as the age of the mastodon. The profile of a decade is here on the flaking paper—for whose quality the library profusely apologizes, and which comes off on the reader's clothes.

Here one reads of the social occasions that brightened the lives of Edna Millay's successors on Macdougal Street: the ads for dinners at John's Restaurant. "Italian dishes—a place with atmosphere where all radicals meet"; the New Masses Ball; "Camp Unity—a resting place for proletarians."

There are tormented examinations of conscience. "Shall the artist passively play the prophetic role of the visionary, or shall he fight on the side of the working class?" "I am but an atom," writes Mother of Three. "It is too late to save me, but I am vitally interested in the sort of civilization that my children and my children's children will have to live in."

There are the ads for *Sane Sex Life and Sane Sex Living;* for *Bishop Brown's Quarterly Lectures on the Science of Moscow and the Superstition of Rome* and for The Workers' Rational Living Library "How is your Stomach (Food, indigestion, constipation); Sex and Health (the Sexual Revolution, Anatomy, Physiology, Menstruation)."

Chambers' wife, Esther Shemitz, has contributed monolithic proletarian cartoons. There are articles by unfrocked priests, unflattering likenesses of Hoover, Ford, Mussolini, and the Pope.

Chambers himself contributes some short stories. "You have Seen Their Heads" takes us to the front lines of the Kuomintang–Chinese Communist Conflict, where we witness gory death in *The Damn Fool* manner: "They stuck the head of Wan Gan-chi beside that of Lin yu-tin." "Can you Hear Their Voices?" is set in drought-ridden Kansas. Chambers has none of Scott Fitzgerald's confusion about the good guys and the bad guys. The Communists are dedicated to an unimpeachable program of free groceries, free milk for babies. The heartless capitalists exult over the death of a baby because the Red Cross will be freed of the onus of feeding it.

This tale was given a Poughkeepsie accent by Hallie Flanagan, guiding light of the Vassar Experimental Theatre in an independently published play. Miss Flanagan added to Chambers' drought-ridden *New Masses* farmers some characters with whom Vassar girls had more empathy. The heroine is Harriet, daughter of a reactionary congressman. Daddy fears that higher education may give Harriet "ideas." Harriet's parents are planning a little coming-out party for her costing $250,000 (topping Barbara Hutton's by a mere $190,000). The whole lower floor of a hotel is to be done over and a musical-comedy troupe imported by airplane for the occasion. Harriet bitterly resents this because Harriet has a social conscience.

The farmers in Chambers' original story are contrasted with the young worldlings at Harriet's party. The reactionary congressman sees to it that no one spoils the farmers by saving them from starvation. Harriet makes a scene and gets off some pretty dangerous remarks. Once she says that when they have droughts in Russia, they don't sit around waiting for handouts from the Red Cross. "I might be a revolutionary," she says; "I look well in red." At one point she bursts into the "Internationale." The orchestra plays "Just a Gigolo." The telephone rings. The number, significantly, is October 1-9-1-7.

Such parlor pinks as Harriet are Chambers' *bête noire*. Lacking the courage to take out a party card, they have nonetheless advanced the social revolution, which Chambers deplores, "in the name of liberalism . . . has been inching its ice cap over the nation for two decades." For years after the Hiss trial it was unhealthy to say that the revolution had not been an unmitigated disaster; that Franklin D. Roosevelt and Dean Acheson were not in the pay of Moscow; that the New Deal was the pragmatist's answer to the contrasts between Harriet and the denizens of the dust bowl.

Fred Cook has gone so far as to hint that Hiss might have been framed by Chambers and collaborators, who found it expedient to discredit the so-called "A.D.A. liberal." This seems like a wish-fulfillment fantasy on a par with what the Republicans used to say about F.D.R. and the Crown Princess of Sweden. Unquestionably, however, the Hiss case did throw a cloud over the now-on-the-one-hand-now-on-the-other-hand, East Coast, footnoted factual New Dealer, of whom Alger Hiss became the unhappy symbol.

It was a pity, for the moderate Left speaks to America's allies more eloquently than the voice of the Far Right. The moderate Left measures patriotism in terms of foreign aid more than in paeans to Old Glory. "High-Tax Harry" did as much to shore up America's defenses as the advocates of "more bang for a buck." Harriet's heart was, after all, in the right place. America's international standing was not advanced in the years when the "100% Americans" refused to forgive her a few youthful choruses of the "Internationale."

To the tangled question of Chambers' break with the party comes a footnote from the author of *The College of the Few.* In his autobiography, published in 1958, Mark Van Doren tells of a visit from Chambers which took place some twenty years before. In October 1938, Chambers had come breathlessly to his old schoolmaster, begging for a testimonial letter to get him started back on the road to respectability. He described his break with the party in the usual purple hues: plots, murders, guilty secrets, the malevolent band of pursuers.

He again slipped out of Van Doren's life until ten years later, at which time Van Doren underwent some questioning on the part of the Hiss lawyers, as one who knew Chambers when.

Of his erstwhile pupil Van Doren wrote, "Knowing Whittaker's flair for the dramatic, remembering his numerous plunges into extremes of conviction contrary to one another and having in mind his cloak-and-dagger air when he slipped down in 1938 to have me help save him from murderous pursuers, I found I could not believe him now, though I granted that he might very well believe himself."[27]

Whittaker Chambers is incapable of understanding the genius for peaceful evolution that is the Anglo-Saxon's greatest strength. It is impossible to imagine Chambers engaged in a friendly political difference. The stakes are too high. "I see why it might not pay the Communists to kill you at this point," he quotes a New Dealer as saying, "but I don't see how the administration dares to leave you alive."[28]

The tragedies which afflicted Hiss and Chambers after the trial attracted little popular attention. Hiss was separated from his wife in 1959, after twenty-nine years of marriage. Chambers suffered in relative obscurity through a heart attack and a fire on his Maryland farm. On July 9, 1961, Chambers died at the age of sixty.[29] The *New York Times* published a glowing tribute to him from Richard Nixon. Alger Hiss, when approached, declined comment.[30] Chambers had spent the latter stages of his literary career as an editor under William Buckley, Jr., on the *National Review*. For both of these campus insurgents, Communist or anti-Communist, the liberal is the enemy. In *The Damn Fool* the muzhiks significantly follow the man with a symbol—be it crucifix or hammer and sickle. The villain is the workaday fellow whose only reaction to Everett Holmes' hideous sacrifice is an unheroic "ouch."

Yet, for all this, Chambers had a sense of history. In the stentorian prose of his *apologia pro vita sua* is the story of a sick civilization. We smell the dying aroma of Edwardian lavender and lace. We hear the well-modulated voices of his childhood drowned out by the thundering encyclicals of Engels and Marx. Chambers seems to have been created for an age of violence. He spoke of the necessity of overcoming his revulsion against killing as "part of what makes me a man."[31] Strange talk for one who has allegedly found peace. One wonders if the mild-mannered Quakers are not sometimes taken aback by the antics of this rehabilitated lost lamb.

In Chambers' story lies the strength, as well as the weakness, of the fanatic. The Communist conspiracy flourishes though the avant-garde have dropped by the wayside along with Chambers. Gone is Harriet at her Roman orgy, the cheery ones mixing red wine and red politics. Yet after the "eleventh defeat without a victory" the Chinese Communists in Chambers' short story have banished the evil war lords to Formosa. Camp Unity, the Workers' Rational Living Library, the ads for *Sane Sex Life and Sane Sex Living* would be funny if they were not so sad.

Pitted against the Hiss supporters is the figure of the fanatic —the counterpart of Everett Holmes flailing about with a crucifix, choosing the monk's cell or the party cell but never the comfortable pew or the Marxist study group. Holmes' creator happened to be able to throw himself with a frightening fervor into the excesses of one revolution as well as to lead the counterrevolution against it with undampened fervor. As with Holmes, convictions were not too important as long as one held them violently. In the shifting tides of public opinion, convictions change. For all Chambers' noisy talk of turning the other cheek, only the violence remains.

II "SING ME A SONG OF SOCIAL SIGNIFICANCE"

"They're not our niggers. Look at their eyes, look at their hair, gentlemen.

"They look like something just broke out of the zoo.

"Guilty or not guilty, let's get rid of these niggers."
Quoted in *Scottsboro Boy*, by Haywood Patterson and Earl Conrad

"I wouldn't have missed it for two million dollars. But wouldn't go through it again for five million." *Scottsboro Boy*

6

Scottsboro Boy

HAYWOOD PATTERSON

On June 4, 1950, the blurred features of a Negro appeared in a dramatic ad in the *New York Times Book Review*. The copy read:

My name is Haywood Patterson. I am living in hiding somewhere among you. I stand convicted of rape. I have served 17 years in Alabama prison farms and jails. I am not guilty. Read my story of my "crime" and my punishment. Know the living hell I have endured—and escaped—in the pages of

SCOTTSBORO BOY

By Haywood Patterson and Earl Conrad

Just published. At nearly all bookstores. $3. Doubleday

Once the name of Haywood Patterson had galvanized public opinion from Harlem to Riga, Latvia. Yet at the time his book was published, hardly one American in a thousand would have had any idea who he was. A war had bred so many displaced persons that everyone had long forgotten the Depression and the young D.P.'s of the hobo jungle.

Haywood Patterson was one of nine children. He was born in Elberton, Georgia, in 1912. When he burst into print at eighteen he had had only a few months' schooling. In addition to the disadvantages of poverty, he was handicapped by being simultaneously Southern and black.

Patterson remembers the years 1924 and 1925 as a time of relative prosperity. His father was then earning between forty and forty-five dollars a week. After 1929, the elder Patterson's salary dropped to fifteen dollars a week, and the boy joined many others of his generation in riding the rods. "Faraway places were in my bones," he wrote. He took his first freight-car ride to Dayton, Ohio. "That opened the world." By the time he was sixteen, he knew all the nearby states—southeast to Pensacola, north to Ohio, west to Arkansas. He knew when the freights left and when they arrived. He could light a cigarette in the wind on a moving boxcar.

On March 25, 1931, Patterson and eight other colored boys were looking for work, bumming a ride on a slow freight between Chattanooga and Alabama. Eugene Williams, the youngest, was thirteen. Charlie Weems, the oldest, was twenty. Patterson was eighteen. Some were in sorry shape. One was half blind. Another was "so sick with the venereal he could barely move around."[1]

On the train a fight broke out between the Negroes and some white boys. All the whites except one were thrown or jumped onto the tracks. The group which had been put off was furious and reported to a nearby telegrapher that the "niggers" had tried to murder them. When the train arrived at Paint Rock, Alabama, the boys were taken off the train and arrested.

Two white girls, Victoria Price and Ruby Bates, who had also been on the freight car, admitted under questioning that they had been raped—each six times. The doctor who examined them discovered evidence of sexual intercourse. The lack of bruises or torn clothing suggested a measure of acquiescence. The boys were, however, taken to Scottsboro, the Jackson County seat. On March 31, 1931, an all-white jury indicted all nine for rape. By April 8, all but one had been sentenced to death. A mistrial was declared for fourteen-year-old Roy Wright because of his extreme youth. A rehearing was denied to Eugene Williams on April 9, 1932. In June of the following year, however, he and Wright were handed over to the tender mercies of the Juvenile Court.

Objectivity was not the keynote of the occasion. A parade of Ford trucks with phonographs and amplifiers invested the proceedings with a carnival air. The defendants were compared to animals in the zoo. Enthusiastic applause greeted each of Victoria Price's revelations. The first two convictions took place to a rousing accompaniment of cheers. A band outside the courtroom played "There'll be a Hot Time in the Old Town Tonight."

Both Victoria Price and Ruby Bates had reputations for being no better than they should be. Local gossip had it that prior to the trials both had distributed their favors impartially to black and white alike.[2] The press, however, built both of them up into symbols of outraged Southern womanhood.

A rumor was spread that one of the girls had had a breast chewed off by a Negro. The *Jackson County Sentinel* gave a piteous description of their condition "after their unspeakable experience at the hands of the black brutes." Headlines described a "splendid capture by Deputy and Posse."

Caught in the limelight, Victoria Price began to blossom as a thespian—identifying each of her alleged attackers with cries of "yonder he sits—yonder he sits."[3]

The situation was complicated by the fact that several of the Negro boys testified to having seen the rape while denying their own participation.

Some details of the girls' story didn't quite add up. The fight started, according to Victoria Price, about ten minutes after the train left a town called Stevenson. The ride from Stevenson to Paint Rock lasted forty to fifty minutes. Allowing time for a fight, for a total of twelve rapes, plus the effort of removing dresses, overalls and step-ins from the two tigresses clawing for their virtue, the rapists would have had to work with the speed of sound. The gravel came nearly to the top of the shallow gondola car, making the locale a bit public except to the most determined of exhibitionists. One of the boys was so far gone with "the venereal" that rape would have been at best an excruciatingly painful experience. The lack of marks on the victims was particularly suspicious in view of the fact that the scratchy assault must have taken place on a bed of gravel—truly a fate worse than death.

Almost immediately agitation began for a new trial. The Communist International Labor Defense wired the governor demanding a stay of execution, and sent poison-pen notes to the trial judge. The I.L.D. imported a lawyer named Joseph Brodsky. The N.A.A.C.P. entered the lists, retaining as their counsel Roderick Beddow, Clarence Darrow, and Arthur Garfield Hays.

A fight forthwith developed between the N.A.A.C.P. and the I.L.D. as to which really represented the boys. The different approaches of the gradualist bourgeois and the Communist fanatic were instantly apparent. The N.A.A.C.P. regarded the boys' vicissitudes as being a problem of color rather than economics—pointing out that the loudest cries for a necktie party came not from capitalist exploiters but from the working class.

The Communists saw in the Scottsboro case an opportunity for "self-determination for the Black Belt"—a solution of the Negro problem which had little to recommend it except that self-determination had worked out nicely for the minorities in the Ukraine.

Out came the shibboleths about the class struggle, the mass meetings, the letters in the *Daily Worker*. On May Day, 1931, 300,000 workers demanded the release of the nine. Police broke up a mass meeting in Harlem. Thanks to I.L.D. publicity, such notables as Thomas Mann, Kay Boyle, and Theodore Dreiser took up the cudgels for the boys.

The N.A.A.C.P. accused the Communists of having abducted members of the boys' families. The Communists charged the N.A.A.C.P. with forcing some of the Negroes to sign statements which they could not read. The boys' mothers were pressed into the service for party fund-raising drives. Bogus mothers, according to the N.A.A.C.P., were used in cases where the real ones were unavailable.

Negro sympathizers of the boys were whipped up to a frenzy by meetings often held in churches, which had the spirit of old-time revivals. The success of the Communists' tactics could be gauged by their effect upon Patterson's mother.

> I love the Reds [she wrote in the *Daily Worker*]. I can't be treated any better than the Reds has treated me. And I am a Red too. I tell the white and I tell the black I am not getting back of nothing else. . . . I hope next time I be to see you all I will be less worried. I never stayed away from my family that long for I think my children don't get along without me. . . . Give all the Reds my love for I love them all. . . .
>
> From one of the Reds, Janie Patterson.[4]

The inhabitants of Scottsboro resented the interest taken in their town by the denizens of "New Yawk and Rusha." The K.K.K. wired threats to the I.L.D. There was to be no nonsense about Negroes being included on the jury which tried the boys. "A Negro juror in Jackson County would be a curiosity—and some curiosities are embalmed, you know."[5]

The battle as to who was to represent the boys raged on. The N.A.A.C.P. enlisted the services of a lawyer named Stephen R. Roddy. The story went that the Communists tried to lure him over to the I.L.D. According to Edmund Wilson, the Communists took Roddy to the mountaintop and showed him the kingdoms of the world, attempting to dazzle him with the vision of becoming another Clarence Darrow. Mr. Roddy proved to be far more interested in how they proposed to pay his fee. They were evasive, and he declined their offer. Thenceforth his name was mud. The *Daily Worker* accused him of being a Klan member, of having conspired to electrocute the defendants, even of having been an inmate of an insane asylum.

Darrow and Hays were willing to drop all organizational

ties and give their services to the boys alone, provided the I.L.D. would do the same. The I.L.D. people refused to sign a statement to that effect. The Communists were successful in persuading the defendants that the N.A.A.C.P. was really a pawn of the "lyncher bosses of the South" and its officers as "sycophantic tools" of the "capitalists."[6] After endless charges and countercharges, the defendants signed with the I.L.D. Communist tactics at Scottsboro might have served as a case study in the Lenin Method.

Whatever ethical problems it posed, the method got results. On March 31, 1932, the I.L.D. secured leave to appeal to the United States Supreme Court. On November 7, 1932, retrials were ordered for seven of the boys on the grounds that they had had inadequate counsel at Scottsboro.

The point was well taken. An attorney for the Alabama Power Company, briefly assigned to the case, summarized the attitude of local legal circles when he said that the power company had enough juice to burn all of his prospective clients.

Once the I.L.D. had staked out its exclusive claim to the "Scottsboro martyrs," it entrusted their defense to competent hands. On March 13, 1933, Samuel Leibowitz, the famous criminal lawyer, took charge of the case. On March 27, 1933, Haywood Patterson's case was separated from those of the other defendants and he was placed on trial at Decatur in Morgan County, Alabama, before Judge James E. Horton.

Patterson's second trial added some significant details to the portrait of womanhood defiled. The Southern court had debated earnestly whether the evidence of intercourse discovered by the examining doctor could be traced to a white man or a Negro. The defense produced a white man named Lester Carter, who with a friend, Jack Tiller, had jumped off the train after the fight. Carter testified that he and Tiller had had intercourse with the two plaintiffs on the previous night in a hobo jungle. This shook Victoria's story of a virtuous overnight stay at the home of a Mrs. Callie Brochies.

The real bombshell was dropped by Ruby Bates, who suddenly reversed all her previous testimony, denying that there had ever been an attack.

She wrote to a male admirer, "I want to make a statement too [sic] you Mary Sanders is a goddam lie about those Negroes jazzing me . . . those policemen made me tell a lie . . . i was jazzed but those white boys jazzed me i wish those Negroes are not Burnt on account of me."[7]

Apparently her admirer was more likely to be horrified by Ruby's involuntary submission to a Negro than by the voluntary offer of her favors to a white.

Ruby said she had told her rape tale for fear of being imprisoned on a charge of crossing the state line with men. She reversed herself completely, appearing at Patterson's second trial as a witness for the defense.

Patterson himself reversed some of his previous testimony. He had originally been among those who had claimed to have seen some of the others commit rape. This he now denied. Originally he had denied participation in the fight. Now he admitted, "I helped in the fight."

Orville Gilley, the white boy who had stayed on the train after the fight, refused to say that rape had taken place. The Jackson County prosecution attributed this to the fact that he was incapable of relating the term "sexual intercourse" to a shorter, less literary Anglo-Saxon word.

Despite serious setbacks, Victoria Price stuck gamely to her story. She was a witness in the grand manner, later popularized at the televised Kefauver hearings by another star performer named Virginia Hill.

She had testified that when the rape had occurred she was twenty-one years old. Asked if she were now twenty-two, she said, "I ain't that educated that I can figure it out."[8]

Belatedly she produced a pair of torn step-ins as evidence of her struggle. Leibowitz wished to know why it had taken them two years to turn up.

At one point she had trouble identifying a painstakingly constructed scale model of the scene of the alleged attack. "The gondola I was in," she said, "was much bigger than that thing."[9]

Despite the body of new evidence in support of the Negroes, Patterson was sentenced on April 9, 1933, to die in the electric chair at Kilby Prison. Judge Horton was apparently assailed by disquieting reflections about the justice of this verdict. A motion was filed with him, demanding a new trial for Patterson. On June 22, 1933, he granted the appeal, with a lengthy opinion reviewing the case, concluding that the conviction was unjustified by the evidence. Patterson reports on the political repercussions of Judge Horton's moment of truth. "They beat him in the fall when he ran for the judge job again. He never did nothing more in Alabama politics after that. He was done."[10]

Haywood Patterson was tried twice more. At Decatur, before Judge William Washington Callahan, he was once again sentenced to death. The United States Supreme Court reversed the conviction on April 1, 1935, because Negroes had been excluded from the jury which had tried him. The grand jury indicted Patterson once again on November 13, but, for the first time within the memory of any resident of Alabama, a Negro was included among the jurors. On January 23, 1936, Haywood Patterson was convicted for the fourth time and sentenced by Judge Callahan to 75 years' imprisonment. Four of the other defendants had been let off by this time. The five remaining boys were taken to Kilby Prison, and Haywood Patterson was sent to Atmore State Prison Farm. In July 1937 a news dispatch predicted that this would end the Scottsboro Case.

Yet for Haywood Patterson the long, degrading battle for survival was just beginning. Patterson's account of his stay at Atmore State Prison Farm, and at Kilby Prison, if true, makes an appalling social document. He charged that medical care was bad, the food worse. Prisoners were not considered sick until they ran a temperature of 100 to 104 degrees. Each prisoner was given a spoon. If he lost it, he was forced to eat with his fingers, or put his face down into the pan to suck in slops which Patterson claimed to have seen a pig refuse.

Medical treatment was rudimentary. Aspirin was administered for all illnesses from head colds to tuberculosis. Ailing teeth were indiscriminately pulled. Since the prison doctor was paid for giving V.D. shots, they were administered to sufferer and non-sufferer alike.

Disciplinary measures ranged from the "whupping" and

hose-piping to the castor-oil treatment and the "dry shave." The dry shave consisted of pulling out all the flesh around the lips of wayward prisoners with a safety razor or dull knife.

Patterson was given one beating so bad that it took two months to heal. When the plaster was removed the scabs came with it, and he went around with his trousers open in the back so that the cloth wouldn't touch his skin.

Crazy people and sane people worked side by side. Sick men were beaten in the fields for not keeping up with the work. Prisoners were not even allowed to learn to read. Knifings occurred every few days, killings on a slightly lower frequency—every few weeks. Mealtimes were often enlivened by some form of violence. A group of convicts once refused to reveal the whereabouts of a gun. Their heads were pushed under water. As soon as they came up again they were dunked like apples in a Halloween tub. The day was brightened by periodic visits from ministers and people who had dropped by to take a gander at the death row. Patterson briefly got religion, but quickly decided that he wanted no part of pie in the sky.

He became adept at working the angles. Publicity had made the Scottsboro boys the glamour prisoners of the cell block. Kay Boyle, Thomas Mann, Theodore Dreiser, and Albert Einstein were rallying intellectuals to the cause, and packages from well-wishers all over the world turned up in their mailbags.

Prison guards helped themselves to goodies intended for the boys. When Patterson, in front of the warden, asked his mother to inform the postal authorities of the disappearance of certain registered letters, the missing mail was quickly delivered to his cell. Southern prison officials, it seems, have a wholesome respect for the Feds.

Behind bars, as elsewhere, money talks. Convict waiters brought breakfast to the boys, and took orders for special lunches. Sympathizers provided them with weapons, which they agreed to part with in exchange for exercise privileges, visitors, and food. Guards, who were paid some sixty dollars a month, were responsive to bribery and would furnish the boys—for a fee—with women, men, and other niceties of life. Patterson made a tidy profit from a prison "store" which bought items from the commissary and resold them on the cell block. Patterson lived in comfort on the proceeds of a lively traffic in such stimulants as benzedrine, shoe polish, shellac, paregoric, and dope. He was able to avail himself of the services of a "gal boy."

The authorities, Patterson contended, were more corrupt than the prisoners. Parole officers took kickbacks from parolees. The prisoners justified the rackets that went on behind prison walls, but the fact was that the biggest racket of all was the prison farm itself. Convicts who were worked to death to raise food never saw the fruit of their toils. The food raised at Atmore went to canned-goods companies whose advertising campaigns did not stress the origins of the product.

The convicts protested this injustice in a manner so eloquent as to make one think twice before opening up a can of vegetables.

The regime at Atmore was not calculated to make recalcitrant natures more lovable. Prison was a cradle for the murderer, the squealer, the deviate, and the nut. "You put men in a sewer, they will get muck on them,"[11] wrote Patterson in *Scottsboro Boy*. In prison, Patterson developed into a tough, dangerous man, whose motto was "Don't mess with me."

Once a crazy convict aroused his ire by setting a pace of work which saner folk were unable to match. Patterson slowed him down with a pine club.

Being leaped on from behind gave Patterson a sixth sense. The person who approached him with a friendly touch on the shoulder was likely to end up with a knife in his ribs.

Once Patterson was stabbed through the lung by a fellow convict. He lived on milk and soup for sixteen days, and had to be fed through a reed. Small wonder that Patterson's radar became sensitive. "You never know what a person has in his mind," said Patterson. "The deep-down part in a man, you never know that."[12]

Once, in an unexpected blossoming of the spirit of fair play, it was suggested that Patterson settle a difference with a fellow convict in the boxing ring. Patterson assured the outcome by threatening to get his opponent with a knife if he didn't throw the fight. The luckless man was beaten almost senseless by Patterson, and, on reviving, was beaten for a second time by the guard for putting up such a spiritless defense.

Toward the end of his stay Patterson was ostensibly tractable, but the "deep-down part" of his mind was plotting his exit from Atmore. On April 12, 1943, he vanished. About fifty miles from prison he was turned in by another Negro. For his sins he was sent to Kilby Prison. He escaped once more on July 17, 1948. This time the deep-down part was working on all cylinders.

Patterson and some of his friends made a break while the dog warden was putting on a sham dog race. Under his convict's uniform, Patterson wore civilian clothes. The dogs followed the other convicts through the woods, and Patterson's friends were caught. He doubled back in the opposite direction with the dogs in hot pursuit. He spoke kindly to them and went into a stream of water. The dogs trotted after him. Patterson got hold of two of them and drowned them. The third trotted prudently away.

Patterson hid in the toolbox of a waiting steam engine bound for Opelika, Alabama. Just as they were raiding the train he crept down between the engine and a box car. He slipped off the train into a white neighborhood, and hid out one night beneath a garage. The following evening he sneaked out and walked all night.

He was aided more than once in his escape by the knowledge he had acquired as a disinherited boy. There was a spot between the engine and the first car where one could travel without being seen. In this hideout he rode to Collegeville, Georgia, where he took a bus to Atlanta. In Atlanta he knew just where the freight yards were. The freight trains were old friends from his hobo days. The car that took him to freedom was a car of the type that had been the scene of his downfall seventeen and a half years before.

The trains with numbers from 6300 to 6600 go to Kentucky and Ohio out of Chattanooga. From Chattanooga he took 6600 to Kentucky, "then jumped into Ohio, riding all night, moving out of the South fast now." The pace of his narrative

quickens with the proximity of freedom. At the end of the line
his sister Mezell waited for him in Detroit. The other Pattersons, Sebell, Julian, Louise, and Ollie, turned out to welcome
the prodigal. There was a big home-cooked meal—the first
decent one he had had since he was a boy. At thirty-six
Patterson tasted his first glass of beer.

In New York he met some of his old supporters and was
persuaded to write his story. His book *Scottsboro Boy* was
published in 1949. Alabama tried to get him back, but Michigan's liberal governor G. Mennen Williams refused to ex-
tradite him.

By 1951 he was in trouble again. He was found guilty of
manslaughter after having knifed one Willie Mitchell in a
barroom brawl. Earl Conrad, who had worked with him on
Scottsboro Boy, said that like all the nine, he was a marked
man. Sometimes he spoke of getting "straightened out" and
settling down somewhere with a wife. But he was beset by
difficulty in holding jobs, racked by stomach attacks, smolder-
ing under an injustice the world had forgotten. His phraseology remained, to the end, that of a fugitive at bay.

"I'll lay out here in my room—and see what you do. Then
I'll make my next move."[13]

This was the thought with which he left the readers of
Scottsboro Boy. But nobody cared enough to bother calling
out the bloodhounds, much to the disappointment of his
publishers, who hoped for the sales figures which accompany
"controversy." In 1952 Patterson died of cancer in the prison
at Jackson, Michigan. He rated a few lines in the paper,
tucked away on page fourteen. He died as he had lived—
behind bars. Atmore and Kilby had failed to provide him with
much of a training in citizenship.

Scottsboro Boy rubbed a little salt in the wounds of Walter
White. White resented the fact that nowhere in the book, not
even in the chronology, was there any mention of Hays, Darrow, or the N.A.A.C.P. The Communist I.L.D. emerges
throughout as the boys' sole, shining champion.

The Southerner Hodding Carter also deplored Communist
exploitation of the case. His article on "Scottsboro Boy" in
the *Saturday Review* was endorsed by Walter White, even

though it gave the impression that somebody would eventually have slapped down any Negro as uppity as Patterson.

Patterson himself suffered from a very human tendency to edit the record in retrospect. Arthur Garfield Hays, writing at the time of the trial, named Patterson as one of the original supporters of the rape charge. No mention of this or of his changing testimony about the fight appears in *Scottsboro Boy*. None of the evasions of a frightened youth are allowed to mar the picture of Mr. Big. No base thoughts about Communist motives disturb Patterson's convenient memory.

Confirmation of Patterson's gloomy picture of the Southern prison system came from a totally unexpected quarter. In 1951, conditions in Louisiana prisons caused Westbrook Pegler to turn his attention briefly from liberals and labor racketeers to thunder at Devil's Island in Dixie. Mr. Pegler can hardly have been prompted by sympathy for the Communist party. He has been accused of many things, but rarely of left-wing bias.

At the end of *Scottsboro Boy*, Patterson surveys his sufferings from the long view:

> I guess my people gained more off the Scottsboro case than any of us boys did. It led to putting Negroes on juries in the South. It made the whole country, in fact the whole world, talk about how the Negro people have to live in the South. Maybe that was the biggest thing of all. Our case opened a lot of politics in the country. People said more about lynching, the poll tax, and a black man's rights from then on. In 1936 when I went on trial for the fourth time they said the South was the number one economic problem. My case helped the country to realize that.
>
> Something I got out of it too. I wouldn't have missed it for two million dollars. But I wouldn't go through it again for five million.[14]

One notices even here the influence of his Marxist teachers. It is still a problem of economics rather than of pigmentation.

Walter White, the bourgeois, the moderate, and the gradualist, points out the true moral of Scottsboro.

> In the intervening years it had become increas-
> ingly clear that the tragedy of a Scottsboro lies,
> not only in the bitterly cruel injustice which it
> works upon its immediate victims, but also . . .
> in the cynical use of human misery by Commu-
> nists in propagandizing for Communism, and in the
> complacency with which a democratic government
> views the basic evils from which such a case
> arises.[15]

Haywood Patterson did not live to hear of the Supreme
Court decision on school desegregation, of Autherine Lucy,
James Meredith or of Little Rock. Once more the eyes of the
world were on the South, as Miss Lucy picked her way across
the University of Alabama campus, through fiery crosses and
rotten fruit; as Central High School announced that if it
opened at all, it would open in the fall "all white." World
Communism was watching as James Meredith—harried by
campus hecklers, by reports of a shotgun attack on his parents'
home—discovered the atmosphere at the University of Mississippi was not conducive to classroom work. The Communist press hammered away at Governor Faubus and 'Ole
Miss as it had once hammered away at Victoria Price. The
problem endured long after the excitement of the depression
years died down: the workers' protests, the rallies of Scottsboro mothers, Ruby Bates's marches on the White House, the
articles for the highbrows by "Bunny" Wilson and Kay Boyle.
    Little by little, change was coming to the South. Little by
little, too, one bastion after another of the Western world was
falling under Communist domination. In Jordan and New
Delhi, in the lands of the White Man's Burden, sat party
propagandists ever on the alert for an issue. It was a race to
see who would move fastest—the Texas students who were
offering two dollars apiece for "coon's ears"; or the Reds
whose helping hands reached down to Janie Patterson and the
tough young hobo in the gondola car.

"The Oval Room where the debutante and her friends had supper was transformed into a sunken garden, circled by a miniature forest of silver birch and tropical flowers and foliage." *New York Daily News,* December 23, 1930

"Mommy had some treatments but they didn't seem to work much." Lance Reventlow, quoted in the *New York Times,* September 13, 1949

7

The Last of the Poor Little Rich Girls

BARBARA HUTTON

"Babs is a serial story, exciting, enviable, absurd, romantic, unreal," said *Time* magazine in 1938.[1] "Generous, luxurious, impulsive, and pleasure-loving . . ." said *Fortune*,[2] "completely lacks a sense of both social and financial responsibility." To tabloid readers of the thirties Barbara Hutton was the glittering denizen of the playgrounds of Europe—avidly pursued through ocean voyage, rumored engagement, custody suit, and divorce settlement. She was more than once compared to Marie Antoinette. Perhaps most telling of all was her own wry, poignant self-appraisal: "When I think of all the silly things I have done—maybe this will all be different tomorrow."[3]

Barbara was the granddaughter of Frank Woolworth, founder of the five-and-ten-cent-store chain. Woolworth had three daughters, Helena, Edna, and Jessie. Helena married Charles McCann, nephew of the Tammany boss, Richard Croker. Jessie married James Donahue. In 1907 Barbara's mother, Edna, married a stockbroker named Franklyn Laws Hutton. Barbara was born on November 4, 1912, when the conjunction of the planets was particularly favorable to capital formation. Barbara lived apart from her contemporaries in a sort of financial stratosphere, thanks to the ruthless old grandfather who had made the Horatio Alger legend come true.

Frank Woolworth was the son of a penniless upstate New York farmer. He combined a genius for merchandising, an unflagging capacity for hard work, and a social philosophy naïvely Darwinian. He opened his first five-and-ten-cent store in Lancaster, Pennsylvania, on June 21, 1879. By 1905 the Woolworth chain was worth $10,000,000. For the year 1939 sales for the 2,015 United States stores alone totaled $318,-839,664. A confidential secretary described Mr. Woolworth as "the most notional individual I ever knew." He was careless about large sums of money and chary of nickels and dimes. Once he allowed checks totaling $212,000 to accumulate undeposited in his wallet; yet he could keep two associates grubbing about on their hands and knees long after hours hunting for a quarter that was missing from his change pocket.

He had learned the value of a dollar the hard way. On his first job he was paid nothing at all for a three-month trial period and advised that if he wanted to be a success he would do better in a clean shirt. With the aid of the shirt, his fortunes soared meteorically to a salary of $3.50 a week. Woolworth courted his wife Jennie in what spare moments were left over after a working day which lasted from 7:00 A.M. to 9:00 P.M. When their oldest daughter was born she was brought down to the store on Saturday nights while her mother helped out behind the counter.

When Woolworth acquired stores of his own, he watched over the business with an eagle eye—wandering about incognito, pilfering things off counters to point up the laxness of the salesgirls; playing a cat-and-mouse game with his competitor Sebastian Kresge—sitting in the semi-gloom after hours cutting the price of chocolate pots from 5¢ to two for 5¢, to four for 5¢, until at last the opposition made no further move and all hands went home. Old Woolworth had an uncanny sixth sense about choosing novelties which would sell, and he made heavy use of "leaders"—items which cost the store more than the customers paid for them—a practice justified economically as "our form of advertising."[4]

Half a century later Defense Secretary Charles Wilson would amuse an entire nation with the words: "What's good for General Motors is good for the country." In Woolworth's day, far more paternalistic statements inspired not so much as a snicker. Woolworth looked upon the five-and-ten-cent stores as "an indirect charity . . . the means of making thousands of people happy."[5] To achieve this effect he had another guiding maxim: "We must have cheap help or we cannot sell cheap goods."[6]

Salesgirls were paid $2.00 to $2.50 a week. Managers began at $6.00 a week and were raised gradually to $10.00. Having made such a heavy investment in them, the New York office wished to be kept posted on the $10.00-a-week men's progress. Woolworth justified the salesgirls' salaries on the ground that white-collar jobs imparted more dignity than, say, domestic service, and that most of the girls lived at home with their parents anyhow. Despite these rationalizations he was forced to admit, in his annual letter in 1895, that the problem of salaries "has come to be the most sensitive subject we touch in an expense report." Shortly thereafter he took the step of granting a week's paid vacation to all who had been with the firm since January 1. Six months later another bombshell was dropped in the form of a Christmas bonus distributed under a veil of secrecy to "qualified" help. The bonus was accompanied by a letter which began: "You must certainly be a good, honest, conscientious and willing worker, or the manager would not have kept you so long."[7] Originally the bonus worked in such a way that veterans of several years with the chain might receive as much as $50.00. On the second year there was a $25.00 ceiling.

If these methods seem a trifle harsh to an age conditioned

to "labor-management partnership," it must be remembered that Woolworth was only abiding by the business ethics of his time. These were the practices which produced the shingled show places of Newport, the private railroad cars of New York Central magnates, the vast neo-Rhenish castles overlooking the Hudson, the Victorian horrors, which a less extravagant generation converted into museums and homes for fallen girls. By the turn of the century Frank Woolworth was ready to build his own big status-symbol, a mansion on Fifth Avenue.

In 1901 he moved to New York with his wife and three daughters. Perhaps the most remarkable feature of his new show place was its huge player pipe organ. As a youth Woolworth had attempted to take up both the violin and the flute but had been foiled by tone deafness. His new home was outfitted with a vast collection of player piano rolls. An evening with the Woolworths was eloquently described in one of a series of articles by John K. Winkler and Boyden Sparkes in the *Saturday Evening Post*. Guests would be escorted up a marble staircase to a great second-floor drawing room paneled with carved light oak decorated with gold. After profound rumblings the room would be filled with lights which turned various hues—nickelodeon-style—to match the industrialist's mood. Conduits led from the organ to various parts of the house—some leading to the newels of the marble staircase, others to the hollow posts of the Woolworths' bed. Still others carried the merest whispers into the Woolworths' clothes closets. Woolworth had commissioned a Hungarian artist to paint portraits of Beethoven, Wagner, Liszt, Mendelssohn, against allegorical backgrounds. A guest might have the strange experience of listening to *Die Walküre* to an accompaniment of lightning flashes and sound effects reminiscent of roulades of thunder, while out of the half-light there slowly materialized an ectoplasmic likeness of the composer.

Every Woolworth dwelling paid similar tribute to the Muse. There was a $20,000 pipe organ in the Glen Cove house which he acquired in 1915. When, in 1916, the house burned to the ground, it was promptly replaced by a $2,000,000 white marble Renaissance palace. In its "million-dollar living room" a $100,000 pipe organ with a particularly impressive set of storm effects was concealed behind an elaborately carved screen. The house also had ten master bedrooms and fifteen servants' rooms. The decorating of the second and third floors alone (in ten different styles) cost $200,000, with three crews of workmen working day and night. It was not to be marveled at that Woolworth's granddaughter soon displayed a taste for conspicuous consumption.

As Barbara was growing up, the old man's last days were drawing to a gloomy close. On June 7, 1918, Woolworth had to apply to court for the care of the property of his wife Jennie, whose mind had become befuddled. Woolworth was himself in poor health, given to sitting for hours at the organ controls, or in a depressing *partie carrée* consisting of himself, his wife, his nurse, and his wife's keeper. An interior decorator attempted to sell him on building a mansion occupying an entire city block. He settled instead, with typical practicality, for a costly mausoleum in Woodlawn.

In these final years, Barbara was to see the most impressive extension of the Woolworth personality: a Napoleonic office in what was then the highest building in the world. A year after her birth the $13,000,000 Woolworth building was completed.[8] Woolworth, taking seriously the sobriquet of a business associate who called him "the Napoleon of commerce," patterned his office on the emperor's palace at Compiègne. A foreword to a descriptive brochure, *The Cathedral of Commerce,* gives an idea of the impact of the skyscraper upon the imaginations of Woolworth's contemporaries.

> When seen at nightfall bathed in electric light as with a garment, or in the lucid air of a summer morning, piercing space like a battlement of the paradise of God which St. John beheld, it inspires feelings too deep even for tears.[9]

Barbara was five years old when her mother died. "I never knew my mother," she was to say later on, "but I have missed her all my life." Two years after her mother's death Woolworth himself died. Barbara was shuffled off to live with various aunts and uncles. She divided her time between the Tom

132 HERE TODAY

Middletons in Burlingame, California, the James Donahues in
New York and Palm Beach, and the Charles McCanns on
Long Island. After her father's remarriage she stayed with
him and with her stepmother in New York and South Carolina. When she was twelve Grandmother Woolworth died,
leaving her heir to over $25,000,000 of the $78,317,938 Woolworth estate.

When she was thirteen Barbara's father asked that her allowance be upped from $12,000 to $35,000 a year. When she
was fifteen he requested $60,000 plus $250,000 to remodel the
family apartment. By the time she was eighteen Barbara had
developed a few modest wants of her own. She requested an
additional $120,000 for a private railroad car, whose main-
tenance would come to $36,000 a year. In 1933, when she
finally came into her money, the value of her patrimony had
been doubled by judicious handling. She was worth roughly
$42,000,000.

In 1930, in the pit of the Depression, Barbara came out. Her
party in the ballroom of Manhattan's Ritz-Carlton Hotel cost
$60,000. There were two thousand guests and four orchestras:
Rudy Vallee, a Russian string ensemble, Howard Lanin's orchestra, and for the long pull, the dependable businessman's
bounce of that hardy perennial Meyer Davis. Argentina, the
famous Spanish dancer, entertained during the supper break.
The decorations inspired the following rhapsodic comment
from the *New York Daily News'* Nancy Randolph:

> Under a sky of soft blue, from which beamed a
> full-tropic moon, there lay an enchanted garden,
> thanks to the combined wizardry of Joseph Urban
> and Max Schling.
> The walls of the ballroom were hung with heavy
> cloth of silver, and the room's paneled mirrors
> covered with Southern smilax. At close intervals
> about the ballroom were tall, live silver birch trees,
> covered with green leaves as in midsummer, ob-
> viously imported from a warm clime [e.g., Cali-
> fornia]. . . .
> Other silver birch trees shimmered under the soft

light of the ballroom foyer and it was here that the debutante and her parents received their guests, in a bower of silver birch trees, palms and blossoming pink rose bushes.

Passing on from the decorations to the debutante's dress of bouffant white tulle, Miss Randolph ended up in a flurry of flesh-colored satin—the material selected by Mrs. Hutton "for this momentous occasion."[10]

Everyone admitted the following day that the Huttons had done well by their girl.

Barbara's doings had always occupied a certain amount of space in the tabloids, but with her party she became hot copy. Three years later a polo-playing prince named Alexis Mdivani pursued Barbara halfway around the world. In Bangkok, Siam, he announced that she had consented to marry him. The prince was the son of General Zachari Mdivani—onetime member of the Russian imperial court and aide-de-camp to the Czar. In 1923, Mdivani, like thousands of other impoverished Russian refugees, had moved his family to Paris. His three sons developed an instinct for survival which quickly set them apart from others of their kind who were eking out a living as waiters and concierges. Alexis' brother Serge married the movie star Pola Negri and later the opera star Mary McCormick. Another brother, David, was at the time the husband of Mae Murray. Prince Alexis had been divorced the previous year from Louise Astor Van Alen, from whom he was reputed to have received a large chunk of the Astor fortune.

The wedding was a city editor's dream. The religious ceremony in the Russian cathedral in Paris was said to have cost $100,000. There were four Orthodox priests in attendance, a Russian choir chanting hymns, and the traditional gold crown was held over the heads of the principals. When the pair emerged from the church, they were greeted by several thousand uninvited guests who had overpowered the police to crowd around the entrance, and it took the bride twenty minutes to gain access to her limousine.

Barbara's wedding to Mdivani inspired the first wave of the social criticism which was to engulf her periodically throughout the Depression. Certain features of the wedding and the honeymoon seemed unduly elaborate to an America where some twelve million people were currently out of work: the half deck of an ocean liner hired to take the newlyweds on a trip around the world; the royal suite rented in a Venice hotel, complete with Veronese frescoes; the bride's largesses to the groom, the pearl shirt studs, the string of polo ponies; the 58-foot motorboat ordered for delivery to the Lido.

Westbrook Pegler sneered at the union of "little Babbie, the darling of the $10-a-week personnel" and the "dream prince from Russia," regretting with heavy sarcasm that he had "not yet had time to visit any of the Woolworth 5-and-10¢ stores to observe the rejoicing." Shortly after her marriage, Barbara's twenty-first birthday and her acquisition of the Woolworth millions pointed up the differences between her standard of living and that of the five-and-ten personnel. Later she was to celebrate her twenty-second birthday by having an orchestra flown from London to Paris, for a party which cost more than $10,000. The prince's comment on the affair smacked of the *après-nous-le-déluge* school of social thought. "We didn't think it fitting to spend too much in these times."[11]

Plump Barbara did not conform to the prince's notion of the ideal woman. He put her on a rigorous diet, so that for three weeks at a time she existed on black coffee. She lost forty-two pounds and her health into the bargain, during her transformation from a "nice, fleshy American girl" to a "sleek, chic European."[12]

The prince frequently abandoned his wife for the more congenial society of polo ponies. During one of these interludes Barbara for the second time met the knight on a white charger. This time it was a Danish nobleman, Count Kurt von Haugwitz-Reventlow, scion of a family which had a hereditary trust fund of more than 3,500,000 kronen plus extensive estates in Denmark and Upper Silesia. On May 13, 1935, Barbara divorced Mdivani in Reno, Nevada. On May 14 she was married in Reno to Haugwitz-Reventlow. On August 1, 1935, Mdivani was killed in an automobile crash in Spain.

Later it was revealed that Barbara had set up over $2,250,-000 in trusts for the prince. Some of the bread cast on the water came back to Barbara. According to the *New York Times,* she declined to comment on the report that the prince had left her £400,000, but intimated that it could hardly be true. It was probable, she said, that the value of his palace in Venice and other property would amount to roughly that sum.

The Haugwitz-Reventlows' marriage began on an auspicious note with a statement from the Count: "No financial matter stands between us. I was never interested in money."[13]

Barbara and the Count decided to make their permanent home in England. Barbara feared she might be a target for gangsters, as America was currently harassed by Dillinger and Alvin Karpis. The Count and Countess moved into Winfield House, a mansion set on twelve and a half acres in the heart of London's Regent's Park. Named after her grandfather's estate in Glen Cove, it was a dwelling to warm the heart of Frank Woolworth.

The Countess' bathroom had heated towel racks, $10,000 worth of green and ivory marble, mirror glass walls, crystal shelves and gold fittings. A world-famous collection of Chinese jade was displayed in her bedroom, while priceless eastern embroideries were encased behind glass panels in the wide corridors. Other chinoiserie included elaborately carved Suchow lacquer, the smallest chair of which took several generations to complete. Young Lance, the child who was born to the Reventlows in 1936, was settled in his own separate six-room apartment—a self-contained affair with three living rooms, two baths, and its own kitchen.

For two years, 28 gardeners had been working on 5,000 privets, planted in a high bank formation. These, with 10-foot spiked iron railings, shielded the Haugwitz-Reventlows from the prying eyes of passers-by.

But domestic felicity was to elude Barbara in Regent's Park as it had in the palace in Venice. The birth of her child nearly wrecked her health. The baby was only three weeks old when a jobless Briton named Alfred Molyneux attempted to extort £200 from the Reventlows with an offer to disclose the details of a fictitious kidnapping plot against him. When caught,

Molyneux offered his American counterparts a commendable object lesson in British courtesy. Writing in his confession of the difficulties of supporting a wife and two children on 30 shillings a week he concluded: "I sincerely regret my action and hope I have not caused the Count and Countess any worry or anxiety."[14]

Where Mdivani had been indifferent, Reventlow was dictatorial. Barbara was beginning to establish a pattern as a marital accident-prone. In the troubled summer of Munich the tabloids exploded with sensational headlines. There was an endless jockeying for front-page position between Hitler's brown shirts and Babs' lawyers.

Even the dignified *New York Times* gave front-page treatment to the Haugwitz-Reventlows' divorce. The *New York Daily News* was having a field day of innuendoes and startling revelations: "Babs Count Rift Seen in Baby Kidnap Guard," "Babs Advised to Hide Son Away From Husband," "Babs, Count, File Danish Divorce Suit," "Bare Threat by Count to Babs' Admirer," "Count in British Court Denies Threat to Babs," "Babs Must Bow to Danish Laws in Divorce Fight," "Prince got $2,251,189 (and ponies); Count Asks Five Million."

The *Times* reported that the Countess had had Winfield House locked against all comers, while police patrolled the grounds. She was said to have made successful application for a summons to obtain temporary custody of the child. In Paris, the Count declined to comment on the news that his wife had got out an arrest warrant against him in Britain. "I suppose," he said irritably, "that one of these days they'll blame me for the Spanish War . . . or suspect me of wanting to steal the Eiffel Tower."[15]

On July 5, 1938, however, Haugwitz-Reventlow came to London to appear in court; and the public was treated to a series of sensational charges made by the Countess' attorney, William M. Mitchell. What Barbara's father had dismissed as a "minor marital tiff" promised to be one of the decade's most sensational divorce cases. Mr. Mitchell reported on an alleged visit to Haugwitz-Reventlow in Dijon, France. The Count was represented as having run the gamut of melodramatic emotions—"temper," "self-commiseration," "moods when he was cold and . . . calculating." Mitchell said that he had offered Haugwitz-Reventlow £50,000 as a "gesture," a "settlement for life," and that the Count had spurned the offer as "laughable and an insult."

Mr. Mitchell reported that the Count had threatened his wife with "three years of hell with headlines," that he had announced his intention of taking Lance "away from England forever," and, as a fat bonus to the tabloid reader, that he intended to return to London and shoot a certain " 'Mr. X' like a dog."

Norman Birkett, attorney for the Count, made much of the mysterious "Mr. X." "It is plain, is it not, that one of the chief features of the case is that this matter of 'the gentleman in London' upset the Count profoundly?"

"Yes, and in my view, childishly," Mr. Mitchell replied.

"Never mind your view," said Mr. Birkett. "Husbands are not like solicitors."[16]

"The development gave London its greatest sensation since King Edward VIII renounced the throne eighteen months ago for love of Mrs. Wallis Warfield. . . ." said the *New York Daily News*. The *News* was not as discreet as the *Times* about identifying the mysterious "Mr. X." It was quickly announced to the world that he was Prince Frederick of Prussia, 26-year-old grandson of the former Kaiser of Germany.

Everything seemed to be building up to a denouement with pistols at fifty paces, yet sensation seekers were in for a big disappointment. On July 22, 1938, the *New York Times* reported that the Haugwitz-Reventlows were seeking a quiet private separation in the Danish courts which could be transformed by legal steps into a divorce. If the current negotiations bogged down completely, divorce would still be automatic after four years' separation.

The agreement covered the future of young Lance, who, at the height of the controversy, had been made a ward of the British court.

The Countess was to have custody of him "for most of the time" during his "tender years." When he came of school age, he was to spend half of his holidays with his mother and

half with his father. The Court waived his right to any part of
his wife's fortune to which he might be entitled under a
Danish law giving him a claim on one-half of their common
property. Owing to the tortuous processes of Danish jurispru-
dence, the decree did not become final until it was signed
by King Christian on March 1, 1941.

A year before the outbreak of war in Europe, Czechoslovakia was more remote to millions of Americans than "the
walled fortress of Winfield House," further than the lawns
and gardens where nurses and detectives hovered over "the
curly-haired Lance" or the Paris hotel which the Count was
supposed to have left on a mysterious mission with "an un-
identified blonde." The drama played out in "society's whispering galleries" was more immediate than the dramas which
were taking place in Bad Godesberg and Berchtesgaden.
What Chamberlain said to Hitler was less interesting than
what Babs' chauffeur might have seen in the rear-view mirror.

There were many critics who felt that the world had more
pressing preoccupations than the testimony of lawyers and
the innuendoes of servants.

> Are you fed up with Babs? [*The Christian Cen-
> tury* asked editorially.] We thought so. So, as
> far as our observation goes, is almost everyone
> else. . . .
>
> Yet most of the press will not allow the public
> a single edition's surcease from the latest misad-
> ventures of the 5-and-10-cent store heiress. Babs
> charges this. Babs' count denies that. Babs' father
> asserts such-and-such. Babs' lawyers plan thus-
> and-so. (Pictures on the back page.) A world
> cataclysm is forming in Europe; the Far East is in
> flames . . . fifteen million Americans wrestle with
> the despair that comes from living on relief. Never
> mind all that. Here's the latest. Babs, Babs, Babs.
> Read all about it! . . .
>
> Here the injustice of a social order which
> pours unearned wealth into witless hands is being
> pounded home as no soap-box agitator, no radical

pamphleteer ever succeeded in making it clear. Every day that the papers continue to play up the silliness of this woman, her senseless extravagance, her lack of patriotism (as shown in her transfer of citizenship to escape taxation), her love affairs, and her indifference to the wage scales of the $14-a-week salesgirls who have piled up her fortune, the day of reckoning is brought that much closer. Keep up that sort of thing long enough and who can tell how soon the lid will blow off? After all, look what Marie Antoinette's "Let them eat cake" accomplished.[17]

Barbara in this period was suffering from what a later generation would call bad public relations. John Winkler and Boyden Sparkes wrote in 1940: "Whenever Barbara's name is headlined in the newspapers, some 2,800 managers of Woolworth stores shudder for their business." The situation had become so acute that relatives prevailed upon Barbara to get rid of her Woolworth stock.

There was no question that many of Barbara's actions were extraordinarily ill-timed. In December 1937 the Woolworth stores were on strike in New York, when Barbara paid a lightning visit to her native land. Her purpose, succinctly stated by *Time* magazine: "to sign away, in a round, schoolgirl hand, her U.S. citizenship."[18] She was still married to Haugwitz-Reventlow, and tax experts pointed out that by becoming a Danish citizen, she had put up a barrier to the collection of inheritance taxes which would have taken about two-thirds of her estate, when it passed on to Lance. Her relations with the tax collector were, throughout the Depression, turbulent. In May 1938 she had finally agreed to pay the United States Government $20,086 in settlement of a deficiency claim of $25,108 on her 1933 return. Her financial problems did not endear her to her countrymen. As the *New York Daily News* pointed out: "The absentee landlord has never been a beloved figure."[19]

Barbara's homecomings were marred throughout the thirties by the presence of unofficial welcoming committees. During

the course of a strike in March 1937, the employees of Woolworth's sent a cable to Barbara asking her intervention for a
living wage. In earlier demonstrations strikers had carried
signs reading, "Miss Hutton counts millions while five-and-ten
girls count ten and twelve dollar salaries."[20] Often the girls
would appear on the dock to meet her. When she returned
from Europe in 1939 pickets followed her to the Hotel Pierre,
carrying signs which asked rhetorically: "We live on $15.60 a
week. Could you?"[21] Once, outside a New York theater, she
was mobbed by an angry crowd, who tore at her clothes and
clawed at her face with cries of "rich bitch." Barbara was
puzzled by these demonstrations. "Why is everyone so hostile
to me?" "Why do Americans hate me so?" she kept asking.[22]
"I'm tired of saying I have nothing to do with the Woolworth
stores."[23]

To a certain extent she was the scapegoat for the economic
sins of a whole era. In half a century, the Woolworth wage
scale had undergone few upward revisions. By 1940 the Woolworth stores were theoretically meeting the going wage, which
varied in different parts of the country from $10 to $23 a week.
In New York the girls pulled down a weekly salary of about
$14 to $16. When Barbara got off the boat she landed in a
country in violent transition. This was the America of Father
Coughlin and Huey Long, of the Union Square orator and
the Wagner National Labor Relations Act. Labor was still on
the barricades, and the New Deal was a fighting word to
conservatives. Businessmen took heart from the fact that certain features of the Roosevelt program had been defeated—
including a tax law proposed by Roosevelt in 1935, which
(had it gone through and had it been in force when she came
into her money) would have reduced Barbara's millions to
seven. The handwriting was on the wall. When the Woolworth
girls went on strike for union recognition, a forty-hour week,
and a $20 a week minimum wage, they were fighting for
what would ultimately be theirs by law.

In the years when collective bargaining was still a novelty,
however, ancient grievances still rankled. In 1892 Woolworth
had retaliated to the threat of a strike with the following blunt
directive:

No doubt they take advantage now while we are
too busy, and think we will pay the advance. All
such girls you should remember when the dull
season comes and give them "the bounce."[24]

When Babs was attacked, critics were really attacking old
Frank Woolworth, and a society which kept the help in line
by talk of the cachet of working for the five-and-ten, or the
economic advantages of living at home with the folks.

The identity of some of Barbara's bitterest critics is significant. The *New York Daily News*, for example, frequently bit
the hand that fed the press releases. Sometimes the *News*
represented Babs as a kind of blot on the nation's social conscience. When, in 1936, she bought Ganna Walska's emerald
collection for $1,200,000, the *News* editorialized: "It is inci-
dents of this kind that light up the whole background of the
1936 campaign struggle between the Old Deal and the New
Deal. . . ."

Sometimes she was attacked on a more personal level, as
when the *News* gloated that "willful Barbara" had had to live
apart from the Count for a year before her Danish divorce
became final. Had she remained an American citizen, she
could have expedited the dissolution of her marriage with
Yankee efficiency through the Reno divorce mill.

Westbrook Pegler reserved some of his most vigorous ex-
pletives for her: "I do not believe that anyone since the day
of Marie Antoinette has been guilty of such dumb judgment
in mocking the sufferings of the poor as the young American
girl . . . who set out to spend her way extravagantly around
a world full of want and woe."[25] Pegler was also to turn his
guns on Eleanor Roosevelt. The *Daily News* was soon to for-
sake New Dealism and to represent F.D.R. in the capitalist-for-
breakfast and private-enterprise-straining-at-its-shackles genre
of cartoon art. The vehemence with which two such conservative critics lashed out at Miss Hutton shows the extent of the
Depression dissatisfaction with the iniquities of "the system."

Miss Hutton was forced to listen to some fairly dubious
poesy composed by the poets laureate of the picket line. For
example:

> Barbara Hutton's got the dough, parlay voo
> We know where she got it, too, parlay voo
> We slave at Woolworth's five-and-dime
> The pay we get is sure a crime
> Hinky dinky, parlay voo.[26]

Or, on the occasion of her renunciation of American citizenship:

> While we're on strike for higher pay
> Babs takes her millions and runs away.[27]

The tone of these two offerings makes an interesting contrast to the more subservient tribute of her grandfather's day, written by a clerk in a store in Milwaukee to commemorate a merger with Woolworth:

> When earth's last ten-cent store has opened, and
>   the new-painted red front has dried,
> And the oldest clerk has her station down near
>   the register's side,
> We will look to new worlds to sell to, perhaps
>   Jupiter, Venus or Mars,
> And the master of all the ten-cent stores will put
>   us to work in the stars.[28]

The Woolworth millions were to come back to America sooner than anyone expected. In September 1939 war was declared, and in October Barbara arrived on the *Conte di Savoia* bringing three-year-old Lance back to the safety of the U.S.A. for the duration. On July 8, 1942, Barbara was married in California to the actor Cary Grant, in a union which Hollywood wits characterized as "Cash and Cary." Grant was the only one of her husbands to date who was gainfully employed and who did not cost her money. (Count Haugwitz-Reventlow had become an American citizen in 1941 and was the trustee of a $1,500,000 fund set up by Barbara for Lance.) In June 1942 Barbara once more took up her American citizenship, and was immediately slapped by the American government with a bill for $3,000,000 in back taxes.

The Grants moved into Douglas Fairbanks, Jr.'s enormous

house in Hollywood. They escaped some of the rigors suffered by humbler folk during the war years. Their sentiments were nonetheless firmly and generously pro-Allied. Mrs. Grant gave ten ambulances to the British Red Cross, donated heavily to the American Red Cross War Relief Fund, and was a staunch supporter of the Hollywood Canteen. Grant, who had become an American citizen himself a week before their marriage, was said to be one of Hollywood's largest contributors to Allied causes.

Even with wartime austerity, the Grant ménage had a mauve-decade ratio of servants to masters. The household consisted of the Grants, Lance, Lance's onetime nurse, Miss Latimer, "Mlle. Tiki," companion and lifelong friend of Barbara; and there was Grant's valet, his secretary, and his chauffeur-masseur, in addition to some eleven household servants. *Look* magazine quoted Grant as saying: "The servants had so many shifts to feed at mealtime that Barbara and I were lucky to get a sandwich." Grant recalls looking forward to Sunday, when the army of retainers went off duty and Barbara prepared tête-à-tête tray dinners of chicken à la king.

By the 1940's, Barbara's marital misadventures had lost a bit of their glamour. Newspaper readers had become accustomed to interchanges such as the following, which took place on August 30, 1945, in a Los Angeles court:

> Mrs. Grant: Mr. Grant and myself did not have the same friends. Mr. Grant did not like my friends. On more than one occasion when I gave parties he would not come downstairs, but would have dinner in bed. When he did come down he obviously was not amused.
>
> Judge Clarke: How did this affect you?
>
> Mrs. Grant: It made me rather nervous.
>
> Judge Clarke: Did you require the services of a doctor?
>
> Mrs. Grant: Yes, I did.
>
> Miss Germaine Tocquet (Mlle. Tiki) corroborated the fact that Mr. Grant did not like his wife's friends.

Mr. Geisler [Mrs. Grant's attorney]: How else did
  it affect her?
Miss Tocquet: It made her nervous, very.
Judge Clarke: That's enough; decree granted.[29]

In the court transcripts and newspaper interviews of two
decades was written a dreary record of failing health and
recurrent domestic tragedy. In March 1947 Barbara married
Prince Igor Troubetzkoy and in 1950 she told a *Time* reporter: "He's one of the cheapest men I've ever met in my
life. He only married me for my money."[30] Decree was
granted on October 31, 1951.

In 1949 Lance was asked by a reporter to comment on his
mother's health. "Mommy had some treatments, but they
didn't seem to work much." Asked if he felt sorry to leave
his mother, who had been in and out of hospitals in Italy,
France and Switzerland, Lance answered with the sophistication of a child grown wise in the ways of litigation: "Yes,
but we have that Massachusetts agreement signed three years
ago (with Haugwitz-Reventlow) so I have to."[31]

Barbara bought a three-story Arabian mansion, El Kasbah,
in the heart of Tangier's native quarter. "Here," she said, "I
will find the peace and dignity I have sought all my life."
She was to live in it only a few weeks out of the next eight
years—in between seven major operations and the periodic
bouts in the hospital which were an aftermath of the Mdivani
coffee diet.

Finally, at Deauville, Prince Charming came into her life
for the fifth and most disastrous time. Porfirio Rubirosa was
a Dominican diplomat whose amours had earned him such
titles as "the most famous foreign corespondent of the year,"
"the big dame hunter," "the boudoir problem of two continents." *Time* magazine described him as "dark" and "politely
feral." Raised in Paris, he had been married in 1933 to Flor de
Oro Trujillo, daughter of the Dominican dictator "El Benefactor." He remained married to her for five years. "The
Dictator," said *Time*, "apparently impressed by this feat, made
him a diplomat."[32]

In 1939 he married Danielle Darrieux, "the most beautiful

woman in the world," and later Doris Duke, who vied with Barbara for the title of the richest. Shortly before his romance with the Woolworth heiress he was named as corespondent in a divorce action and accused of indiscretions involving the wives of Richard Reynolds, Jr., the tobacco heir, and Robert Sweeney, the British society golfer. When he met Barbara in Deauville he was squiring Zsa Zsa Gabor, one of three Hungarian beauties, around the watering spots of the continent. He was removed temporarily from his diplomatic post in Paris by El Benefactor. At the time of his marriage to Barbara he was reinstated, his wild oats forgiven and forgotten.

Rubirosa had Mdivani's fatal fondness for polo. His pronouncements on the subject of his earlier marriages did not augur well for Barbara's future. "I married them not because I wanted to, but because women want to marry. Women don't want to be concubines."[33] Rubirosa, who appeared to have a substantial income from undisclosed sources in addition to his salary, made pious protestations of financial independence: "What property she has is hers, and what property I have is mine."[34]

On December 29, 1953, he visited Barbara in her hotel suite. On emerging he announced that they would marry the following day.

The wedding, a civil ceremony in Spanish, was conducted by the Dominican consul general, Dr. Joaquín Salazar, at his Park Avenue apartment. Rubirosa's former brother-in-law, Major General Rafael Trujillo Martínez, was best man. As she entered the apartment Barbara said: "Oh, this is impossible."

She had just been released from Doctors Hospital, and her hand shook as she held the champagne glass. Periodically tears welled up in her eyes. She asked her son Lance to hold her hand. Fortified by a Scotch and Soda, she was able to murmur "*si*" when asked if she took Rubi as her husband. After the contract was signed she said to the bridegroom: "Aren't you going to kiss me now? The press has waited so long."[35]

The Rubirosas were embarrassed by periodic bulletins from

Miss Gabor, who was photographed holding an eye patch to a black eye. She let it be bruited about that during Rubirosa's courtship of Barbara he was simultaneously proposing to her (Zsa Zsa) by telephone. "In Spanish," she told a *Life* reporter, "Rubirosa means a red rose, but to me it's a black eye. He said to me, 'If you do not marry me now I will marry Barbara Hutton.' I said 'That is a smart idea.' He said, 'Why won't you marry me?' And I said, 'If I must tell you the truth, I am in love with George.' [Zsa Zsa was currently seeking a divorce from actor George Sanders who was quoted by *Life* as saying: "She is discarding me like a squeezed lemon."] And so then Rubi hits me. I am the luckiest woman who ever lived. He might have broken my head or my nose. A man only beats a woman if he loves her."[36]

Miss Gabor was frank about the Rubirosas' marital prospects. "See how unhappy they look. I give them six months. I love George, Rubi loves me, Barbara loves Rubi, but who loves Barbara?"[37]

Surprisingly, Miss Gabor erred on the side of charity. The newlyweds set off in an 88-passenger plane for their Florida honeymoon. Barbara was wearing a leg cast, as she had broken an ankle in a fall in the bathroom the morning after the wedding. Rubirosa spent his days playing polo, while Barbara spent hers ailing in bed. By March 13, 1954, well before Miss Gabor's six months elapsed, the bride had had enough. She came back to New York City while Rubirosa went to Paris to join Zsa Zsa.

Rubirosa's post mortem on the marriage was typically chivalrous:

> I was a bachelor and very happy between my divorce and marrying Barbara and I did not want to change. I fell in love with her. It was fine and it was fun. And then she said "Let's get married." I said no, because I was afraid she would change. But she said "I promise not to change." But she did change. It was no good. She stays in bed and reads all day. It's a very boring life. I like outdoor sports.[38]

With her wedding to Rubirosa, Miss Hutton renounced her United States citizenship for the second time, to become a citizen of the Dominican Republic. With the breakup of the marriage, friends expressed the hope that she might at last "put down American roots." But force of habit prevailed. She wed Baron Gottfried von Cramm, another titled foreigner. "Gottfried," she said, "is the only one who has really wanted me to love him. I won't say my previous husbands thought only of my money, but it had a certain fascination for them." In November, 1955, she married von Cramm, whose occupation was given by *Time* as a "tennisocialite," and whom, as *Time* commented, she "has seen often since."[39]

Like her grandfather before her Barbara rested up from the struggles of her youth in the company of faithful family retainers. For Miss Latimer and "Mlle. Tiki," her "second mother," were more constant than any of the dream princes.

She hit the headlines briefly when her son Lance was married to the actress Jill St. John. Such columnists as were still functioning during the New York newspaper strike reported a rift between them.

Miss Hutton's name has been linked with such romantic-looking young men as Philip Van Rensselaer and playboy Jimmy Douglas. She drifts from hotel suite to elegant house— Tangiers in the summer, Venice in late September, Cuernavaca in January and February, New York and Paris in the spring. Imported piece by piece from Japan, in the 19th century mogul tradition, her Mexican pied à terre in Cuernavaca is a monument to the lure of the Far East. Four hundred people worked for two years to transplant sloping rooves, temple bells and gold tiles. The improbable presence of rice fields, the view of the romantic volcano Popocateptl, create the illusion of looking at the Fujiyama for her houseguests. A measure of Oriental serenity is a by-product of the gold tile. A friend has said of this haven that it seems like a tranquil spot to end one's days.

The Venetian palace had been put up for auction. Winfield House had been given to the American Embassy in London. Her paintings had gone to the National Gallery in Washington. Her yacht, *Troubador*, had been sold to a Greek shipping

company after being requisitioned by the British Admiralty
at the outbreak of the war. Two continents were strewn with
the wreckage of her home life.

As she reached middle age, she had finally got her countrymen on her side. Sociologists no longer quibbled over her
jewel collection, her wardrobe of more than a hundred saris,
the life-sized gold horses' heads studded with precious stones
which graced her hotel suite in Paris. For this, if for nothing
else, she could thank Porfirio Rubirosa. As Eleanor Harris said
in an article for *Look* Magazine: "For Barbara there was one
happy result of the nightmare marriage. In the eyes of many
fellow Americans, she had finally become an underdog."[40]

She had earned the right to the eccentricities, the impulsive
generosities of the very rich, because she had also become
something of an anachronism. In the 1950's times were good.
Many of the battles of the shopgirls had been won. A generation living "high off the hog" was inclined to be indulgent
of extravagance. In the new climate of moderation Barbara
Hutton was free, if she wished, to settle $1,500,000 on a hus-
band. (Over the years this had been established as roughly
par for the course.) No one was inclined to say her nay. The
leveling of the social pyramid was being accomplished on a
far larger scale, by the less capricious methods of the Internal
Revenue Bureau.

It was idle to speculate on what her life might have been
had she felt the impact of the Depression or the war. She
might have been caught in the Fitzgerald migration of homecoming expatriates. She might have been forced to add further
culinary triumphs to that Sunday night chicken à la king.
She might also have been spared some of the hazards of love
in the high surtax brackets.

On the occasion of her fifth marriage she had one sentiment
for the reporters: "I'm so tired." The frail expatriate was exhausted from the search that had led for so long to another
house, another country, another spa, another man. It was a
reminder to her critics that the gods have their troubles too;
and that there are certain drawbacks to being one of the last
survivors of capitalism's Paleolithic Age.

" 'No,' she said emphatically, 'You *can't* take my picture.' " *New York World-Telegram*, December 28, 1938

"Nobody is interested in an ex-glamour girl"— Brenda Frazier in *Time*, April 14, 1952

Brenda and Cobina

BRENDA FRAZIER AND COBINA WRIGHT, JR.

Eight years after Barbara Hutton's debut the Ritz ballroom was sparsely decked with flowers. Sheaves of lilies, gilded palm fronds and transparent leaves were grouped against the panels of the wall. The rhythms of Emil Coleman alternated with the gypsy melodies of the Haas band. Candid camera men plied their forbidden trade behind pillars and posts. The "dance-list lads" and "junior lovelies" of the Sunday supplements were only slightly repressed by the socially impeccable phalanxes of old Newport.

Such assorted society column familiars as "Kitty" de Rothschild, Mrs. James P. Donohue in the "priceless Burden pearls," Mrs. Vladimir Behr "ablaze with diamonds," made the occasion (in the words of the *New York Journal-American's* Cholly Knickerbocker) "the diamond-est party I've attended in years."[1] Some two thousand guests paraded past the striking dark-haired debutante, Brenda Diana Duff Frazier; and the following morning the *New York Daily News* applauded— "Bow's a Wow."[2]

A few weeks before, a blonde society singer named Cobina Wright, Jr., had made her professional debut at the Waldorf Sert Room. One observer described her impact upon the audience as follows:

> When she stepped out into the huge room she hesitated a moment and, as she stood there, the audience paid her the tribute of sudden, complete silence, followed by a sort of audible sigh, that slight, well-bred intake of breath that can sometimes be startled out of a group by an unexpected thrill. For she was a vision in a gown of light gray tulle. . . . She looked almost like a Madonna.[3]

The critic's transports were understandable. She happened to be the young chanteuse's mother. Cobina Wright, Sr., made much of the contrast between the two evenings—the magnificent $25,000 debut that launched Brenda Frazier, the more modest bow of her own hard-working little Cobina.

There was no doubt that each of the debuts had paid off. The press, which did not suffer from the softening myopia of mother love, greeted Cobina's singing with adjectives somewhat less extravagant than Cobina senior's. Everyone was agreed, however, that her clothes were pretty. Brenda's debut introduced the public to the season's most photogenic face.

Compared with Barbara Hutton's $60,000 splash, Brenda's party was a modest affair. Cholly Knickerbocker, two days before, had been promising his disciples a ballroom "festooned with large groups of gold and moonlight cellophane leaves . . . moonlit mirrors placed at either end of the room, massive groups of vivid red and exotic white flowers, and stunning ostrich-feather Christmas trees."[4] He was disappointed to find nothing but tasteful Constance Spry floral arrangements. Once the glare of the diamonds had worn off, he proceeded to chide the debutante's mother for her cheeseparing, incidentally providing a clue to tabloid criteria of beauty. "Constance Spry's decorations were far from effective, due to their simplicity."[5]

Whatever Mr. Knickerbocker's feelings about the décor, he was to make as much capital as anyone else of the season's number one debutante. *Journal-American* reporters were to be found jockeying for position the moment Brenda chose to show her face. It was a face that assailed the public from the covers of *Life* and the corridors of Jay Thorpe. She made news when she was sketched under a hairdrier, where she put on horn-rimmed glasses or looked startled; when she sat at a table in the Rainbow Room with Douglas Fairbanks, Jr.; when she dined off lettuce leaves and champagne at Armando's; when she was mobbed by admirers at the Easter parade; when she was named by Ida Bailey Allen as the "all-American girl"; when she was questioned on such weighty matters as "What would happen if a socialite won a $150,000 sweepstakes ticket?"

The newspapers quickly sensed the copy possibilities of linking the names of Brenda and Cobina; and soon they were brewing up a fictitious feud between the girls. It remained only for Bob Hope to call two shopgirl comediennes on his radio program Brenda and Cobina to turn their names into household words.

They were perfect foils for each other. Cobina's blondeness made a striking contrast to Brenda's dark hair. Both, at some point in their schooling, had attended Miss Hewitt's Classes. Both belonged to the charmed circle of Hewitt students which included Diana Barrymore, Esme O'Brien and "Vivi" Fairchild.

Both shared modest intellectual aspirations. Cobina claimed to enjoy reading plays—her favorite playwrights being Noel Coward and William Shakespeare. A *New Yorker* profile noted that Brenda rarely read, "though professing a fondness for history and biography."[6] In her set this did not bar her from having a reputation as a thinker. Brenda's friends recalled with some awe that "she talks about life and things."[7]

Both girls had had tempestuous family lives. Brenda was the daughter of a wealthy Midwestern broker named Frank Duff Frazier. Her mother was Brenda Williams-Taylor, daughter of Sir Frederick Williams-Taylor, onetime general manager of the Bank of Montreal. Brenda acquired two stepbrothers and a stepsister in 1926 with her mother's second marriage to a lawyer named Frederic N. Watriss, who died on April 10, 1938.

She had been buffeted about in one of society's great custody battles. Her mother got a divorce from Mr. Frazier, a Yale man, on grounds of desertion. The custody suit began when Brenda was three. At eleven Brenda hit the headlines as the center of a scandalous financial row between her parents, each of whom tried to prove that the other was unfit to take care of her. She lived in the limelight of notoriety until her father's death in 1933.

Brenda's father's will contained the proviso that if Brenda elected to live with her mother his money would go to Yale. *The New Yorker* quoted Mrs. Watriss' adverse reaction to this notion: "Yale is a lovely institution, but I don't want it to get Diana's money." She accordingly contested the will—and successfully, with the result that Brenda was to come into her father's money at the age of twenty-one. His death automatically made her the beneficiary of two trust funds set up by her paternal grandmother, Mrs. Clara Duff Frazier.[8] Eventually Brenda's patrimony was valued at a grand total of more than four million dollars, with the whopping allowance awarded her mother for Brenda's maintenance and support. The slim beauty was perhaps the 1938 season's richest financial catch.

Brenda had had the schooling appropriate for a girl of her station. Miss Porter's School in Farmington, Connecticut, took up where Miss Hewitt had left off. Sargent's *Handbook of Private Schools* described this institution as dedicated to "a Victorian attitude of genteel superiority and culture."[9] Later she went to Munich, where, again according to *The New Yorker*, "a baroness . . . for a reasonable fee saw to it that Brenda and four young English companions were tutored in German and given a discreet taste of continental atmosphere."[10] She burst on the New York social horizon with a smattering of French and German and the ability to carry on simple conversations in these languages with headwaiters.

Cobina Wright, Jr., Brenda's opposite number, had had a

harrowing series of financial crises in addition to a fashion-
ably plural parentage. Her mother was an indomitable Oregon
girl, born Elaine Cobb. When her father died, Elaine Cobb
was shipped off to an aunt in Back Bay who was dead set
against her girlish aspirations for a singing career. Aunt Ellen
was of the generation which believed that a lady's name appeared in the paper only three times: when she was born,
when she married, and when she died. She also shared the
Victorian belief that the stage was the road to ruin.

Like many of her generation, Aunt Ellen made, to no avail,
the Victorian's last fluttering stand. Elaine was more than a
match for her, and soon she was singing in Mainz with Aunt
Ellen in nervous attendance. Later Elaine appeared in *The
Magic Flute*, after a hair-raising escape from a seducer which
seemed to justify all of Aunt Ellen's direst apprehensions.
Early in her singing career, Elaine Cobb shucked off her
identity. She was reborn under the professional name of
Madame Cobina.

When Cobina came back to New York she met Owen
Johnson, the author of *Stover at Yale*. He shared with her "a
magnificent idea of outlay and boundless faith in income."
They were accordingly married. They were divorced at the
time of the First World War. In Cobina senior's autobiography their union is dismissed rather summarily as "one of
the earliest career versus marriage stories of our explosive
century."[11] Later she was to marry William May Wright, who
is alluded to variously in her autobiography as "the storybook
socialite with the Midas touch," "the Bright Boy of those
fabulous roaring twenties," "my great love,"[12] "the owner of
the longest car in the world," or, simply, "my multi-millionaire
husband."[13]

Stockbroker Wright presumably had an even more boundless faith in income than Mr. Johnson. "In our case it was always Bill who said 'What do *you* want now?' and agreed with
me, whatever it was, and set out to get it for me. We both
wanted everything bigger and better. That was the tempo,
the watchword of our times.[14] Amidst all our money and
extravagance, time was the mistress of us all. How to fill each
minute was one of our problems. Speakeasies were in full

swing. Women now smoked, drank, got divorced whenever they felt like it, flirted and laughed as their men heaped fortune upon fortune and gave away mink coats and diamond bracelets and thousand-dollar bills as party favors. All tinsel, all unreal, all, I suppose, materialism at its nth degree. . . . In a way, it was all very human, and there was about it a gaiety and color that made it almost irresistible."[15]

Cobina junior, the child of this marriage, spent her earliest years in one of the most flamboyant ménages of a flamboyant age. On Long Island's North Shore the Wrights built a peach-pink stucco house called Casa Cobina, complete with a play-house for the child, a small golf course, and gravel to match the walls of the house. Cobina senior turned to entertaining with a vengeance, and at her famed Circus Ball Elisabeth Marbury, Clifton Webb, and Gertrude Lawrence, dressed up as tightrope walkers and peanut vendors, congregated to eat "Park Avenue hotdogs with ball-park mustard."[16]

Cobina senior had a custom-built folding table in "the longest car in the world," where she wrote articles, read, and claimed to study. And when the Wrights went to Europe, Cobina senior took along thirty trunks. "There wasn't one I could do without, not one."[17]

Later a Hollywood publicity department quoted in *Collier's* was to add to the picture of little Cobina's opulent youth a few additional flourishes of its own:

> She had a specially built miniature automobile in which she was driven to the polo matches at Sands Point, Long Island, N.Y., by a midget chauffeur. She took her little friends sailing on her father's yacht, was attended by fourteen servants and lived in her choice of two houses between trips to Europe where she was admired by Noel Coward, the Duke of Westminster, and all the heroes and heroines of the Sunday supplements.[18]

Cobina junior was, however, soon to be expelled from fairyland. On one disastrous day in 1929 Daddy returned from the Stock Exchange with the news that he owed the bank $90,000. His wife, accustomed to hearing his day's accomplishments relayed in terms of a $3,000 to $15,000 profit, did not understand that their fortunes were foundering. Wasn't her husband "the best man on the floor"? How could such a small amount mean disaster? It must all have been "a clerical mistake." Mr. Wright reassured her with the news that "there's a mild panic on."[19]

All over America people were asking themselves the same questions. All over America families were sharing, to some degree, the experience of the William May Wrights, who "awoke one morning millionaires and went to bed the same night penniless."[20] Cobina senior remembers ladies offering fur coats for sale in hotel lobbies; yachts, polo ponies and custom-built Rolls-Royces being sold for cash. Mr. Wright sold his seat on the Exchange. As the extent of the "mild panic" became apparent, others on the Street blew out their brains. A little later the Wrights gave what they called their "last party"—the final fling before they joined the ranks of the *nouveaux pauvres*.

Around the time of the crash Cobina senior had had the first hints of impending domestic catastrophe. The Wrights' divorce case hit the front page along with the Lindbergh kidnapping and the Vanderbilt custody suit. When it was over, Mr. Wright married a Miss Myrtle Gardner. The two Cobinas were left to shift for themselves.

In the early days of the Depression they set up housekeeping as non-paying prestige guests of the Waldorf-Astoria. Cobina senior turned her hand to a variety of enterprises. She started a Saturday night supper club at the Waldorf. She attempted to revive the Circus Ball. She resurrected the ocean liner *Leviathan*, and unsuccessfully attempted to convert it into an "entertainment boat." She became a night club singer at Mon Paris.

As the thirties wore on, Cobina junior began to develop into something of a beauty. At fifteen she appeared at the Trianon Room of the Hotel Ambassador as a "mystery singer." At sixteen she modeled for *Vogue* and *Harper's Bazaar*. She won a singing contest which entitled her to a two-week engagement at the Whitehall Hotel in Palm Beach at a hundred dollars a week. She was offered a raise if she stayed on another month. Her mother considered that this was good "experience," and apparently Miss Hewitt also gave her blessing. This lenient institution of learning was quite accustomed to carrying on correspondence courses with young ladies of fashion whose parents had removed them from school for the winter season in Florida. Later Cobina junior appeared in a summer stock production of *Stage Door*, and went with her mother to Europe, where she had a whirlwind romance with Prince Philip of Greece. When she turned seventeen her mother decided against a formal debut for her. "A debut would be sheer nonsense, a farce. She might better learn to cook and take care of her own clothes."[21]

For this decision Cobina senior was branded as a "rebel." If Cobina's mother eschewed the formal debut, she made as many cluckings as any debutante's mother over Cobina's first night in the Sert Room. She taught her singing, worked on her diction, coached her, made contacts, designed her clothes, and acted as her duenna. "More and more," she said, "I regarded her success as the key to my own peace of mind, and I cannot deny that I took much joy in it—more perhaps than she did herself."[22]

Young Cobina was aided in her career by her mother's extensive acquaintance. A shipboard friendship paid off years later, "when the power wielded by the great Col. Robert McCormick of the great, far reaching *Chicago Tribune* and its syndicates was behind my penniless little Cobina. . . . For the Colonel . . . arranged a radio program for my daughter, because 'a wild little girl I knew on shipboard turned out to be a valiant woman.' "[23]

This liaison between the press and the Four Hundred—unthinkable in the days of Ellen Cobb—was evidence of the social upheaval brought about by the Depression. The wolf had visited the door of many of the Wrights' acquaintances. Such erstwhile members of the leisure classes as Grand Duchess Marie of Russia were working at Bergdorf Goodman. The Marquis of Milford Haven was selling hot-water heaters.

A few years before, Mrs. Stuyvesant Fish had caused headlines and riots by driving in the park with Lillian Russell. The *Social Register*, which still paid homage to the ideals of Ellen Cobb, dropped the thespians from its pages like hot potatoes. Cobina senior was ousted from the 1935 edition,

along with Michael Strange, Rosamond Pinchot, and Grand
Duchess Marie. For all of this, society was invading the arts
as well as the ribbon counter and the steno pool.

The crash had brought about a discrepancy between social
aspiration and fiscal reality. Maury Paul, then the *New York
Journal-American's* "Cholly Knickerbocker," had a touch of the
social philosopher. On October 25, 1938, he devoted his
column to the shake-up of the classes that had taken place
since 1929. "Social Revolution Taking Its Toll of Wealth from
Families Once on the Top Shelf of Affluence" ran the headline. "Confiscatory Taxes Reducing Great Fortunes to Vanish-
ing Point." "Baker and Pyne Clans Are Among Those Who
Have Seen Depletion of Their Riches via This Route." He
went on to describe others who had shared in the plight of
the two Cobinas:

> Social Registerized matrons on the other side of
> fifty, accustomed all their lives to unlimited wealth
> and luxury, are now punching time clocks as sales
> ladies in department stores, gown shops, etc.; . . .
> post debutantes reared as "heiresses" are holding
> down jobs as models and press agents; there are
> two members of the Union Club eking out an ex-
> istence as floorwalkers . . . and I know of at least
> six men whose names are enrolled at the Racquet
> and Tennis Club, who are all but panhandling on
> Fifth and Park Avenues.

He went on to describe the case of one Andrew McKinney,
who gave his address in the *Social Register* as The New York
Yacht Club to hide the fact that he had long since disposed
of a fashionable 75th Street house. Once the owner of a large
steam yacht, he dropped out of the *Social Register* early in
the Depression, and his true address was at last revealed to
be Welfare Island.[24]

A new class had emerged in an inverse ratio to great houses
and enormous staffs. "This is 1938," Mr. Paul philosophized on
November 14. "A bloodless revolution has taken place. No one
cares about the moribund, passé 'Old Guard.' Interest today
centers on 'Café Society,' the 'Glitterbug Set' and the 'Inter-

nationals.' "[25] These assorted "glitterbugs" and "internationals" shared a common love of the limelight—which led Cleveland Amory a decade later to give them the sobriquet of "publiciety."

In another mood Mr. Paul betrayed a nostalgia for the dying aristocracy. On October 19, 1938, he regaled his readers with the intelligence that "Few Ladies of Fashion Lunch at Home." Among those who did he listed Mrs. Cornelius Vanderbilt, Mrs. Hamilton Twombly, Mrs. W. Watts Sherman, Mrs. Payne Whitney.

> I suppose you will dub me a snob for ringing in those Grade A "Old Guard" names after telling you about "the Ritz Regulars" and the "Cosy Colonyites." Never forget, however, I may write about "Cafe Society" but my heart belongs to Grace, "Florrie," Sophia and Helen.[26]

In presenting a code of behavior for debutantes Mr. Paul was troubled by the same schizophrenia. At the beginning of the 1938 season he issued a series of directives to mothers of what he referred to as "buds":

> Bringing out a daughter is serious business [he warned ominously]. The task calls for the use of brains and tact if daughter is to be catalogued as a success and dance through her first season without having her reputation torn to shreds or her heart broken by the unpardonable actions of her jaundice-eyed sisters.[27]

After this alarming beginning, he proceeded to catalogue various "don'ts" to help one avoid the social abyss:

> Don't invite debutantes your daughter has never met to entertainments you give.
> Don't allow your daughter to attend ballet or other evening entertainments minus maid-chaperone.

Don't send your daughter into the ballroom over-dressed or underdressed.

Don't allow your daughter to indulge in ostentatious jewel displays during her first season.

Don't sanction the use of your daughter's name as a program girl at charitable entertainments until you have investigated and ascertained who is back of the enterprise.

Don't allow your daughter to indulge in spectacular stunts even in the name of "sweet charity."

Don't fail to keep the grade C and D debutantes at a safe distance.[28]

Peppered as they were with references to "bounders," the "maid-chaperone," "Sunday afternoon at homes," Mr. Paul's thou-shalt-nots had a curiously Edwardian flavor. Yet when it came to coverage of debutante activities Mr. Knickerbocker's nostalgia for the past inevitably gave way to his nose for news. Brenda and Cobina violated the Knickerbocker code on nearly every count; but as in the older set, the birds of paradise made better copy than the little brown wrens.

Mr. Knickerbocker, for instance, defined a Grade A debutante as one who had gotten into the Junior Assemblies. Out of 400 applicants for this exclusive dance 143 were chosen, and the rejects were presumably kept at arm's length by every self-respecting mother. Brenda did not make the Assemblies, but Mr. Knickerbocker remained unperturbed. Two years before, he had spotted her as "a young miss we'll hear from"; and he reveled in the triumphs of her debutante year as confirmation of his prophetic gift.

Miss Frazier and Miss Wright took lightly his injunction about avoiding the spectacular. When Brenda's picture appeared in a Woodbury soap ad, accompanied by Mr. Knickerbocker's personal endorsement, nobody kept her at arm's length. It was understood by the most undiscerning mother that Brenda posed with a sort of papal dispensation.

When it came to lending one's name to sweet charity, no one was more active than Brenda. Some fifteen worthy causes drew sustenance from her glamour. As debutante chairman of the Velvet Ball, Brenda was to enjoy a distinction vouchsafed to few. She may not have made the Assemblies, but she made the cover of *Life*. The Velvet Ball was a typical function of what *Life* described as "the new commercial society." As such it was something that one of Mr. Knickerbocker's "grade A" debutantes might have been expected to shun like the plague. To be sure, the Velvet Ball did clear $12,000 for the New York Infirmary for Women and Children, but *The New Yorker* referred to it baldly as "a promotion stunt for the velvet industry."[29]

Besides the women and children, the Velvet Ball had innumerable unofficial beneficiaries. The Ned Wayburn Studio, for example, was called in to instruct the girls in the waltz and the polka-mazurka. Mr. Wayburn scored a coup for his instructresses by dressing them in cellophane hoopskirts. Other arrangements for the occasion were made by June Hamilton Rhodes, onetime business manager for Ruth St. Denis, and currently a publicist for velvet, jewelry, and orchids. She attired her prettiest Velvet Ball debutantes in velvet evening gowns lent by Fifth Avenue department stores. The girls were liberally covered with jewelry and orchids to give her other clients a gratuitous plug.

Mr. Knickerbocker notwithstanding, the methods of modern commerce were being used for the merchandising of the finishing school product.

> The modern debutante [said *Life*] has become as well publicized and commercialized as a fan dancer or a new hairdo and for good reason. The old and rather stodgy New York society is practically extinct except as names of telephone exchanges. The $50,000 private parties of the lush debutante era collapsed of their own weight and extravagance, and the post-depression debutante is presented, not only to her family and intimate friends, nor to New York's plutocracy, but to the general public. . . . But what makes Brenda the outstanding debutante is that with her long hair,

her vivacity and splendid figure, she is superbly photogenic, and publicity is the life blood of the new society. Apart from that, her chief distinction is that she never wears a hat, does wear shell-rimmed glasses, a great deal of jewelry.[30] [Another tabu smashed without a murmur from Mr. Knickerbocker.]

Thus did the fates conspire to thrust fame on what some uncharitable critic referred to as "the most unproductive public figure of the era next to Charlie McCarthy."[31]

In a year when debutantes gave fashion shows in the Rainbow Room, went roller-skating for Altman's or sold at Saks, Brenda's hayride down Broadway still came under the heading of "a spectacular stunt."

It was sponsored by the Coq Rouge and Radio Station WOR. The proceeds were to go to the National Bureau of Blind Artists. Station WOR supplied a small wagon, a team of horses, some hay, and fifteen minutes of radio time. The Coq Rouge supplied the debutantes—including Brenda, who was attired in an ocelot coat, dark blue slacks, white shoes and socks. The group progressed down Broadway to the strains of "Turkey in the Straw"—regaling passers-by with cultured halloos, cries of "free drinks, free meals, free supper, free floor show," and "don't look so glum, the Depression's over." When they reached Times Square, a man gave an imitation of a hog caller. Brenda gave a carefully rehearsed squeal as a rubber mouse was produced from a handbag; and an announcer explained to the listening audience that Brenda was colorful.

As a result of such activities, Brenda acquired quite a popular following. When she hired Burrelle's Press Clipping Bureau, she was swamped with more than 5,000 items about herself. She was deluged with requests for money, interviews, and other favors. Newspaper readers avidly devoured the most trivial details of her private life. They were fascinated by the news that the social pace had begun to tell on her as evidenced by her seemingly unending succession of head colds. They were let in on such housekeeping secrets as the domestic champagne served at her debut; the amount spent on breakage; the amount spent for detectives to keep an eye on light-fingered guests.

When she went to Nassau to visit her grandparents, she was "lost" to friends and press for twelve hours, and the *New York World-Telegram* treated her temporary silence as they would a major news blackout from Paris or Rome.

"Will she announce her engagement to Sir Edward Astley in Nassau?" the *Telegram* queried anxiously.[32] Suspense mounted with every hour she remained incommunicado. When her followers at last re-established contact with her on the gangplank of the steamer *Munargo*, the papers re-created a farewell scene to rival anything in grand opera. Young men who came down to see her off found their names in headlines. "Harry Wilson Sadly Bids Brenda Goodby. Fears Competition in Billy Livingston who was on Board the *Munargo* as Miss Frazier's Fellow Passenger."[33] Her departure was rendered more dramatic by last-minute feelers from the Coast. A talent scout had made a special trip from Hollywood to get her signature on a contract, only to have her reply: "I'm definitely not interested."[34]

As the ship got under way, the *Telegram* provided its readers with a dope sheet of Brenda's suitors.

> Billy is the unofficial victor of the first round with Ogden (Hammond) looming up as a serious challenger and Sir Edward Astley, already in Nassau, predicted the winner.
>
> Before the boat started, Billy, holding the trump card, made a gallant gesture. He praised Harry Wilson, saying he was a swell fellow and then explained that he wasn't trying to get the jump on Harry. "I'm just going down for my health," he remarked.[35]

It was also reported that Brenda threw poor Harry a crumb by lending him the Frazier Lincoln for the day and giving him the job of escorting her mink coat back to her hotel.

When Brenda arrived in Nassau, her fans had to subsist for a fortnight on pictures of her dressed as a Hindu princess, doing the hurdle dance with Billy Livingston. They learned that Sir Edward Astley was a late scratch in the race, who "just didn't rate at all."[36] New York recovered with surprising rapidity from the emotional catharsis of her departure. Soon the perfidious *Telegram* was headlining the startling news that "Life Goes on Without Brenda."[37]

This saturnalia of publicity did nothing to decrease Brenda's popularity. A comparison of Brenda and one of her fellow debutantes, Miss Rosemary Warburton, pointed up the futility of playing the game according to Cholly Knickerbocker's rules. Society columnists wanly tried to pit Miss Warburton against Miss Frazier in a contest for the position of the year's top debutante. By November, Barclay Beekman of the *New York Daily Mirror* had thrown in the towel, and was complaining: "I just can't keep her name out." As E. J. Kahn wrote in *The New Yorker:* "He didn't mean Miss Warburton."

Miss Warburton was the prototype of the Grade A debutante. She was a member of the all-important Junior Assembly. She was kin to the Vanderbilts. Cholly Knickerbocker characterized her party as "a case of quality, not quantity. . . . Only those debutantes whom Rosemary knows personally have been invited, for, contrary to the usual custom, no 'canned' debutante list was used when the invitations were issued."[38]

Yet when Mr. Paul was rating the season's debutantes in brief, the chips were down. . . . He described Brenda as "glamour spelled with capitals," while he wrote of Rosemary Warburton, "her modesty is refreshing"[39]—an appraisal roughly as satisfactory as being lauded for one's sweet expression.

Brenda's mother seemed somewhat offended by her daughter's fame. Cobina senior basked in Cobina junior's reflected glory. Young Cobina spent her season also triumphantly in the public eye. *Life* elected her as the glamour girl of 1939. She was on the July cover of the *Ladies' Home Journal.* The Fashion Academy elected her "the best-dressed girl in the supper clubs." Like Brenda, she took lightly Cholly Knickerbocker's advice to the *jeune fille* about ostentatious jewelry— posing as the "Jewel Queen of the World's Fair" with $95,000 worth of pearls and diamonds. The Society of Illustrators nom-

inated her as "the most attractive and talented New York girl
of the 1939 season." She was also named as "the perfect blonde
television type" and "The most beautiful girl at Palm Beach."
At the World's Fair she was one of eight working girls who
vied for the title of Miss Manhattan. Cobina, representing the
Fifth Avenue Association, won the prize, triumphing over the
more proletarian representatives from the 6th Avenue, 42nd
Street, 34th Street, 23rd Street, Washington Square, and
Central Mercantile Associations, as well as a girl from the East
Side Chamber of Commerce. A dramatic school student was
the runner-up, while a Schrafft's waitress won third place. The
occasion was only slightly marred by rumblings from the other
contestants who did not consider Cobina a working girl. She
had movie offers from Warner's and M.G.M. Later she did
performances at Loew's State with Eddie Cantor. She appeared on the Bob Hope radio show and the Rudy Vallee
show. She did a dramatic broadcast of *Fifth Row Center* on a
coast-to-coast hookup—the program arranged by Cobina
senior's old shipboard acquaintance, Bertie McCormick, in
deference to the "valiant woman." She opened in a play called
Lorelei, which closed a few nights later. She broadcast over
WJZ, explaining why she had written a magazine article de-
fending Brenda Frazier. ("We glamour girls must stick together.")[40] She was nominated by the National Dunking Association as "a gracefully correct dunker."[41]

But Cobina junior's greatest contribution lay in the cachet
she conferred upon the society singer. After her singing debut
in the Sert Room, New York supper clubs bloomed with aristocratic talent. Adelaide Moffet, daughter of a Standard Oil
multimillionaire; Lois Elliman, daughter of the real estate
Ellimans; Audrey Gray, niece of the Duchess of Marlborough,
were only a few of the well-bred voices one could hear by
dropping in at the late floor show. Lunch tables resounded
with finishing-school accents lamenting the unfamiliar problems of breaking even on a salary. Typical was the plaint of
Mrs. John J. ("Jeannie") Roberts, who sang with a quartet at
Le Mirage, and was shocked to discover that she cleared $5.00
a week after taxis, and that she was forced to join a union
which took $16.50 out of her first week's pay check.

After Cobina junior's triumph in the supper clubs, there were still new worlds to conquer, and it was inevitable that Cobina senior should turn a longing eye toward the coast. 20th Century offered Cobina junior a contract at $250 a week, climbing to an outside figure of $5,000. In Hollywood Cobina junior was squired about by Robert Stack, George Montgomery, and Sterling Hayden. Cobina senior's efforts to further her daughter's career were considered a bit bald even for a town not given to understatement.

Kyle Crichton wrote in the *Saturday Evening Post* that "Cobina Sr. launched a campaign on behalf of Cobina, that for subtlety and finesse has not been surpassed since Grant's investment of Vicksburg."[42] The publicity buildup included photographs in magazines, a masked ball at Ciro's, tours of night clubs in the company of escorts calculated to catch the eyes of columnists. When the aspiring star landed parts in *Moon Over Miami* and *Murder Among Friends*, cynics said that "Hollywood was pushed."

Cobina's screen career was to die a-borning, as were her hopes for a royal marriage. When Prince Philip of Greece was planning a visit to America, newspapers speculated wildly on the real reason for his trip. One paper ran a picture of the starlet, asking rhetorically: "Hollywood fame or H.R.H. Princess Cobina?" The answer, alas, was neither.

The trip was called off on account of the war. Instead of coming to America the Prince went into the British Navy. Instead of Cobina he married Princess Elizabeth of England.

The royal wedding ceremony would have seemed shabby beyond belief in the palmy days of Casa Cobina. Prince and princess sat down to a dinner which sounded like the menu for a children's party: creamed chicken, ice cream, pitchers of orange juice and, as a special concession, a few small bottles of champagne.

Belts were being worn tighter everywhere, and Brenda and Cobina felt the wartime pinch. They married within a few months of each other, and their weddings made a startling contrast to the ballyhoo of their season as glamour girls. On June 18, 1941, Brenda married John Sims (Shipwreck) Kelly, an insurance broker and former University of Kentucky foot-

ball star. They were married in the presence of twenty-five
close relatives and friends. The reception took place in the
Crystal Room of the Ritz Carlton. Brenda had one attendant,
and the best man was dressed in a sergeant's uniform. There
were less than 250 guests and only one gate crasher. The
Journal-American no longer clamored for more flowers. "Due
to the times, nothing could have been in better taste than the
simplicity of the reception which followed yesterday's equally
unostentatious wedding."[43]

While on vacation in California Cobina met Corporal
Palmer Beaudette. He was the son of wealthy parents in
Pontiac, Michigan, heir to a fortune amassed by his grand-
father, O. J. Beaudette, a designer of auto bodies.

> A whirlwind courtship? [wrote her mother.] It
> certainly was. But everything that summer and fall
> was like a whirlwind, and after December 7th a
> full-blown tornado. Girls married boys they had
> known three days who were "about to die." Most
> of Cobina's friends were married or about to be
> married. Every emotion was intensified by the
> weight of insecurity and terror. "Live for today,"
> they all cried. "Who knows about tomorrow?"[44]

Corporal Beaudette came to visit Cobina in Hollywood and
overstayed his leave. He made headlines by chartering a plane
to take him back to camp. Shortly after this the corporal and
Cobina announced their engagement, and another simple wartime wedding took place, this time in New York's Rockefeller
Church on Riverside Drive. After a brief wedding trip, Corporal Beaudette returned to Fort Benning, Georgia, to become
a lieutenant.

Kyle Crichton credited Cobina's husband with having
brought an era to an end by removing her from circulation.
"With one mighty stroke he has killed the age of glamour. . . .
We can now get on with the war."[45]

The glamour era did die with Pearl Harbor. The soft
cadences of rumba music in the Ritz were replaced by the
harsh strains of "Rosie the Riveter"; by raucous songs about

defense workers with "sweeties on the swing shift"; by radios blaring the welder's early morning complaint, "Milkman, keep those bottles quiet." Lonely girls dispatched V-mail letters to A.P.O. addresses. Housewives plowed through reams of federal prose to discover when the next meat coupon came due. Girls in offices lined up every morning in the cigarette queue. Clerks in stores rebuffed every request with the discourteous stock retort: "Don't you know there's a war on?"

And Brenda and Cobina slipped into obscurity—their thirst for publicity apparently slaked. On June 9, 1942, Brenda Frazier quietly turned twenty-one. It might have been considered an occasion for bacchanalian rejoicing as she got control of her handsome patrimony; yet she entertained at a small dinner party. "Since her marriage," said the *New York Times*, "she has dropped out of night club life, her social activities confined to war work."[46]

She lived on in obscurity until March 13, 1956, when her husband filed suit for divorce against her. They had been separated since 1951, and had one child, Brenda Victoria.

At the time of the separation Mrs. Kelly described her publicity build-up as "the worst thing that can happen to you. . . . It's all so superficial. It means nothing." Nothing was more anticlimactic than the life of a superannuated glamour girl.[47]

Brenda has put all this behind her. She lives in obscurity in Massachusetts, her health, like Barbara Hutton's, somewhat impaired by her years of service to the press. Occasionally someone who looks like her will appear in her old haunts, giving people the smug feeling of having gotten a glimpse of a Garbo. It is not Brenda, however, but a double.

Gossip columnists report that she has been amicably separated from her second husband, Robert Chatfield-Taylor. Brenda's daughter by Kelly was, in 1963, in her final year at Miss Hewitt's Classes, and presumably a candidate for the heady delights of the debutante whirl. Mrs. Chatfield-Taylor, significantly, did not want her to have a coming-out party. Recognizing the pitfalls of stage-managing a child's life, the ex-glamour girl felt that college would do more for Victoria than Ordeal by Flashbulb.

There were still one or two who looked back with nostalgia

to Brenda's year of triumph. The bare shoulders and curling hair of the glamour-girl era were still in view in 1958, when society turned out for the Cuban Gala at the Waldorf. Eugenia Sheppard of the *New York Herald Tribune* took this as evidence of America's abiding love for Brenda Diana Duff Frazier and was inspired to a somewhat unhappy turn of phrase. "The Brenda Frazier formula of 1938 . . . ," said Miss Sheppard, "has never been bettered for balls."

Cobina Wright junior also retired into domesticity eventually to become a mother of three. Shortly after her marriage, Cobina senior provided a characteristic note of drama by rushing to join the young people at Fort Benning, Georgia. She refused to leave her daughter's side until she was sure "the United States itself was not going to be under attack."[48]

Yet the Second World War defied all this doughty romanticist's attempts to dramatize it. It was a dreary and grubby affair—an age of overcrowded trains and overpopulated army towns, of babies howling in Quonset huts and neighbors' fights overheard through paper-thin walls; of hasty furloughs and poignant farewells in railroad stations; of tear-streaked faces and girls badly dressed in maternity clothes.

Cobina junior joined the vast army of women who traveled undramatically from camp to camp as chief cook and bottle washer to a soldier husband. Cobina senior was left with hardly a name to drop, though she did later recall to her readers the tense days "when we hung by our radios breathlessly awaiting the precise analyses of my old friend H. V. Kaltenborn."[49]

What a contrast to the First World War, when Cobina senior set off for France fancying herself in the roles of "Florence Nightingale, Joan of Arc and Nurse Edith Cavell off to do battle."[50] How drab the life of an army wife was in comparison to Cobina senior's vignettes of her days as a grass widow with the A.E.F. Cobina senior surrounded by servicemen imploring her to sing; Cobina senior reminiscing about some of her old comrades in arms; Louise Cromwell Brooks, "the jazz girl," whose "merry philosophy was a 'beacon light' to the officers who 'singed their wings at her gay flame' ";[51] Elsie de Wolfe, who remarked to her maid at the Ritz on returning from her duties as a nurse, "Delouse me—and then let's pray";[52] Cobina senior "lightly but earnestly loving a 'great many young men,'" receiving letters from the "poetic Prince de Savoia," whose prose style was as supercharged as Cobina's own:

> "During my lone vigils in this treacherous and warring sea, as the bow of my Sparviero (The Hawk) plows through it looking for the enemy against whom to throw itself, my thoughts often fly to you, and my heart fills with emotion at the memory of another sailing which made me happy because of the presence of the beautiful Golden Blonde Vision."[53]

Cobina junior's generation produced no memoirs to compare with those of the Golden Blonde Vision. Few were inspired to wax lyrical over the war that produced the A-bomb. The society that emerged from it had its spiritual roots in Levittown and not in the Casa Cobina.

The war had accelerated the leveling process started by the crash and the Depression. A Brenda Frazier or a Cobina Wright could never contemplate the world from a lofty pinnacle of wealth, certain that their money would insulate them from the struggles of the common herd. The servants who left the kitchen for the defense plant had made an anachronism of the girl who couldn't boil water. As Cobina junior could testify, even an auto body heir had to show up for reveille.

The barriers of class began to crumble on that fateful day when Father Wright came back from the Stock Exchange. They had crumbled a little more when Cobina opened at the Waldorf, when Brenda endorsed a beau or a soap, when the Wrights, junior and senior, appeared in a public restaurant wearing Daniel Boone hats. The bars went down a little more when the "Vivis," "Vahs" and "Mimis" of Brenda's year got wartime jobs as nurses' aides, as hands schooled to the receiving line turned to emptying proletarian bedpans.

By 1950 Cholly Knickerbocker no longer informed his readers when a socialite was gainfully employed. There were no more banner headlines in the society column about "Coco's" baby-sitting service, "Nancy's" bold experiment in moving to her own apartment, or "Didi's" job with the phone company. Many a reconstructed blueblood, living on the memory of money in a servantless world, could smile at Cholly Knickerbocker's 1938 headline: "Extra!! Socialites Wash Own Dishes."[54]

Cobina senior, faced with her daughter's apathy to a career, emigrated to Hollywood and turned her formidable literary gift to writing a gossip column. It was typical of the new age, when debutantes regaled the reading public with descriptions of what they had for lunch, that Mother should be syndicated.

The cruel differences between a Doris Duke and a Haywood Patterson, a Barbara Hutton and a Woolworth ribbon clerk were becoming ever smaller. As Brenda and Cobina whirled about the dance floor to the music of Emil Coleman and Alexander Haas, they bore unwitting witness to the declining prestige of a Hewitt accent. No longer did the ladies of the manor live off the sweat of the dime-store girl's brow. The best the modern debutante could hope for was to start out even with the shopgirl in the competition for the National Dunking Championship.

"What the hell you wanna do? Make people think we're crooked?" Quoted in *Victory in My Hands,* by Harold Russell

". . . that the human soul beaten down, overwhelmed, faced by complete failure and ruin, can still rise up against unbearable odds and triumph." *Victory in My Hands*

9
The Blessing in Disguise

HAROLD RUSSELL

On Armistice Day, 1918, little Harold Russell asked his father what all the shouting was about. His father replied, "Don't ask why. It doesn't make any difference why. Never again in your lifetime will you see another celebration like this, my boy. There'll never be another war."

Shortly after these prophetic words, the elder Russell died. The family had moved from Nova Scotia, where Harold was born, to Cambridge, Massachusetts. There, in 1933, the boy graduated from Rindge Technical High School.

Since the age of ten Russell had helped to augment the family income. He had hoped to win a scholarship to M.I.T., but failed. When the scholarship fell through, he took a job as a counter man in a meat store at fifteen dollars a week. As apprentice to a meat cutter, Russell was taught the intricacies of the "short weight" and the "chicken switch." He learned to weigh his hand along with the meat, to "clip" chops, to add the customer's address in inadvertently when totting up a column of purchases. He became an expert at making the hundred and one little "honest mistakes" which have one thing in common. They are never in the customer's favor. He was once harangued by his superior when a woman caught him short-weighting her —not for having cheated her, but for having done it so clumsily. "What the hell you wanna do?" the superior had railed. "Make people think we're crooked?"

This innocent persiflage went on to an accompaniment of inspirational slogans from the management: "Keep up the P.C." (percentages); "Pleased Customers Mean Higher Percentages." Employees were constantly reminded of the meat vendor's Hippocratic oath. "Your relationship to your clients is akin to that of a doctor to his patients."

Russell made modest progress, rising finally to the position of market manager. He was neither enthusiastic nor unenthusiastic about his job. He was hounded by a vague sense of failure, which was heightened by an unsuccessful courtship. It was Pearl Harbor that resolved his nagging doubts about the worth of a lifetime devoted to butchers' malpractice.

Russell enlisted in the army, and was inducted on February 12, 1942. In his autobiography, *Victory in My Hands,* he was disarmingly frank about his motives.

> It had nothing to do with patriotism, with duty. I had enlisted because my whole life had been a failure up to that point. Joining the Army had given me a glamorous alibi for running away from a job that offered little, a girl I had failed to win, a life that meant nothing. It gave me a chance to be a quitter and a hero at the same time.

He was sent to Camp Croft, South Carolina, for his infantry training. Parachute school and demolition school took up his education where the chain store left off, teaching him such helpful bits of information as the use of parachute knives and the most effective ways of kneeing adversaries in the groin. He became a demolition school instructor, eventually achieving the rank of sergeant. Shortly after D-Day his outfit was alerted for overseas duty; but Russell was never to have the prepaid tour of exotic places. He was one of the saddest kind of war casualties, for he acquired his battle scars without setting eyes on a single enemy.

On June 6, 1944, at Camp Mackall, North Carolina, Russell helped to lay out an obstacle course with nitrostarch charges. Another man was supposed to run a demolition platoon over it; but his girl was coming to see him and he asked Russell to relieve him. Russell paid a high price for playing the Good Samaritan. A defective fuse on a charge of explosives went off, wounding him in the chest and stomach, and blowing off both his hands. An Elgin watch which he was wearing at the time came through the explosion unscathed—a fact so extraordinary that the manufacturers flatly refused to believe it.

The following day Russell's hands were amputated three inches above the wrist at Walter Reed Hospital in Washington, D.C. He was fitted for a pair of hooks. In the hospital he had to relearn the use of his head and shoulder muscles. Tying a shoe or holding a beer bottle was suddenly a herculean feat. He eventually worked up a typing speed of twenty-five words per minute by the hunt-and-peck system. After passing an examination in dressing, eating, writing, shaving, dialing phone numbers, and brushing his teeth, he was judged ready for the tender mercies of the outside.

Though instructed in the mechanics of motion, he was unprepared for the slips of the tactless. Two waiters in an Italian restaurant collided, dropping large bowls of spaghetti because they couldn't take their eyes off his hooks. A woman who had known him at the meat market urged him not to worry over his hands. "They never really belonged to you. Every time you weighed meat you sold part of them." A woman in a movie house who clasped Russell's hand in a spontaneous welling up of patriotic feeling, shot up with a scream when she discovered that what she had thought was warm flesh was actually cold steel.

Russell understandably developed something of a chip on his shoulder. To a man in a bar who asked him how he had lost his hands, he retorted, "Maybe you'd like to tell me how

you lost your teeth!" To a cab driver who asked him if he
missed his hands he riposted, "No, of course I don't miss
them. Now I don't have to spend money getting them mani-
cured."

During this reconstruction period, he enrolled in Boston
University. Like so many of the liberally educated, he set his
sights on some undefined goal in "advertising."

He also agreed to make a movie for the army called *Diary
of a Sergeant.* Originally designed as a morale builder for
amputees, the film came to the attention of Samuel Goldwyn.
It so happened that, out on the Coast, Goldwyn had gotten
the idea of doing a film about veterans and their difficulties in
adjusting to postwar civilian life. He had commissioned Mac-
Kinlay Kantor to write a novel on this theme to serve as a
scenario for the movie. Kantor came up instead with a long
narrative poem in blank verse. The general tone of the play
could be deduced from the following description of the hero,
a spastic named Homer Wermels:

> Nineteen years old; but twenty soon;
> His yellow hair was tufted at his ears.
> He had a sweep of whitish fuzz around his chin
> And bright blue eyes that looked with love on life
> Because he'd never thought to taste it more.
> He dragged his foot; his shoe was built so thick
> He'd drag it twenty days before the sole wore
>   down. . . .
>
> So they took off; three points, tail down
> And Homer Wermels drooled and dripped. . . .
> One thing about spasticity; you always seem to
>   drool.

Mr. Goldwyn had understandable misgivings about the box-
office appeal of this work. Russell's film gave him the idea
of having the part played by an amputee. Accordingly he
issued the command which sent equerries of the film industry
scurrying about as if in response to the whim of a Tudor:
"Get me that man."

When the call from the Coast came, Russell thought the whole thing was a practical joke. The signing up of William Wyler to direct the picture and Robert Sherwood to rewrite the script, plus an impressive array of talent, finally convinced him of Mr. Goldwyn's serious intentions. Fredric March, Myrna Loy, Dana Andrews, Hoagy Carmichael, Teresa Wright, Virginia Mayo, Steve Cochran, and a newcomer named Cathy O'Donnell were to be among Russell's costly co-workers. The amputee's unfortunate surname "Wermels" was changed to a more euphonious "Parrish."

The Best Years of Our Lives was something special in the way of pictures. Wyler insisted upon naturalness at all costs to the distress of the "cosmeticians," who were constantly frustrated in their attempts to "touch up" make-up and "freshen" hair-dos. . . . Whenever something happened by accident it was left in the script—as when March drank a Bromo-Seltzer out of an empty glass. Russell couldn't get sufficiently steamed up about hitting Ray Teal, who was play- ing the part of a Fascist. Wyler told Russell that Teal really was one and Russell struck him with conviction.

On the set Russell was exposed to the vagaries of the artistic temperament. There was the little girl who played Russell's sister who refused to speak to anyone else because a screen credit made her the queen of the "Kiddie Car Cabal." There was Hoagy Carmichael in the role of a bartender, and his agent who kept trying to elevate the tone of the bar to a milieu more in keeping with the dignity of a grand old man.

Russell's own personality was left virtually intact. The only alterations were a diet of leafy vegetables to reduce his weight and diction lessons intended to modify his Down East drawl. In at least one case, Boston triumphed over Hollywood. After Russell pronounced the word "cars" "ca's" throughout nine retakes, it was ultimately changed to "automobiles."

For the most part, the pear-shaped vowels went the way of Max Factor. The result was that Hollywood rarity—an adult picture.

Russell was at this point engaged to a childhood sweet- heart. Their impending wedding plans, plus the fact that Russell couldn't find a place to live in Hollywood, provided the publicity department with a heaven-sent "angle"; "Waiting twenty-three years to marry his dream girl, and now he can't because he can't find an apartment."

The studio solved this omnipresent problem of the postwar newlywed.

A kindly publicity man was equally helpful in arranging the "sordid details" of the wedding ceremony. He did his work so well that, as Russell recalls, "Rita and I were practically reduced to playing bit-parts at our own wedding." Steve Cochran and Virginia Mayo were cast as best man and maid of honor because they commanded more linage than any homely intimate of the bride or groom. The forgotten man of the wedding ceremony described some of the other "sordid details" which were thoughtfully taken care of. "Jack set up picture and story coverage of the ceremony and the wedding party that followed it. He hired the hall, invited all the guests, chose the breakfast menu and stage-managed the entire affair from start to finish. He did, however, let Rita and me fix the date—February 27, 1946."

When the picture was finished, Goldwyn hugged Russell and congratulated him on his "simply gorgeous performance." Myrna Loy's maid conferred the final cachet by asking for his autograph. Russell retired with some relief to Boston and a brief vacation from being a "personality."

The publicity juggernaut in his case was to make a sneak attack on the public. When the picture opened in November 1946 at the Astor Theatre in New York, Russell was warned not to come within a hundred miles of the proceedings. All publicity releases on him were killed. "I was to stay under wraps until the critics stumbled over me *if* they did."

A week after the New York premiere, this unconventional thinking paid off. Russell received a royal command from Louella Parsons to appear on her radio show. He was flown to the Coast to appear on the program for three minutes. Miss Parsons was kind and motherly and insisted on picking up canapés and putting them into his mouth.

Russell was then flown back East for the Boston premiere and for the local-boy-makes-good treatment. The picture received rave reviews, and the following day he experienced the first mixed blessings of fame. There were people who called up requesting small loans and seats for "tonight's performance." There were invitations to speak before groups representing every shade in the political spectrum, from the American Legion to the Communist Party.

Goldwyn sent him around on a nation-wide personal-appearance tour, during the course of which he was told not to mention the picture unless he was asked about it. His appearances were to be in connection with some local charitable cause. "But by an amazing coincidence," he noted, "it turned out that *The Best Years* either was just about to open or just had opened wherever I went."

The Best Years of Our Lives won eight Oscars plus the Irving Thalberg Award. Russell's performance earned him a special award for "bringing aid and comfort to veterans through the medium of motion pictures" (presented to him by Shirley Temple); an Oscar for the best supporting performance of 1946; and the *Look* award for the best dramatic performance of 1946.

After the ceremonies Pat O'Brien clapped him on the back and declaimed, "That's us Irish! Yes, sir! You can't beat us Irish, can you Russ?"

"That's right, Pat," murmured Russell. He tactfully refrained from mentioning to Mr. O'Brien that he actually came of Scotch-English antecedents.

Mr. Goldwyn's exuberance knew no bounds. In a speech thanking the members of the cast he asked rhetorically how could he forget all those splendid men and women who had made this triumph possible? "Then," Russell recalls, "he proceeded to call the roll of all those 'unforgettable' names, including that great actor and musician, 'Hugo Carmichael.'"

Later the fair-haired boy was permitted to throw a little party of his own and to sign the Goldwyn name.

Back in Boston he came to know another treat reserved for the famous. He was awakened in the middle of the night by a call from Toots Shor's in New York. Pat O'Brien spoke for a few minutes, and was followed by Joe diMaggio, Mayor O'Dwyer, Hank Greenberg, Ted Husing, Paul Douglas, and finally Toots Shor himself. None of them did more than greet

Russell and ask how he was, a query to which he never had a chance to reply before another reveler was put on. The call took two hours in all. After that, it was safe to say that he had arrived. Drunken telephonitis from Toots Shor, however irritating, established the party at the other end as a member of an Olympian brotherhood.

As Charles Lindbergh discovered two decades earlier, a man who is successful in one field becomes in the eyes of the public an authority in all others. The Oscar gave Russell an omniscience on March 14 that he had never enjoyed on March 12.

This popular reaction to Harold Russell's fame was a common one. His reaction to the popular reaction was most uncommon. He decided that he might as well talk about something important as long as he had the public ear.

Russell's war experiences had brought him from absorption in the fortunes of the Braves and the Red Sox to a growing consciousness of the world around him. On an Atlanta street-car he noticed that an old colored woman was standing up, though a seat beside him remained unoccupied. He asked her why and she told him.

Later in Raleigh, North Carolina, he was riding on a bus, when a Negro lieutenant sat down with several white officers. The driver saw him in the rear-view mirror and shouted, "Get the hell where you belong, you nigger son of a bitch." The lieutenant got up without a word and sat down in the back of the bus. A white sergeant got up, grabbed the driver and lifted him out of his seat. "You dirty goddam white bastard," he said, clipped him on the chin, and jumped off the bus. The Negro lieutenant remained prudently seated in the rear.

Russell's education was further advanced by a Nisei G.I. who had lost a right leg, arm, and eye at Cassino, and had a Silver Star, a Bronze Star, and a Purple Heart. He was informed while on furlough: "We don't want none of you yellow Jap bastards in this town."

Hitherto Russell had not believed in the existence of prejudice, though he himself had briefly suffered under the sobriquet "dumb Canuck." In traveling around the country on his personal-appearance tour, he decided to speak up against disunion and hatred. The more he spoke the more he realized that there was no pat way of legislating brotherly love into being.

He discovered that there were those who took exception to his gradualist approach.

> Their solution for the problem of racial preju-
> dice and religious bigotry was simple and disas-
> trous: Crack the bastards' skulls with a club and
> pour knowledge and tolerance into their brains.
> . . . The lion and the lamb must be made to lie
> down together . . . and if they wouldn't, why then
> . . . just pass a law! Get the cops after them!
>
> Drag 'em into court, sue 'em, fine 'em, toss 'em
> into jail. We shall have the brotherhood of man
> even if we have to slaughter half of mankind to
> get it.

After protracted negotiations between his agent and the Goldwyn people, the crown prince was absolved from his vows to the studio. The Goldwyn representative was not authorized to raise Russell's salary. Russell's agent was not authorized to sign him again at the old figure. There was a flurry of coast-to-coast telephone calls so dear to the hearts of the executives in The Industry. Both factions stood back like tennis partners deliberating who should take a shot. At last the ball plunged unreturned down the center of the court. Russell signed with William Morris.

The terms were attractive: at least $35,000 for him, with a fair chance of making another $25,000 or $30,000. His first appearance at the Oriental Theatre in Chicago was not much of a success. An official of the Anti-Defamation League of B'nai B'rith heard him speak and offered him a job. Russell canceled all his bookings with the Morris Agency to take it.

During 1948 and 1949, Russell visited forty-six states, working with teen-agers. He appeared on the scene in Gary, Indiana, to speak against racial hatred less than a year after the "school strike" in which fifteen hundred high school students had refused to attend classes with Negroes. He was enthusiastically cheered, though the students had booed the same theme when it was presented by the erotically titillating figure of Frank Sinatra.

In 1947 Russell joined the American Veterans of World War II. He became the national chairman of its Youth Opportunity Committee. Later he was elected national commander. He was re-elected when a constitutional bar against second terms for national commanders was lifted—an amendment which applied only to him.

In 1950 Russell became head of the World Veterans' Federation. He visited the capitals and villages of nations from England and France to Thailand and Japan. Medical techniques and rehabilitation programs, unknown until Russell appeared, materialized in the far corners of the earth. The World Veterans' Federation now boasts more than nineteen and a half million members. Russell's efforts have helped to transform it from an idea on paper into a world force.

Russell settled down in Natick, Massachusetts, with his wife and two children. In the concluding pages of *Victory in My Hands*, he wrote of his experiences:

> People frequently marvel at the things I can do with my hooks. Well, perhaps it is marvelous. But the thing I never cease to marvel at is that I was able to meet the challenge of utter disaster and master it. For me, that was and is the all-important fact—that the human soul beaten down, overwhelmed, faced by complete failure and ruin, can still rise up against unbearable odds and triumph.

World War II left its mark in many ways. In addition to the ugly problems it left in its wake, it acted as a great social catalyst. Because of it, scions of old New York families brought home fiancées from small Midwestern towns. Woolcaps from Alabama were subjected to a series of broadening influences from the wine cellars of French chateaux to the furnaces of Buchenwald. The banker's daughter found the barriers of class less real in Neosho, Missouri, as she listened to the sex problems of an army post, or was elected to break the bad news to the buck private's wife.

Because of the war a boy who couldn't win a scholarship acquired the most priceless by-product of the liberal arts—a sense of perspective. Harold Russell not only survived his disability; he also survived his fame. With a measure of good humor he weathered a Hollywood build-up, a White House presentation, and a breath-taking exposure to "big names." He left the Coast without getting the illusion that he would inherit the mantle of Olivier. He realized that but for the ballyhoo, he might still be clipping chops in a Cambridge meat market. He lived a truly "inspirational" story without, after the time-honored fashion of the *Reader's Digest*, recommending disaster to all.

He was also that rarest of do-gooders—a middle-of-the-road crusader.

After the war every branch of the arts reflected his conscience pangs on the subject of minorities.

The nation's movie screens blossomed with hearty Catholic priests, and nuns in boxing gloves and jeeps. Best-sellers were populated with Jews and Negroes, whose humanity was lost in the larger aspects of The Problem. Drugstores offered 25-cent editions of *Brave Little Sambo*, where a familiar nursery tale was purged of embarrassing references to pigmentation.

Russell, however, stepped in and did something. Others were content to tell their children that there was something not quite nice about the unexpurgated version of Eeny, meeny-miny-mo. He pursued his goals without resorting to the methods of the brass-knuckled men of good will. Occasionally a life foredoomed to mediocrity was raised to unexpected levels of achievement in those days of the B-29 and the Molotov cocktail.

The picture which made him famous is filled with vignettes that were dated a year or so after V-J Day. They strike a chord in anyone who lived through World War II. G.I. Fredric March becomes suddenly inarticulate, as the baby son he left behind discourses learnedly on Japanese family patterns and the fact that brotherly love is humanity's answer to the Bomb. There are the young men "nervous out of the service" coming home to the neat hedgerows with the same sick feeling they had before they hit the beach. There are the awkward silences in the hearty reunions with "the folks." There are jobholders suddenly elbowed out of a soft berth by the servicemen they were buying drinks for a few months before. There is the wife's involuntary cry, "I've never seen you in civilian clothes before." The parenthetical cry of a million horrified women was deleted: "Oh my God, the color of those pants!"

Husbands walk in unexpectedly on their wives. Myrna Loy wishes she had been given the time to put on her face. Dana Andrews surprises an improbably sluttish Virginia Mayo with a dark-haired stranger who is having little trouble readjusting to civilian life.

This is a picture where the happiest couples have bitter quarrels, where heroines look like real women who are occasionally startled in pin curls.

Russell's performance initiated the public into the problems of the amputee. Audiences winced as he dropped a beer bottle, and got off his crack about the manicure in response to some civilian *lapsus linguae*. They caught him in embarrassed reunion with Wilma, his girl friend. "The Navy," as a buddy remarked, "didn't teach him to put his arms around her." They saw him smash his hooks through a window when cornered by curious neighborhood kids. They were there in his bedroom as his fiancée watched the man she was going to marry become as helpless as a six-month-old, in the moment when he removed his hooks.

Grueling as these details were, the impression they gave was one of purpose and strength. Even then, however, the problems of tomorrow were in the making. Some years later a Warner Brothers executive was to say, "Of course no one would dare make that picture nowadays." In 1946 it was already becoming unhealthy to express such heretical reservations as Fredric March and Dana Andrews did about "the land of unlimited opportunity."

"If the next war comes we won't have to worry, we'll all be blown up the first day," one character remarked. In those days of America's atomic monopoly, nobody really believed it. Yet the deterioration of the free world's might was symbolized in a shot of the B-17's gathering dust in a junkyard.

"I hope she really is a swell girl," Russell's friends say, as they watch him turn away from Wilma. For every swell girl there was one in real life who wasn't. For every Harold Russell who ended up in the arms of Miss Right, there were two strangers glaring at each other over the breakfast table with a future juvenile delinquent having his first trauma in the playpen.

The Best Years of Our Lives expressed a fleeting state of mind superbly. There were other movies which did not do it as well. A glut of Grade B revivals on television recalled the days when Hollywood went to war. They were movies about noble Seabees and noble nurses. There were movies in which the general's daughter fell in love with a private named Kalamazoo down at the local canteen. Stern but lovable papa always conferred his blessing on their mésalliance after discovering Kalamazoo under the living room sofa. "The Stars and Stripes Forever" swelled in the background.

A whole generation of bobby-soxers thrilled to the talents of Van Johnson and Sonny Tufts. They stared fascinated as Veronica Lake patriotically blew herself up with a hand grenade. Every Saturday afternoon they saw one Grumman Wildcat demolish the whole Japanese navy, as the sinister little yellow men in heavy glasses went screaming down to Davy Jones's locker.

As works of art these films had little to recommend them except a common sense of dedication. The dedication disappeared in the postwar period as more pressing problems reared their heads—when the Chevrolet dealer with the new spring line announced for the first time that he could offer a *choice* of colors.

The dedication was showing almost for the last time in *The Best Years of Our Lives*. Harold Russell spoke for a civilization with a star in the window, which had briefly discovered the truth of the old saying that "you never know what you can do until you have to."

"I remember Mother whispering, 'Shirley I think they're going to give you something. If they do, say "thank you." ' That's when they gave me my little Oscar. I thanked them and said 'Can we go now Mommy?' "
Shirley Temple in *Modern Screen,* April 1949

"I have no sad memories. I never had to work very hard. We all just seemed to play games." Shirley Temple in *Time,* January 27, 1958

10
The Good Ship Lollipop

SHIRLEY TEMPLE

On April 23, 1928, in Santa Monica, California, little Shirley Jane Temple was born. Her doting mother nicknamed her "Presh," short for "Precious." A few years later she lisped her first dramatic lines, *"Oui, mon cher."* The world was waiting for her—a world already weary of breadlines and not yet attuned to the goose step; a world which found Shirley's dimples a welcome antidote to Hitler's mustache and Chamberlain's umbrella.

Shirley's mother, Gertrude Temple, may have had some inkling of Shirley's future. She soon noticed that Shirley didn't walk like more earth-bound children. Shirley skipped and danced like a fairy child. Arriving many years after her two older brothers, Shirley's appearance marked the fulfillment of Mrs. Temple's fondest dream—"a little girl to lead by the hand."[1]

According to the fan magazines, the tot had from the first the air of one called to a historic destiny. *Photoplay* reverently recorded the first hint of her greatness. "In the palm of her little right hand is a peculiar marking. It was the first thing the nurses noticed the day Shirley was escorted into the world. 'What does it mean?' they asked. And then someone said in a rather awed voice, 'It's a sign of fame, great fame.' "[2]

Where Shirley's fate line left off Mrs. Temple quickly took over. In 1934 she reminisced in *Motion Picture*, "Long before she was born, I tried to influence her future life by association with music, art and natural beauty. Perhaps this pre-natal preparation helped make Shirley what she is today."[3]

Other movie mothers gave their offspring a similar uterine nudge. Jackie Cooper's mother channeled her thoughts to the same end. "When I knew Jackie was coming, I wanted him to be somebody. With every bit of will I had, I focussed my hope on his future."[4]

Shirley's prepartum preparation was followed up with dancing lessons. At dancing school she attracted the attention of a scout from Educational Pictures. She won a contract to appear in a series of shorts called Baby Burlesks. Her first French phrase was addressed to a diapered male colleague in a take-off of *What Price Glory?*

Like all child stars, Shirley embroidered a bit for the fans on the cosmic moment of her "discovery." Her recollections vary in successive versions of autobiographical reminiscence. In an autobiography written in conjunction with the editors of *Look*, the talent scout routed Shirley out from behind the piano.[5] In *My Life and Times*, another version of her life, written when she was a literate seven-year-old, she tells the public:

> . . . I didn't do anything at all except walk past Mr. Lamont. That's what all the children there did —just walked past him. I don't know why he picked me out. I didn't even *know* he'd picked me out until three or four days later when he telephoned Mom and told her to bring me around for a screen test.[6]

A third version given to a reporter from the *New York Times Magazine* apparently represented Miss Temple's final thinking on the subject.

> I remember when I was three and unknown . . . and some character who turned out to be a talent scout came into the dancing school and I hid under the piano . . . He stood around for a while watching, and then he said, "I'll take the one under the piano."
>
> There are times . . . when it pays to hide your bushel under a piano.[7]

One of Shirley's selected short subjects attracted the notice of the song writer Jay Gorney. Leo Houck introduced him to the Temples in the lobby of a Beverly Hills theater. Gorney sent his find to the Fox studio, where she was auditioned for a part in *Stand Up and Cheer.* According to her mother, "she had such rhythm in her toes that she got the job."[8]

She proved to be so popular that she was responsible for the merger between 20th Century and Fox. She was loaned to Paramount for *Little Miss Marker,* after which her weekly salary jumped to about $1,250 with option raises. She was featured in *Baby, Take a Bow* and *Now and Forever. Bright Eyes* gave her star billing and a special Oscar as the outstanding personality of 1934. With the much-publicized modesty of a screen child, she later characterized the Academy Award Dinner as a rather "boring" affair.[9]

Between 1934 and 1939, the treacle flowed freely, in *Rebecca of Sunnybrook Farm, Curly Top, Poor Little Rich Girl, The Little Colonel, The Littlest Rebel,* and *Heidi.* In the banner years between 1934 and 1938, she had fourteen straight smash hits. In 1935, 1936, 1937 and 1938 she was the number one box office favorite. At the age of ten she grossed over $300,000 and hobnobbed as an equal with the Roosevelts. And well she might have, since she was pulling down a bigger salary than F.D.R.

The market became glutted with by-products of her fame:

Shirley Temple dolls, dresses, and accessories. In 1935, as a result of *The Little Colonel,* she was made honorary colonel by the American Legion. Her favorite poems were compiled into a slim volume for school children. James Farley commissioned her to be honorary Sponsor of National Air Mail Week. She became a captain of the Texas Rangers, an honorary G-woman and a mascot of the Chilean navy. To other South American admirers she was known as "Ricito de Oro" or "golden curls."

In one of the bleakest decades in American history, Shirley provided a million-dollar ray of sunshine. The Depression hit the Temple household a few years after it hit Cobina Wright. One day Mr. Temple stayed home from the bank. "I asked him why," Shirley reminisced in *Pictorial Review,* "and he said President Roosevelt had closed the banks and he couldn't get to work.

"But *I* was working . . . I was only three years old but I was working! I was in the movies! And a few months later I was making more money than Daddy or Mom or anybody else ever dreamed of."[10]

Stand Up and Cheer took the public on a jolly voyage to Never-Never Land. It involved a Secretary of Amusement who was appointed to cheer people up, and a bunch of crooks, bent, for some obscure reason, on prolonging the Depression. After seeing it, Winfield Sheehan, one of Shirley's legion of "discoverers," realized that cheering people up was fraught with vast commercial possibilities.

"In a little while, darling," he enthused, "you're going to make millions of people happy—sick people, sad people, poor people—yes, and rich people and young people, too. . . . They'll all love you. You're going to be the most loved little girl in the whole world."[11]

Shirley exercised her talent for making people happy on lachrymose old gentlemen around the studio, to whom she told riddles. She brightened the final hours of a dying boy of fourteen with an autographed picture and a long-distance call. Cheer rang up the register in one Temple hit after another. Her mother directed Shirley's natural buoyancy into channels both proper and profitable. In *Little Miss Marker*, Shirley appeared as the companion of gangsters, and was forced to come out with an unladylike "Aw, nuts." A disapproving Mrs. Temple was assured that "her plays, from *Bright Eyes* on, will be more suitable to her cheery, winsome personality."[12]

Thenceforth Shirley's parts were tailor-made for her, with a specified number of tap routines and an abundance of such cheery, winsome lines as "Daddy, I don't want to go away." To provide her with a vehicle, Kipling's *Wee Willie Winkie* underwent a convenient change of sex. Ricito de Oro was shielded from the slightest hint of grossness. A naked baby picture was suppressed by the Hays Office because it "suggested nudity."[13] The title of *The Bowery Princess* was changed to *Dimples* because it was unseemly to find Goldilocks wandering around Skid Row. A hula scene was expurgated from *Captain January* as too suggestive. As Susannah of the Mounties Shirley smoked a pipe. She was forced to be sick, as the public would not tolerate the slightest hint that their darling reacted favorably to stimulants.[14]

Shirley was invariably a force for good—a Little Miss Fixit who brought sweethearts together, found wives for the lovelorn, made crooks go straight, and snatched parents back from the brink of divorce.

A typical plot was that of *Kathleen*, in which she appeared during a temporary lull in her career, when the formula was losing its magic.

Kathleen's mother was dead. Her governess was a martinet. Kathleen's psyche came under the scrutiny of what *Newsweek* called an "improbably good-looking" child psychologist played by Laraine Day. With the aid of Kathleen, Papa was brought together with Miss Day and saved from the clutches of Gail Patrick. (As any moviegoer of the thirties was well aware, the ominous appearance of Miss Patrick always presaged trouble.)

Shirley danced and chuckled through endless variations on this theme. She was from the first a little pro. She was a quick study, always knew her lines perfectly, and was known as "One-take Temple." She had played the part so often she could do it with her eyes shut.

She could turn on the charm when cued by her mother: "Sparkle, Shirley." She was equally adept with the waterworks. She imparted her secret to the public in almost as many versions as the "accident" of her discovery.

"Crying is fun when you're not really sad," she told an interviewer from the *New York Time Magazine* in 1941. "The way I do it is usually just to look awfully hard at something. It's easier if I'm holding a dog or a kitten. I guess it's the way they feel—so soft and furry. But if the scene doesn't permit that, then I just stare hard, maybe at a piece of furniture or at my mother" (she giggled and Mrs. Temple tried to frown) "but I don't try to think of sad things or why I'm supposed to be crying. You see, I'm not really trying to be sad inside at all."[15]

Time, in 1958, wrested a more humorous copy angle out of Shirley's tears. She could cry on cue "by thinking of my pony, Spunky, and how he flunked every screen test." She would stop crying "by thinking of Ching-Ching, my Peke, and all the money he was making in my movies."[16]

In 1949, she once more told the story of her life to *Modern Screen* under the title "So Dear to My Heart." Inexplicably included in her treasure trove of fond memories was a stupid technique of stimulating the tear ducts worthy of the Marquis de Sade.

"They asked Mother to go off on some excuse or other. Meantime they told me there'd been a terrible accident, that a 'big man with green eyes had taken Mommy away.' Well, I got hysterical. Even after she came back it took me a long time to quiet down. They couldn't shoot the scene anyway because I was crying harder than what it called for. After that, no matter what reason they gave Mother never left me again."[17] In her buffer capacity, Mrs. Temple received a sizable Depression salary of around $250 a week.

When she was working, Shirley considered that she was playing a game of make-believe. "What are we pretending today?" she would ask her mother. There was nothing make-believe, however, about Shirley's pay check.

Prior to Shirley's success, the Temples had, as *Pictorial Review* put it, lived "simply and happily after their limited fashion." The *Wunderkind's* career changed all this. The Temples moved twice, each time to a better neighborhood. The two older brothers had the opportunity of going to college, with Shirley paying the tab.

On the studio lot, Shirley moved into a bungalow known by its previous tenant as "La Maison de Rêves." There she lunched and napped, away from the exhausting attentions of her public. At home she acquired a French tutor and a chauffeur, and a glass-brick playhouse the size of an average Westchester home. This was decorated with the dolls which poured in from admirers all over the world. It had a hidden movie projector and a private soda fountain. "All in all," said Mrs. Temple, "it is a cozy and lovely little home we have made for her."[18]

Mrs. Temple was launched by her daughter on a career of belles-lettres. Pediatricians wrote her for her copies of Shirley's diet. The household magazines burgeoned with articles by Mrs. Temple on the secret of keeping Shirley unspoiled. Beauty editors asked for the secrets behind Shirley's petal-soft skin.

To Shirley's fans, Mrs. Temple imparted some of the star's beauty secrets. "A normal, healthy nervous system is a good foundation for good looks and a happy life."[19] "I have to shampoo her head regularly to keep her scalp clean and active."[20] Occasionally Shirley herself put in a childish treble. "Of course I don't use any of those creams or stains on my nails, and there's never anything in my bath but water— and me!"[21]

Shirley was portrayed as the possessor of a seraphic disposition. According to her mother, she had none of the antisocial tendencies to be found among children made of common clay. She did not write on walls, wake up in the middle of the night, tear books, or scratch her little playmates. A maid was reported to have been stunned by Shirley's insistence on making her own bed, despite the presence of competent help which she was paying for. To *Parents' Magazine,* Mrs. Temple explained that the merest ugly look was sufficient to keep the cherub in line.

With *American Magazine,* she took a less permissive tone.

"She is not running the Temple household. When she is disobedient and I am too tired to be sensible, I sometimes give her a spank or two. Some psychologists, I am told, say that corporal punishment is undesirable, but it works."[22]

Fans eagerly devoured every such detail of Shirley's home life, however banal. Her childish witticisms were received with the same respect as the epigrams of La Rochefoucauld.

Everyone tittered delightedly when she expressed a fondness for ice cream with "chocolate gravy," when she described her stand-in variously as a "step-in" or "stand-out," or when she wound up her evening prayers with a fervent "Thank you, God, for sending me Tarzan."[23]

Her pets basked in her reflected glory. Corky, her Scottie (reported by one source to be stuffed), was featured in an autobiographical piece, with Miss Temple addressing various remarks to him for confirmation. He was also the recipient of the following poetic tribute:

> My nicest dog
> Is christened Corky
> I wish they'd let him
> Make a talkie
>
> Now if his name
> Were only Carky
> I'm sure they'd want him
> In a *barkie*.[24]

Occasionally Shirley was credited with a competence outside her special field. Once she received a call from Japan from someone who thought she might make the Japanese and Chinese see eye to eye. Another amateur diplomat thought she might bring about harmony between Hitler, Churchill, Stalin, and Roosevelt. Modestly Shirley admitted that such an entente probably wouldn't work.[25]

In 1945 she told the *Herald Tribune* Youth Forum that movies were the "biggest single factor in shaping young minds" and that she considered them a potent force in spreading democratic concepts among America's former enemies.[26]

After Churchill, Roosevelt, and Stalin had had their innings it now apparently remained for Shirley to deal the final body blow to the Axis.

Unspoiled as she was said to be there were moments when she was not entirely impervious to her fame. In August 1934, long before Shirley became a manipulator of cabinets, a writer from *Motion Picture* called on her mother. Mrs. Temple was adding her two cents' worth to that of Mesdames Collins, Weinbrenner and Cooper (mothers of Cora Sue Collins, Baby Le Roy and Jackie Cooper respectively), on the vital subject of how to make your child a movie star. "Why didn't you ask me the questions?" Shirley suddenly demanded in a surprisingly deep voice. "I'm the star."

The Temples had an occasional premonition that the gravy train would one day stop rolling. The first inkling was confided in *Pictorial Review* in 1935 by Shirley to her canine confidante Corky. "Suppose I'm not so cute when I grow up as I am now, Corky? Suppose people don't want to see me in my pictures any more? Everybody at the studio says that there's nothing to worry about. . . . They say I've got 'natural talent' like those little boys and girls who learn to play the piano and violin at concerts."[27]

Despite such reassurances, Shirley, like all child stars, had to face the grim specter of puberty. By 1939, she had slipped to sixth place in the fans' affections. By 1940 she was out of the first twenty-five. *The Blue Bird* in 1940 failed to make a profit, and in the same year *Young People* brought Shirley's release from the remainder of her Fox contract. At fourteen, with between two and three million dollars in the bank, she retired to Westlake School for Girls, to sit out the awkward age.

The public which had worshipped at her feet now pounded on the studio door. Shirley had started a new children's crusade. Tactless mothers had long sought to curry favor with the Temples by pointing out that their little Johnny or Mary could perform Shirley's routines more competently than Shirley. In 1922, Jackie Coogan's mother had described the parents' solemn obligation to the talented child. "It is the duty of all parents to see that the little ones are given a fair start. . . . If the child wants to act he should be permitted to act.

. . . There is always room, and lots of room for talent, once it is brought to light."[28] When, in the early thirties, Hollywood actually sent out a call for children, many mothers took Mrs. Coogan's admonition to heart. Every studio was plagued by the soft pounding of childish fists, and by the endless parade of tiny applicants who had chosen their life's work at the age of three.

Shirley's retirement gave new heart to the movie mother. Darryl Zanuck had a teletype installed in his office to receive the deluge of messages from candidates for Shirley's job. Despite announcements that Jane Withers had already been picked as the new Crown Princess, thousands of dollars were expended on teaching the little folks everything from waltz clogs to bird imitations. Harried studio cops worked overtime listening to impromptu auditions; beating back bands of performers with zithers and combs; battling the column of gifted and adorable children, and children described by *Collier's* as "neither gifted nor adorable but only a trifle damp about the nose." When central casting got a call for a juvenile bit part they sent someone down to raid the queue for some anonymous Dolly Dimples or Bobby Bounce.

Time was marching on. In 1942 Shirley received her first screen kiss in *Miss Annie Rooney* from fellow child star Dickie Moore. Pictures of the event were suppressed by Mrs. Temple. Mrs. Temple was not one to give out such vital statistics lightly. Shirley's early records had been altered to make Shirley appear a year younger than she was. It was not till her "twelfth" birthday that "Presh" herself learned that she was really thirteen.[29]

With the first screen kiss Shirley entered the precarious domain of the junior miss. She emerged from retirement with a Selznick contract in 1944. The terms were generous. Mr. Selznick graciously permitted her to take two yearly vacations of three consecutive weeks, to go to college, to marry, and to have children.[30] College proved to be unnecessary. Shirley's I.Q., said to be just short of genius, never manifested itself in the field of academic achievement.

In the forties she passed several chronological landmarks that had devastating effects on the psyches of her fans. In

1945, at the age of seventeen, she married a serviceman named John Agar, son of a midwestern meat-packing executive. In 1946, she partook of her first screen drink in *The Bachelor and the Bobby Soxer*. Word of this leaked out to the W.C.T.U. Bowing to a storm of protest, Shirley reacted with a hideous grimace. In 1948, her daughter Linda Susan was born. In 1949, *Modern Screen* gave the fans the biggest shock of all. "No longer child or adolescent, Shirley the woman is publicly kissed by her husband."[31]

This chronology shows the extraordinary lag between reality and illusion. A girl who is old enough to choose a husband should also be old enough to decide whether or not she wants a preprandial cocktail. A kiss from Mr. Agar created as much of a stir in the fan magazines as the arrival of little Linda Susan. A visitor from Mars, dependent for biological information upon the literature of the West Coast, might well conclude that the two events were without causal connection.

In 1943, *Life* took a picture of Shirley in the company of Mary Pickford. The caption writer bracketed the two as "has beens."[32] Their careers make a fascinating parallel because both were doomed to inhabit the same sexless hinterland. Both had gotten a maximum of mileage out of haloes of bobbing curls. They had starred in many of the same vehicles: *The Little Princess, Little Annie Rooney, The Poor Little Rich Girl, Rebecca of Sunnybrook Farm*. Married and divorced at the height of her career, Miss Pickford had played in picture after picture as a child about to slip into adolescence. She had flopped in an "adult" role in 1924, after which she rarely stepped out of character again. The ages at which the Misses Temple and Pickford became too old for rompers give a sidelight on the flexibility of the term "youth" in Hollywood.

As a junior miss, Shirley never quite recaptured the audience whom she had beguiled with such merry tunes as "The Good Ship Lollipop" and "Polly Wolly Doodle." Interviewers postdated Shirley's witticisms to fit the nauseating idiom of the teen-ager. The *New York Times Magazine* described her as a "chic chick." Her views on a variety of subjects were relayed to her public.

Her ideal mate was described as an improbable combination

of Van Johnson and John Kieran. The dignified *Times* reported on her dating mores: "I'm supposed to be home by one, but Los Angeles is kind of spread out"; on her "searing passion" for Mayor La Guardia: "He kills me," she said fondly, "but definitely"; on her suitors: "They're not really men yet, but they're on their way"; on her own acting: "Gurgling just isn't the answer any more."[33]

As an authority on teen-age etiquette, Shirley lent her endorsement to such tips as "Learn to attract attention without startling people." "Be careful what you write—then you'll never rue what you've written." "Even in your own bedroom, do not go around partially clothed."[34] Goldilocks had grown up and the public was left with a vague malaise about where that left them. She had been far better off in the days when gurgling *had* been the answer.

Shirley's Selznick pictures presented an image which simply wasn't box office. Shirley was played up as the "average American girl" with her shirttail hanging out. In one picture Little Miss Fixit nearly broke a romance between Ginger Rogers and Joseph Cotten. In *Kiss and Tell*, she kissed two servicemen at a U.S.O. dance. This event was accepted as her first official screen kiss, by a public which, by some Freudian defense mechanism, blotted out the abortive peck from Dickie Moore. On her twenty-first birthday, in 1949, *Modern Screen* released a still of her *real* first screen kiss with an air of now-it-can-be-told, that might have attended the postwar revelation of cloak-and-dagger operations of the O.S.S.

Shirley always retained the loyalty of one devoted group of fans—the servicemen. In her mail from the front there were communications, some eerie, some touching, that showed the impact of events upon her sunny little world. One veteran who had lost a leg in the war wrote Shirley to ask if his sweetheart would care. Another mailed her a picture of herself that he had found pinned up beneath that of Adolf Hitler. Still a third sent her one of her baby pictures he had taken off the corpse of a Japanese sniper whom he had killed. Appended was a note: "Sorry to treat a fan of yours so badly, Shirley."[35]

Shirley's courtship and marriage followed a pattern all too frequent during the war years. With the wisdom of the hindsight she had gained at thirty, she made the following rueful comment about her marriage to Agar. "At that young age a girl does not have enough judgment to trust herself when she is swept off her feet by a comparative stranger. My own early marriage was based partly on the competitive spirit among the seniors in the girls' school I went to: Who would be the first to get a ring, be engaged, get married, have a baby? I wanted to win the race. That is a dangerous basis for marriage."[36]

Yet on Shirley's twenty-first birthday, the adoring fans had taken quite a different view. In an article entitled "Three Loves That Thrilled the World," Hedda Hopper adds an eloquent footnote to the meeting of Shirley and Jack.

> What Shirley wanted wasn't a foreign title or a glamour playboy or a millionaire social snob. . . . The fact that she was Shirley Temple, the world's most treasured Valentine in person, didn't warp her direct mind or honest heart. Jack Agar was the first and only true love of her life.
>
> He was a buck private when Shirley first looked up into his blue eyes. . . . He hadn't a famous name or too much money . . . but he did have the same solid American background that Shirley had, the same sincerity and sweetness (yep, men have it too). . . . He was 22. Shirley was 15. But Juliet was less than that when she died for Romeo's love . . .
>
> Too young? She was grown up—birthdays not counting—after they'd looked in each other's eyes.[37]

(Lesser loves that thrilled the world, listed by Miss Hopper, included those of Héloïse and Abélard, Beatrice and Dante, Edward and Mrs. Simpson.)

The Agars were married in the Wilshire Methodist Church —after what Miss Hopper described as a "typical, tender boy-girl romance" punctuated by "too too short leaves" and "sweet sorrow partings." The typical tender romance was sanctified before five hundred old friends, and a crowd of five thousand outside the church, to the tune of Irving Berlin's "Always." Typical family friends included Earl Warren, David O. Selz-

nick, and Darryl Zanuck. The typical wedding was said to
have been the biggest affair of its kind since the Vilma Banky-
Rod La Roque nuptials of 1927.[38]

Among Mr. Agar's virtues listed by Hedda Hopper were his
disarming shyness, modesty, and reserve. In a later edition
of *Modern Screen,* Shirley revised her opinion about the *je ne
sais quoi* which had brought them together. She wrote that
she had been drawn to his sophistication, which she had attempted to match by appearing in an Adrian suit.[39] Whatever
his lure, marriage gave Mr. Agar a foot in the studio door.
The couple co-starred in *Fort Apache.* Agar too had a Selznick
contract, for talent will out, though he, like so many others,
"hadn't planned on an acting career."[40]

The home life of the Agars was the subject of much rhapsodic comment in the fan magazines. The vision of little
Linda Susan "cradled in her pink bassinette" inspired Miss
Hopper to transports about the "kind of love that makes the
world go round."[41] *Photoplay* caught the Agars in one of
those contrived domestic crises so dear to the heart of the
sweetness-and-light girls—should Shirley tell John that she
had had her hair cut? This burning problem was resolved by
little Linda Susan, who let the cat out of the bag by snatch-
ing a scarf off Shirley's head. "But John was grinning! 'You
can't get away with anything now there's another girl around
can you?' he asked. Shirley shook her head. 'Or tell about
husbands either!' "[42]

The lapse between the final copy deadline and the time
a fan magazine hits the newsstands often finds the stars whose
home life is being extolled married off to somebody else. In
February 1949 *Motion Picture* was dedicating an issue "To
Our Valentine." As late as June 1949 the young Agars were
still photographed enjoying the simple delights of domesticity.
But there was ample evidence that the Agar household was
being rocked by problems more serious than the length of
Shirley's hair. "Don't let lies hurt you," cautioned *Modern
Screen* in 1949. Only a month later the "lies" were confirmed
by the hard-eyed reporters of the Luce publications. *Life*
reported that Shirley was seeking a California divorce on the
grounds of mental cruelty.

The doings of the stars force the unfortunate columnists to

perform mental gymnastics like those of apologists for the party line. Once the Agars' split-up was recognized as a *fait accompli*, the fan magazines rushed to press with the post mortems. *Motion Picture* brought out an article entitled "We Tried to Make Our Marriage Work." In January 1950, *Modern Screen* described the "secret tensions which brought the world's most cherished romance to a tragic end." Columnist Jack Wade cited the immaturity of the couple. "At 17, Shirley was too young to get married, and at 24 Jack was too young to marry an American institution."[43] This leaves the reader speculating as to the whereabouts of the poised confident Shirley "adult beyond her years" described by the same magazine nine months before. *Look* magazine made Agar and his mother the villains of the piece. Elsa Maxwell in *Photoplay* conceded more ground to the gossipmongers than Mr. Wade. Where Mr. Wade pooh-poohed the possibility of in-law trouble, Miss Maxwell quoted a girl who worked closely with Shirley as saying, "She'll marry early, you'll see—to get away from her mother." Others pointed belatedly to a certain infantilism in the Agars' choice of Shirley's former playhouse as a setting for their lares and penates.

Whatever the causes, the fans took the news hard. "When Shirley announced she was divorcing John Agar," Elsa Maxwell said, "she ended more than a marriage. She also ended an American dream."[44]

Whatever the vicissitudes of Shirley's private life, her screen kisses still made history. In February 1950 *Screen Stars* devoted a double page spread to the preparations for Shirley's second screen kiss. It was to take place in *A Kiss for Corliss* (Dickie Moore was still not included in the official total). Untouched by four years of marriage, motherhood, and divorce, the spotless lamb was gently prepared for the sacrifice, or what *Screen Stars* referred to as "the second great osculatory event in her life."

Shirley's second marriage, to California television official Charles Black, proved more durable, though it received considerably less publicity. Mr. Black did not conjure up images of Romeo or Abélard. For a time Shirley retired temporarily from pictures to live the life of a prosperous housewife in

Atherton, California. She raised Linda Susan, Charles junior, and Lori (the latter two, her children by Black) with little more than the aid of a cleaning woman and occasional baby sitters. Her statements to the press at this time indicated that she had learned a good bit in ten years. For a time her on-screen kisses and off-screen marital problems lost the power to change the destinies of American girlhood.

Yet at twenty-nine the old trouper once more sniffed the heady smell of grease paint. She was signed as hostess on NBC's successful *Shirley Temple's Storybook*, which revived such old nursery favorites as *Beauty and the Beast, Rumpelstiltskin, Dick Whittington,* and *The Legend of Sleepy Hollow*. Shirley's working days were restricted to three a month. Her part in the program was restricted to a few introductory remarks and to singing the program's theme song, *Dreams Are Made for Children*. The proceeds were sufficient to keep her in baby sitters for some time to come.

In *The Legend of Sleepy Hollow*, Shirley took the role of Katrina van Tassel, with unhappy results. The script was riddled with the quaint inversions of subject and verb, the questioning "ain't" which represented a misguided effort to reproduce Teutonic speech patterns. Mrs. Black did her part in compounding the felony, having gone to some pains to change such a straightforward line as "Don't stand up for me" to "Don't for me upstanding be." Shirley was scheduled to play Minnehaha in *Hiawatha*. Of her performance as Katrina, one cynical veteran of the entertainment world remarked laconically, "She'll be better as an Indian."

As John Crosby once pointed out, acting is the least important part of appearing on T.V. Shirley was inspired to revive three defunct businesses—Shirley Temple dresses, Shirley Temple coloring books, and a plastic-and-nylon reincarnation of the old Shirley Temple doll, 130,000 of which were sold with the first pressing. Shirley also planned a Shirley Temple story book and Shirley Temple activity sets for youthful knitters. Once again she walked in the footsteps of her illustrious prototype Miss Pickford—whose bobbing curls concealed a mind that worked like a cash register.

The company that controlled Shirley's old pictures showed

four of them on TV. The ratings were so high that they were put into circulation at local movie houses. She also appeared as a guest artist on the Dinah Shore show, where she portrayed a doll come to life in a childish dreamland. Such artistic triumphs fostered the illusion that America's best-loved little girl was immune to the ravages of time.

When Shirley was twenty-one, just before she went through the divorce mill, *Modern Screen* had assured its readers that their innocent darling was quite changed. "Curly Top" was described as "cute, round, sunny, sweet, merry and bright. Her face retains the agate brown eyes, the naturally delicate eyebrows, the pen point dimples beside her mouth. Only lipstick and powder feature her makeup, and she uses clear nail polish. . . . Smiles, chuckles and merry mannerisms punctuate her personality. She carries herself ramrod straight, walks briskly, talks breezily."

Shirley had gone chuckling back to the Fox lot, where her return was good for an afternoon of the dampest nostalgia. She wandered "in a memory mist to all the old familiar corners. . . . After a rendition of the 'Good Ship Lollipop,' an early Temple hit, she wound up all dewy-eyed and drippy."[45]

Nine years later, the first facial wrinkles had yet to appear. Shirley was to write in *T.V. Guide* in May 1958, "I guess I'll always be Shirley Temple to them—the little girl with the blonde curls and the lisp singing 'Polly Wolly Doodle' and 'The Good Ship Lollipop.' I guess I'll just have to accept it."

It was an image that had little to do with reality. It was as if the public and Mrs. Temple had ganged up on Shirley to keep her a baby forever. The sort of liberties which Mrs. Temple took with her daughter's age were standard practice among movie mothers. Margaret O'Brien's mother once professed her interest in keeping "the child a baby as long as possible." Elizabeth Taylor's mother said she was in no hurry to let Elizabeth quit her adolescent "dream world." Even after her twenty-first birthday Shirley, decked out in pink lipstick and Shy nail polish, was still being photographed amid her dolls. Instead of looking over the head of the child star to the adult he will become, the fans prefer to wax dewy-eyed over the early mewlings of the infant.

When Shirley reached adolescence, romantic love reared its

head. Romantic love is an emotion only remotely connected with sex—or, for that matter, life. It is connected rather with moonlight and popular tunes, maternal tears and sweet little weddings. It is immediately recognizable to people who have known each other for five minutes. Dear little babies often result from it, through some process never fully defined by its disciples.

Romantic love must always be impervious to financial considerations. Hedda Hopper ridiculed the idea that Shirley would reciprocate the slimy advances of a "foreign title," a "glamour playboy," or a "millionaire social snob." Nothing but a "typical tender boy-girl romance would do for the world's most treasured Valentine." It is questionable how typical you can get on a two- to three-million-dollar trust fund, or how impressive Shirley's financial sacrifice was in view of her capital assets. The statement reflects a popular belief that a girl is mercenary if she devotes any consideration *before* marriage to what she will live on. Far better for her to recognize the importance of finances after marriage, when the realization may possibly land her in Reno. It is part of the philosophy which subordinates young people's attitude toward sex, children, a career, and the monthly grocery bill to the burning look that allies them with all the great lovers of history.

Romantic love is an emotion appropriate to the goody-goody child grown up. There is no counterpart in everyday life for the screen adolescent's hygienic first loves and earth-shaking osculatory events. Louella Parsons was horrified at Shirley's desire to play the girl who got in trouble in *An American Tragedy*. The world's most treasured Valentine's handling of such a role is horrible to contemplate from an artistic standpoint alone. For the millions who accepted Shirley as a substitute daughter, it might have brought the facts of life too close to home for comfort.

Nevertheless the children of dear-little-girl-and-boy-land are exposed at an early age to situations which make extraordinarily trying demands on them. With one hand the screen parent pushes the child into the intrigues of one of the world's most cutthroat industries. The other hand exercises a soft, inexorable pressure pulling him back toward the womb.

As a child star, Shirley chose her forebears wisely. The

Temples were many cuts above more predatory screen parents. Shirley was not an oppressed screen child. She looks back on her childhood as a ball. She would be happy to repeat it if she had the chance. The Temples banked her money; shielded her from the adulation of a world where she commanded as much attention as the Big Four; and spared her the fate of Jackie Coogan, who ended up balding and broke in his thirties, burlesquing his great role in *The Kid*.

The disquieting thing about Shirley's little wonderland is its reflection of American upbringing. A child born in 1930 faced a world that was barely recognizable to a child born in 1900. Nobody would realize it from a look at the triumphs of Mary Pickford and Shirley Temple. For two generations harried mothers turned from the disquieting image of their own offspring to find solace in Goldilock's pretty *moues*.

Shirley was able to pocket her winnings and live with the image of Goldilocks. Another ex-child star, Deanna Durbin, could not. As a young singer Deanna had suffered as the innocent, sweet-throated thrush. She complained to an interviewer from the *New York Herald Tribune* that she was forced into a personality that had nothing to do with herself, the personality of the "ideal teen-ager."

> My fans sat in the dark, anonymous and obscure, while I was projected bigger than life on the screen. Fans took home an image of me, and studio press agents filled in the personal details. They invented most of them, and before I could resist, this world-wide picture of me came back stronger than my real person and very often conflicted with it.

Deanna did not believe that her contemporaries ever bought the idealized image.

> My fans were the parents, many of whom could not cope with their own youngsters. They sort of adopted me as their "perfect" daughter. . . . They could, with their tickets, purchase twice a year new stocks of sweetness and innocence. . . . The

> mere fact that today . . . they still apparently are wondering about "their" sweet synthetic star only shows what an escape from reality I represented for them.

She was convinced that she was redeemed by her failure in the years when the war shattered briefly the world of make-believe and platitude.[46]

Shirley, riding high on the fairy tale revival, had no such heretical thoughts. She was merrily writing articles on how television changed her life. A cynic might reflect that *"plus ça change, plus c'est la même chose."*

For Shirley the wonderland had not changed much since 1941. Shirley, then slipping into dangerous adolescence, had spoken for thousands of palpitating fans, looking forward uneasily to the malaise of menopause. "I wish things didn't have to change. I like the way they are now."[47]

III THE TAMING OF THE AVANT GARDE

"My mother died on me when I was nine years old.
What does she expect me to do? Do it all by myself?"
James Dean, quoted in *Look,* October 16, 1956

"James Dean is going to die soon." Vampira, quoted
in *Whisper,* February, 1956

11

Round and Round the Guilt-Berry Bush

JAMES DEAN

Jimmy was a combination of many things, a sky-
rocket, an idealist, a cynic and a dreamer, a thun-
derbolt, an uninhibited extrovert and a little lost
boy. Through the almost unbearable beauty of his
acting, he reached out to us all, and I don't believe that anyone who ever saw James Dean act
could remain unmoved by him.[1]

Dear Jimmy
    We love you.
    We love your expressive lips kissing like no one
else's, or half open searching for air as if the world
smothered you; or twisted bitterly, or in the heart-

breaking smile that should have come more often. . . .

We love—oh Jimmy, most of all, we love your
meteor spirit, lighting a dark sky too briefly. That
spirit, courageous, rebellious, proud, and yet lost
and gentle and lovable; the essence of tormented
youth—of a generation to which we too belong
and which we can therefore understand.

Jimmy, there is only one more thing. We want to
tell you, and it is—that something that is loved
can never die.[2]

These were typical of the tributes which poured in when
the twenty-four-year-old movie star James Dean died in a
wrecked racing car near Paso Robles, California. Humphrey
Bogart, whose years in Hollywood had made him somewhat
cynical, remarked, "If he'd lived he'd never have been able
to live up to his publicity."[3]

As a figure in a school picture, there was little about James
Byron Dean which suggested the future object of a death
cult. In the welter of childhood photographs which appeared
after his death he had the touching, naïve quality of the class
big shot in a small town.

Dean was born in a Midwest town on February 8, 1931. He
was the son of Mildred Wilson Dean and Winton Dean, a
dental technician. The family moved to Los Angeles when
the father was transferred to a veterans' hospital there. When
Dean was nine his mother died of cancer. His father remarried, and the boy was sent to live with his aunt and uncle,
Ortense and Marcus Winslow, in Fairmount, Indiana. In high
school he was popular and went in heavily for extracurricular
activities: acting, debating, and athletics. After high school
he went West to join his father, who was still with the Veterans' Administration. Dean began college in Santa Monica,
and later transferred to U.C.L.A. Here he began to emerge
as an *enfant terrible,* when he was thrown out of a fraternity
for "busting a couple of guys in the nose."[4]

He had started out as a pre-law major but soon discovered
that acting was his real forte. He joined the night class of

actor James Whitmore. Whitmore gave him the excellent advice to save his pennies and go East. Dean accordingly left U.C.L.A. and headed for New York. He was, by this time, a dedicated man. "Acting," he said, "is the greatest. Man, every town has got its successful lawyers, but how many successful actors has it got? The first time I found out acting was as big a challenge as the law, I flipped. I was a gone cat."[5]

The life of an impoverished young actor in New York was a tough one—of "making the rounds," working as a busboy, getting odd jobs in TV. William Bast, who describes himself as the "man who knew him best," writes of sharing Dean's ramshackle living arrangements at this time. He recalls sleeping on sheetless beds, eating vermicelli with bugs in it, and relieving the torments of a stifling New York summer with mock bullfights reminiscent of the garret scenes in *La Bohème.*

Jimmy had succeeded in getting admitted to Actors Studio, the organization which had launched such other stars as Julie Harris, Marlon Brando, and Montgomery Clift. Under the tutelage of Lee Strasberg, Actors Studio paid homage to the Stanislavsky Method. It stressed deep concentration and "living the part." It was also associated with intense young men in blue jeans and leather jackets, who talked about "the raw stuff of experience," mouthed their lines with a curious mumbling delivery, and shuffled about the stage in a stance which led one wag to describe the Method as the school of the "tilted pelvis."

Dean had had a taste of the Method in James Whitmore's group on the Coast. He and Mr. Bast had had to be separated during the course of a scene which both were "living" so vividly that they threatened to do physical violence to each other. In New York Jimmy was appalled by the cutthroat criticism indulged in by fellow Method actors. After his first appearance he did not go back for a long time. "I don't know what happens when I act—inside," he said, "but if I let them dissect me like a rabbit in a clinical research laboratory or something, I might not be able to produce again."[6]

In addition to appearing in such TV dramas as *Stars Over Hollywood, the Kate Smith Show,* and *T-Men in Action,* Dean landed two Broadway roles. One was in a short-lived play

called *See the Jaguar*. The second was the part of a black-
mailing Arab boy in *The Immoralist*. His efforts on Broadway
won for him both the Donaldson and Perry awards, and
brought him to the attention of the director Elia Kazan.
Dean's agent, Jane Deacy, submitted the boy's name to Kazan
for a role in John Steinbeck's picture *East of Eden*. It was a
characterization tailor-made for Dean's personality—that of
Cal Trask, a youth "with a disturbed psyche, a boyish exuberance, a desperate need, an infinite longing for love and
acceptance."[7] He landed the part and became a star overnight. With stardom came the first explosions of the famed
Dean temperament. On the one hand his professed distaste
for publicity caused him to appear at press parties in blue
jeans, and on one occasion to tear a picture of himself off the
wall of the Warner Brothers' commissary. On the other hand
his behavior was calculated to invite the spectator's gaze. If he
was not getting sufficient attention in a restaurant, he would
beat a tom-tom solo on the table top, play with his spoon
against a water glass, pour sugar into his pocket, or set fire
to a paper napkin.

He had a fondness for such practical jokes as sticking carrot
strips in his ears and pouring water on waiters. The harried
patrons of the Warner Brothers Green Room were treated to
the sight of a young Dean eating his lunch with a cracker in
each eye, bending over a table with his collar over his head,
or turning up for lunch with no shirt at all.

Dean dressed sloppily and tended to be consistently late for
work. During the filming of *Giant,* he failed one day to appear.
Vast crews of technicians cooled their heels as the meter
ticked up to the tune of $32,000. George Stevens, director of
Giant, blew up at Dean. Even those who had been well disposed toward him, such as Elia Kazan, were tried by the behavior of the *Wunderkind.*

William Bast recalls his demeanor during his first meeting
with his West Coast agent, Dick Clayton. "He squirmed in
his seat and he scratched himself, he put his feet on the desk,
and he picked his teeth. But Clayton refused to give in to his
game."[8] It was a tribute to Mr. Clayton's equanimity that the
two later became warm friends.

Shortly after *East of Eden,* Dean met the young Italian star Pier Angeli, and experienced what was generally conceded to be the great love of his life. The girl's mother, however, did not approve of Dean as a suitor, and he was reputed to have waited outside the church while Pier Angeli solemnized her marriage to the singer Vic Damone. The depth of Dean's affection for Miss Angeli might be gauged from the fact that she succeeded in getting him into a shirt, a tie, and the habit of a fortnightly haircut.

Much of his unhappiness at the breakup of this romance was projected into his second starring picture, *Rebel Without a Cause.* He threw himself into this role "with an anguish that projected itself beyond the screen and became the aching hurt of every kid who had ever been hit on the nose."[9] His eccentricities were tolerated by hard-boiled members of an industry with a growing respect for a "hot property."

If he tried the patience of his co-workers, few denied the existence of his talent. *East of Eden* and *Rebel Without a Cause* were followed by *Giant.* Dean brought off a *tour de force* in the role of Jett Rink, a power-driven ranch hand who, by the end of the picture, is rich, broken and middle-aged. Dean learned to ride horseback, rope cattle, and play the guitar, though the script required none of these things, because they would increase his understanding of the part. Dean climaxed what was considered by many to be his greatest role, in a superbly acted drunk scene, with Rink passing out and coming hazily back to life to deliver a speech to an empty auditorium.

Around the time he was making *Rebel Without a Cause,* Dean bought a motorcycle. He was discouraged from using it because the studio considered it too dangerous. Shortly after this he bought a Porsche racing car. He took it to Palm Springs and entered it in the road races, winning first place in the amateur class and third place in the professional class. After he completed *Giant,* he made plans to enter his car in the road races at Salinas. He and Rolf Wuetherich, a German mechanic, set out for Salinas with Dean's friend Sanford Roth following in a trailer.

At 3:30 P.M. on September 30, 1955, Dean was flagged down

for doing sixty in a forty-five-mile zone. At 5:58 Dean was turning onto Highway 41, which runs through Salinas. He roared toward the intersection at an estimated speed of between seventy and eighty miles an hour. He did not see Donald Turnupseed—a twenty-four-year-old college student who was even then making a left-hand turn onto the highway. The ensuing crash fatally injured Jimmy. Wuetherich sued the Dean estate for damages, which included a broken jaw, a broken leg, and a broken hip. Turnupseed escaped with minor bruises.

The funeral took place at the Quaker Meeting House in Fairmount. The Reverend Xen Harvey delivered an oration, "The Life of James Dean—A Drama in Three Acts": "The career of James Dean has not ended. It has just begun. And remember, God himself is directing the production."[10]

Almost immediately the legend began to take shape. "When news of what had happened in the dusk near Paso Robles reached a numbed and unbelieving world," said a writer in *The James Dean Album*, "it was as if the curtain of night had fallen in a million aching hearts."[11]

Quickie magazines were rushed out following his death. Dean reconstructed the accident "in his own words" for millions of avid readers. In *Rave Magazine*, he described posthumously the sensation of driving to his rendezvous with death.

Elsewhere there were lengthy interviews with "those who loved him." Movie magazines were crammed with information about him, solicited from such intimates as James Whitmore, Perry Lopez, Dick Clayton, Nick Adams, Hedda Hopper, Nick Ray, and Leonard Rosenman.

Pier Angeli was tripped in the lobby of a New York hotel, by irate fans who resented her jilting their idol. She was featured prominently in the thumbnail sketches of the women in Dean's life. The gallery included "Pier Angeli . . . the only girl to whom Jimmy Dean gave his heart" (other authorities expanded this category to include his mother). . . . "Elizabeth Taylor . . . a deep, strong friendship." . . . "Natalie Wood. . . . It was just fun." . . . "Jane Withers . . .

never involved romantically. . . ." "Ursula Andress" (a glamorous Swedish actress with a penchant for existentialist philosophy), who "came closest to winning Jimmy's heart after Pier Angeli walked out of his life."[12] . . . "Lil Kardell . . . the secret love that haunts Jimmy Dean."

The James Dean Fact Sheet "lovingly assembled" data on his birth, death, hobbies, musical preferences, favorite writers, and pet hates. Fans learned of his ambition to play Hamlet, his fondness for bullfights, bongo drums, photography; for Jean Genet, Curzio Malaparte, Gerald Heard; for Bach, Schönberg, African chants, Frank Sinatra, and the aria "One Fine Day" from *Madame Butterfly*. They discovered that he was studying German, and one periodical mentioned the fact that he spoke English.

Three books about Dean were in preparation—one by William Bast, one by Dean's father, one by Nick Ray, the director of *Rebel*. Busts of the dead star were available in three price brackets—$5.00, $30.00, and $150.00. At least six Dean records were on the market. A death mask of the star was displayed in Princeton University along with those of Garrick, Booth, Thackeray, Keats, and Beethoven. A long, wicked knife was sold under the name of the "James Dean Special."

A couple on the Coast reassembled the wreck of Dean's car and displayed it for an admission price of fifty cents. As many as five hundred fans made a pilgrimage to his grave in a single day. Some disciples claimed to have been unable to eat or sleep for a year after Dean died. One fan cried every night after his death and claimed that she went "to sleep on sixteen mags containing articles about him."[13]

His studio was deluged with an estimated eight thousand letters per month. The James Dean Memorial Foundation in Fairmount received up to a thousand letters a week. Most of the letters asked for souvenirs and pictures . . . for such Deaniana as the red zippered jacket he wore in *Rebel Without a Cause*, for a lock of hair, a piece of the Porsche, a bit of sod or a blade of grass from his grave.

Though he died in 1955, Warner Brothers was still receiving birthday cards for him in 1957. Typical was the one inscribed

"I really love you. Now that I told you how I feel about you I remain deeply greeved. Until we meet, if ever. With much love."[14]

Schoolteachers assigned to their classes the task of gathering data on Dean as if he had been Zoroaster or Abraham Lincoln. "I would appreciate it greatly if you would send me some pictures of Jimmy Dean," wrote a realistic girl of Queens Village, N.Y. "Pictures are very necessary in our reports to receive a satisfactory mark."[15]

Letters poured in to George Stevens, director of *Giant*, warning him not to cut a single shot of Dean from the film. Nick Adams, who appeared with Dean in *Rebel Without a Cause*, was asked to write the President of the United States suggesting that we set aside a Jimmy Dean Day. There were letters lamenting the fact that Dean had not received an Academy Award:

> I only hope that this year Jimmie will be honored . . . You can't realize how much it hurt me last year when Jimmy didn't receive the Award. I can never forget the people responsible, but I sincerely hope this year they will redeem theirself.[16]

Dean's appeal was by no means confined to his own country-men, as the following communication clearly shows:

> Last year I saw the film *Jenseits von Eden*. This one motivated me to write you a letter. I was so inspired of the headliner James Dean that I saw the film two times. Also his partner pleased me very good. Please do not think that I have a craze. Now . . . I only will demonstrate you that I James Dean real adore.[17]

Some of Dean's fans had a curiously morbid turn of mind. Body and serial number plates and pieces of glass from the death car were stolen shortly after the crash. Sanford Roth, the photographer in the trailer behind Dean, was offered large sums for the two shots he got of the actor's body, but he refused to release them. Among the rumors which sprang up after Dean's death was one that Jimmy was not really dead at all but was living out his life, hideously disfigured, in a sanitarium. Many fans continued to address letters to him in the second person, and their communications were studded with references to "resurrection," "reincarnation," and "immortality." Hollywood spiritualists did a land-office business with the myriads of fans who continued to worship his astral body.

It was a curious coincidence that Dean himself had been much preoccupied with the occult. As a boy in Fairmount he wrote a high school composition posing the question: "Why are we compelled to live in one world, to wonder about the other world?" In Los Angeles there were kindred souls, pondering similar questions. Before his death, Dean became interested in such West Coast exponents of Oriental philosophy as Christopher Isherwood, and (in the words of *Photoplay*) "the Hindu philosophy of immortality and the search for an absolute."[18]

His interest in the subject of death was outstanding even in a city known for its preoccupation with the afterworld. A noose hung in Dean's living room, and a favorite Dean prank was to stick his head into it. He was given to morbid reflections such as those recalled by his Boswell, Mr. Bast:

> Death. It's the only thing left to respect. It's the one inevitable, undeniable truth. . . . In it lies the only nobility for man, and beyond it, the only hope.[19]

Photographer Frank Worth wrote in *Photoplay* of dropping in on Dean one evening and hearing some of the star's tape recordings. "They gave me the creeps. They were all about death and dying—poems and things he just made up—about what it might be like to die and how it would feel to be in a grave and all that. . . . I just got out of there, fast." The tapes were wiped clean after the boy's death.[20]

It was inevitable that some question should arise as to whether Dean had a secret wish to die. It was pointed out that he had taken out a $100,000 accident policy shortly before the fatal day. When he was killed, however, he had not gotten around to naming a beneficiary, and the money went to his father as the next of kin. A remark that he had made shortly before his death was widely quoted: "My fun days are over."

A rash of magazine articles appeared with such titles as "The End or The Beginning" . . . "The Truth Behind the Rumors that Jimmy Dean Committed Suicide."

Magazines about Dean with a supernatural slant became overnight best sellers. Typical was a publication called "Jimmy Dean Returns." This purported to be the story of Judy Collins, a girl whose picture, "withheld for reasons of privacy," was admittedly that of a professional model. In Judy's version, Dean was alleged to have had a prophetic vision of his own end, and had promised her "Sometime, somewhere, somehow, I'll come back to you."[21] He made good his promise by sending a message in automatic writing, telling Judy that she was his only love, apologizing for not calling her when he left New York for Hollywood, reliving the accident, and describing the departure of his spirit from his mortal remains.

Dean was also said to be in communication with Maila Nurmi, a self-styled dabbler in the occult arts who gave spooky characterizations over television under the name of Vampira. She and Dean and other Hollywood eccentrics had forgathered at Googie's restaurant for what came to be known as the Night Watch. Among these odd ones, according to William Bast, Dean dabbled in Lotterism, a philosophy of cultivated eccentricity reminiscent of the Dadaists of the twenties. After his death, Vampira, companion of these nocturnal vigils, claimed to have heard from the deceased "through the veil."[22]

A scandal magazine, provocatively entitled *Whisper*, accused Vampira of having engineered Dean's death by black magic. In an article called "James Dean's Black Madonna," *Whisper's* leg man described this feat as "a story so chilling, so gruesome and macabre," that "more than once in the course of tracking it down" he was "tempted to drop it cold and run."[23]

The leg man claimed to have discovered Vampira in a milieu reminiscent of "some witch doctor's shack in Haiti." She had rigged up an altar with a picture of Dean, a picture of herself, and a sign saying "Ye must be born again." She had announced to a group of friends that she was using the altar for black magic against Dean.

"But why?" a friend asked.

"Because I am a witch."

On the day of Dean's death she was said to have sent him a picture of herself standing in front of an open grave. "Darling," the inscription said, "come join me."

The photograph of Dean had been pierced by a small golden dagger. At the hour of Dean's death, the dagger suddenly fell to the floor. "A coincidence," editorialized *Whisper*, "that seems like something out of a weird tale of the supernatural."[24]

Vampira was not alone with her voodoo dolls and her black-cat-in-the-graveyard approach to the dead star. Nick Adams was approached by one of Dean's lady fans for some of Dean's scarves, shirts, belts, and tape recordings. When Adams refused to hand them over, she embellished his house with signs—a burning wax triangle and a wax doll with its head burned off. Because of the unsettled character of some of Dean's admirers, Adams took to sleeping with a loaded gun, and police checked his house eight to ten times a day.

If fans seemed drawn to Dean because of his urge to self-destruction, they were equally intrigued by other neurotic elements in his personality. In two of his pictures, *East of Eden* and *Rebel Without a Cause*, Dean seemed to be acting out many of his own inner conflicts. Indeed, he consciously approached the art of acting as a patient might approach the psychoanalyst's couch:

Acting is to me the most logical way for a person's neuroses to manifest themselves [he once

said]. Actors act so that they may express the fantasies in which they have involved themselves. The
problem for this cat is not to get lost.[25]

His first picture, *East of Eden,* was based on a Steinbeck
novel, which was, in turn, based on the story of Cain and Abel.
It was about two brothers—one good, one bad—a mother
who deserted her family, and a father who gave out his love
like a school principal on Prize Day. As the "bad" brother,
Dean gave a compelling performance of a boy convinced of
his own evil—an outcast trying in vain to win his father's affection.

> Everything about Dean [said William K. Zinsser
> in his review of the film for the *New York Herald
> Tribune*] suggests the lonely, misunderstood nine-
> teen-year-old. When he talks, he stammers and
> pauses, uncertain of what he is trying to say. When
> he listens, he is full of restless energy—he stretches,
> he rolls on the ground, he chins himself on the
> porch railing, like a small boy impatient of his
> elders' chatter.[26]

Mr. Bast describes his reaction to Jimmy's performance:

> I watched him, driven by the overwhelming need
> to gain the love of his father and those around him,
> striving desperately to disprove his inbred belief
> that he was bad because of his mother. There was
> so much of Jimmy in that film, so much of the
> young man I had known for so long and had grown
> to love as a friend, so much of the lost, tormented,
> searching, gentle, enthusiastic little boy; so much of
> the bitter, self-abusive, testing vengeful monster.—
> And it had all been rolled up into one brief hour
> and a half and thrown at us with the impact of
> Cinemascope and stereophonic sound. And when
> my ears were filled with the thunder of applause
> from the audience, I . . . bent forward in my seat

and bawled, like a Jew of old seeing the Promised
Land for the first time.[27]

In *Rebel Without a Cause*, Dean once more played a troubled youth. This picture, like *The Blackboard Jungle*, attempts
to present American youth in its true colors instead of in the
usual candy-box pink and blue.

Once more Dean was struggling to communicate with an
unfeeling father. The hero of the movie arrives in a new
school, and, on his first day, undergoes a series of vicissitudes
that make the carryings-on of F. Scott Fitzgerald's scarlet
juveniles look like something out of Elsie Dinsmore.

First, the hero, played by Dean, is run into jail for being
drunk and disorderly. There he meets two other misunder-
stood teen-agers, played by Sal Mineo and Natalie Wood. He
and Natalie Wood have an immediate rapport as she is having
trouble communicating with *her* father. Sal Mineo warns
Dean against Natalie's boy friend Buzz. The children are
released from jail. The class makes a trip to the Los Angeles
Planetarium, and Buzz lives up to his unsavory reputation by
slashing the tires of Dean's car with his switch-blade knife.
In front of the Planetarium a fight takes place between Buzz
and Jimmy. It is broken up and the boys decide to resolve
their differences by holding a "chickie run." This zipped-up
version of the Heidelberg duel involves driving their cars in
the direction of a cliff. The first person to jump out of his
car is stigmatized by his fellows as "chicken."

Dean goes home and reveals the plans for the "chickie run"
to his Milquetoast father, who does nothing to put a stop to
them. Natalie Wood's father has much the same reaction, and
the "chickie run" goes off on schedule with Natalie as time-
keeper. Jimmy manages to leap clear of his car, while his rival
plunges over the cliff, having presumably established his man-
hood. Jimmy describes this latest development to his parents.
Their reaction is a somewhat understandable wish to leave
town.

Jimmy accuses them of having caused his badness and goes
off to meet Natalie in an alley. Sal Mineo, who idolizes Jimmy,
is beaten up by some of Buzz's henchmen. Grabbing his gun,

he risks his life to warn his idol that he is next on the gang's list. The gang catches up with Jimmy, Sal shoots and finally runs off to the Planetarium, where he remains at bay with police and parents closing in on him. Under the glare of the searchlights, he panics, and is killed by a policeman's bullet. The authors of *The James Dean Album*, in a synopsis of the film's plot, describe what they evidently consider to be a happy ending. "Almost too late, the parents come to understand their children."[28]

It was a melancholy commentary on an era that many young people saw their troubles reflected in this chilling document. Dean once more turned in a highly creditable acting job. One felt almost churlishly Victorian for thinking that with two of the young people dead, to say that the parents came to their senses "almost" too late was to subscribe to an extraordinarily liberal concept of child rearing.

In any case, Dean's performance inspired a wave of pilgrimages to the Los Angeles Planetarium. Letters poured into the studio from teen-agers to the effect that "you are one of us. When I watched you in *East of Eden* and *Rebel Without a Cause*, I was seeing myself."

One of the keystones of Dean's success was this ability to inspire audience identification in the young. Over and over his fans wrote in how their idol understood their strivings, their rebellion. They too had evidently experienced the conflict between the "testing monster" described by Mr. Bast and the "lost little boy," who appealed to women with a fondness for taking in stray dogs and cats.

When the testing monster had the upper hand, Dean was a disturbing figure. Lee Strasberg said of his disciple:

> His behavior and personality seemed to be part
> of a pattern which inevitably had to lead to some-
> thing destructive. I always had the strange feeling
> there was in Jimmy a sort of doomed quality.[29]

This appraisal had a special authority, coming from a man whose work gave him more than a nodding acquaintance with contemporary neurosis.

Dean subscribed wholeheartedly to the practice of spicing up his acting with the juices of human experience.

> His heart and soul and mind [said Mr. Bast] had been opened to run the full course, to digest, without regard to the personal discomfort, . . . whatever scrapings he could salvage from the bottom of this human garbage pail,—our modern world.[30]

Dean's love of the scrapings led him to paint pictures full of such gamy symbols of neurosis as a man struggling to keep himself from melting into a mire of sewage. It led him to abandon any shred of self-discipline that might have made life easier for those around him, whose interest in the garbage pail was less passionate. It led him to take up with such strange companions of the Night Watch as the girl who, when introduced to strangers, responded by absently licking a string of beads which she had dipped in a strawberry malted milk.

Bast recalls that such eccentrics helped him to "situate that portion of him he knew to be totally unconventional,"[31] to play the paranoiac, the sadist, the murderer, and the thief.

> He had made out of his minutest drives and compulsions, vivid and real personality attributes, experimenting with himself, as though he were nothing more than a laboratory guinea pig. He had done this in order to increase his capacity to understand and interpret human behavior.[32]

Having done so, he was sometimes hard put to it to exorcise the demons he had raised in the name of art.

If many of his fans were unhealthily attracted to the testing monster, more of them were in love with the lost little boy. Their letters stressed his shyness, his sweetness, his insecurity, his search for the eternal verities, and above all his search for love.

Elizabeth Taylor, troubled by his lack of a love object, supplied him with one in the form of a Siamese cat named Marcus. The star rushed home from the studio to feed Marcus, and otherwise turned over his life to him; and thus, wrote Mr. Bast, "a few cockeyed ounces of beige fur began the amazing process of taming the erratic Dean."[33]

To anyone familiar with the irrational behavior of Siamese cat owners, Dean's sacrifices on the cat's behalf have a quality of *déjà vu*. In any case, Dean got rid of Marcus, some time before his death, doing his psychiatric interpreters out of their drama of love and its search for an outlet.

If Marcus was grist for the mills of amateur psychoanalysts there was an even richer gold mine in the boy's relationship to his parents.

Dean paid a few disastrous visits to the doctor who psycho-analyzed Marlon Brando. He thereby played into the hands of detractors who saw him as a mere carbon copy of Brando. Dean was not pleased by the compliment. "I have my own personal rebellion," he said, "and don't have to rely on Brando's."[34]

Dean's analysis was not successful. It was generally conceded that many of his troubles began when his mother died and his father moved to Los Angeles. Dean was most attached to his mother. She had bestowed on him the romantic middle name Byron, had subjected him to dancing and violin lessons, and had impressed upon him the importance of success. His father admitted in print that he had never felt close to the boy, having been away from him during most of his formative years. Around this family situation the psychoanalyst built a drama of acceptance and rejection. The only problem appeared to be who was accepting or rejecting whom.

William Bast gave one interpretation of the familiar Freudian triangle:

> He [Dean] knew that he must try to alleviate
> the resentment within him by accepting his father,
> by including him more and more in his daily life,
> by giving to him the love he had so long withheld.
> . . . But even while he was trying to accept his
> father, the psychiatrist was pointing out the many
> reasons why he had not, and . . . should not ac-

cept his father. The confusion that resulted had
him fluctuating between complete rejection of his
father and complete acceptance.[35]

The mother in the gospel according to Bast was responsible
for Dean's terrifying perfectionism:

> The dead seriousness of Jimmy's approach to
> competition made the simplest games too unpleas-
> ant and the important games too frightening.[36]
>
> Constantly dogged by an undefined, obscure ob-
> ligation to his departed mother, he chased his own
> tail through life in a futile attempt to find relief
> from the pressure of that unfulfillable obligation.
> Arriving at the topmost point of attainment in each
> field of endeavor, he would abandon that field and
> turn his efforts in another direction—and on and on
> he went 'round the guilt-berry bush destined never
> to stop until he was stopped.[37]

Dean himself substantiated this interpretation: "My mother
died on me when I was nine years old," he blurted out in the
midst of a temper tantrum. "What does she expect me to do?
Do it all myself?"[38]

Hollywood Love and Tragedy, a movie magazine, provided
a totally different motivation for his conflicts:

> Fiercely James Dean banged the door leading
> from his doctor's office and wandered slowly down
> the stairs and onto the street.
>
> Desperately he tried to reconcile his mind to the
> outcome of those past fifty minutes under analy-
> sis. . . .
>
> He was deeply confused.
>
> He had every right to be.
>
> For in that office, on that hot summer day, Jimmy
> was being led to believe that he felt a true love for
> his father Winton Dean, and that the motives for

his actions, his moods, and even his talent stemmed
from a subconscious desire to have his father's love
in return.

At this point, the testimony of an anonymous friend was
invoked, to the effect that Dean had really wished to achieve
greatness to please his aunt and uncle, Marcus and Ortense
Winslow.

Had Jim not received this [the Winslows'] love,
I would say it was probable that he would try to
seek his father's. Under those circumstances, however, I would say it was NOT.

This friend left in low spirits, having unsuccessfully tried
"to blow away the cobwebs of confusion" from Dean's mind.[39]

Others who inclined toward the mother theory were ever
anxious to provide Dean with a mother-substitute. *The James
Dean Album* suggested that Dean's relationship to his agent,
Jane Deacy, was like a relationship of mother and son. William
Bast spoke of a mother-image named Diane who, after a
brief romance had rejected him, "throwing him back to the
bloodhounds that tracked him through the labyrinth of his
subconscious mind."[40]

Dean's hold on the teen-agers was as fascinating to the
clinicians as the tangled relationships of his family life. A
New York psychologist, quoted in *Coronet* on the subject of
the Dean cult, described the adolescent hysteria as "a curious
case of juvenile frustration, sex-substitution and hero-worship
running like electrical lines into a centrally convenient fuse
box."[41]

Look Magazine prefaced an article on the Dean cult with
a brief Baedeker of the teen-age psyche:

The teen-ager who appears to conform, yet rebels
successfully against conformity and gets away with
it—that fellow is a hero. James Dean not only got
away with it, he got so rich in the process that he
was his own boss; nobody could tell him what to
do.[42]

Cary Grant, movie idol of a suaver era, lamented the fact that the teen-age taste in rebel heroes had made insufferable rudeness, blue jeans, and a week's growth of stubble mandatory equipment for courtship.

In defense of the Hollywood heel-hero, *Photoplay* magazine tried its hand at lay analysis. The staff writers buoyed themselves up on these unfamiliar waters with quotations from the psychoanalyst Robert Lindner, author of *The Fifty-Minute Hour, Must You Conform?* and *Rebel Without a Cause.*

The urge to rebel was a healthy one, *Photoplay* explained, as basic as the instinct to eat and sleep. "There are two ways in which this instinct, this need to rebel, is carried out by teen-agers today. One is to act out their hostilities by acts of violence and delinquency; the other is to merge, herdlike, with a group and be directed by a group mind."[43]

It was understandable, therefore, that troubled youth should sympathize with the plaints of the rebel heroes—with Marlon Brando in *The Wild One,* who, when asked what he was rebelling against, replied: "What have you got?"; with Sal Mineo, in *Crime in the Streets:* "Aw lemme alone can't you? Just lemme alone"; with James Dean's anguished efforts to communicate with his father in *East of Eden:* "Pa, why don't you love me?"[44]

Photoplay then went on to prove to its readers that the rebel heroes led off-screen lives straight out of the pages of *Sermons for Young People.* "While Presley, Mineo, Dean, and others are idolized for appearing to fight against society and against authority, in their private lives every one of them is a complete conformist. They are hard-working, church-going and home-loving, ambitious for fame and success . . . and their rude or shocking behavior is reserved strictly for the occasions when they are in front of a camera or a microphone."

Photoplay archly listed the "vices" of the rebel heroes. Marlon Brando was described as "devoted and big-brotherly to his lovely sister, Jocelyn." Sal Mineo was ticked off playfully for his fondness for second helpings of dessert and Seven-Up floats. Elvis Presley was said to turn the other cheek to critics with the words, "Oh, I don't mind. After all, they criticized Jesus Christ, too, didn't they?" To Jimmy Dean was attributed the following bit of 4-H Club philosophy: "When you fail, you try again, that's all. You never let them lick you —never."[45]

The authors seemed quite unaware that they had just cut the ground out from under Dr. Lindner. Their efforts made one wonder if psychoanalysis should not be hastily given back to the psychoanalysts. *Photoplay*, however, had succumbed to a trend too powerful for any man of science to buck—a trend which made movie magazines read like copies of a psychiatric review. One could no longer pick up an article entitled "James Dean's Hidden Heartache" in the expectation of reading some simple talk of star-crossed love. Instead, one became enmeshed in problems of "insecurity," "failure to communicate," "compensation," and "neurotic guilt." Besides being called upon to decide whether Elvis Presley was worthy to appear in James Dean's life story, fans were invited to unravel the riddle of the Dean personality. "Was he doomed?" "Did he have a self-destruction complex?" "Was he searching for love?" There was a wide cross-section of opinion from which to pick. Freud, Adler, Zilboorg, and Harry Stack Sullivan had been joined by a host of new authorities: *Photoplay, Hollywood Love and Tragedy, Modern Screen.*

Clinical diagnosis was the order of the day as Hollywood paid homage to Vienna and Zurich:

> The dark brooding and gnawing loneliness were
> not the real Jimmy Dean. They were the dragons
> in himself which he sought to slay. They arose out
> of the unhappiness of his childhood and reached
> like terrible claws into his adult life.[46]

One movie magazine hit on the salient fact about James Dean and the new mid-century look in idols:

> For the first time, America's youth has chosen
> the figure of a disturbed man to represent their
> sufferings and longings.[47]

Rudolph Valentino had been worshiped after his death; but in his lifetime he was not given to putting his head in nooses or trying coffins for size. His followers did not go in, as Dean's did, for voodoo trappings and demoniac bric-a-brac. "A Century of Progress" had supposedly left these things behind, though the Valentino ectoplasm still had the power to stir the sensitive feminine heart.

The hero worship of Lindbergh had been tinged with a national mood of self-confidence. His appeal was to the would-be conqueror in the cockpit, rather than to the sufferer on the couch.

The "torments," the "insecurities," the "searches" of Dean's fans—the commonplaces of the fifties—had been, only thirty years before, an exciting novelty. For the age just past had been content to lock its misfits in the garret. The Victorians had little patience with young men dogged by the Eumenides because of the loss of a parent or a childhood subjection to unwelcome lessons on the violin.

Yet Dean's fans were the spiritual heirs of the juveniles of *This Side of Paradise*. The social upheaval which produced the hip flask and Fitzgerald's "speedy" girls from Baltimore had had such latter-day by-products as knife fights and "chickie runs," Milquetoast fathers, and teen-age sex clubs.

Lew Bracker, one of Dean's closest friends, said of the Dean cult: "If Jimmy were here and saw what was going on, he'd die all over again without the accident . . . It's a creepy, almost a sick thing. It's something in Jimmy the teen-agers saw, maybe themselves. Everybody mirrored themselves in Jimmy's fame and Jimmy's death."[48]

Dean's face looked out above the purple captions of poorly proofread magazines: "Even in those days you could sense that he was troubled." . . . "And when resting, there was a part of him that never relaxed. He seemed to be listening to something none of us could hear." . . . "Sometimes he would stare into space, as if he knew his future. He looked like he was astonished by it, but never afraid."[49]

It was a face that had a special message for the lonely ones; for the squealing adolescent outside a movie theater; for the faithful in the medium's parlor; for the browser in those secondhand magazine stores which are the stamping grounds of the furtive smut seeker.

Despite the inanities of certain followers, despite his own idiosyncrasies, Dean was a figure to be conjured with. He commanded respect for his ability as an actor, for his grim perfectionism, for the authority he brought to the role of the "crazy, mixed-up kid."

> "I think there's only one true form of greatness for a man," he once said. "If a man can bridge the gap between life and death, I mean, if he can live on after he's died, then maybe he was a great man. . . . To me the only success, the only greatness . . . is in immortality.[50]

The immortality he desired so fervently came in a strange and roundabout way. It came through the mirror he held up to the face of a frightened people who were collectively undergoing a dark night of the soul.

12

The New Iconoclasts

WILLIAM F. BUCKLEY, JR.

"A brilliant boy named Buckley came to Yale in 1946," ran
the editorial in the *Yale Daily News*. "He came steeped in
stifling orthodoxy. He came bristling with dogmatic preconceptions. He came, a child of the Middle Ages into a hotbed
of twentieth century intellectual ferment. . . ."[1]

His more charitable class historian characterized him as the
Class Bright Young Man who "neatly undercut tolerance, tom-
foolery and everything to the left of Senator Taft . . . for better
or worse—and perhaps significantly—we had none to match
him."[2]

William F. Buckley, Jr. was one of the ten children of a
Texas-born oil magnate. The senior Buckley had strong opinions on the subject of education. He was an ardent foe of "the
blight of liberalism and communism." He established a school
in Connecticut dedicated to exorcising the spirit of John

Dewey. The six or so students schooled in the Buckley method were exposed to the same educational philosophy that the Buckley children had received. They learned that Cleveland and Theodore Roosevelt were among the last American Presidents of ability and patriotism; that certain recent Presidents were thoroughly unscrupulous (guess which one in particular). At the time of the senior Buckley's death, the school disbanded and the tutors were packed back to their native shores.

William junior carried on his father's work of fighting the liberal blight. He came to Yale as a World War II veteran. He won the highest honors the university had to offer. He was tapped for Skull and Bones. He became chairman of the *Yale Daily News*. He was a brilliant and colorful addition to the debating team. Under his aegis, the *News* offices resounded with cultured conversations in exotic tongues. Before Buckley took over, the *News* editorial page was devoted to complaints about the maid service, thefts in the locker rooms, and the scalping of tickets to the Princeton game. It was Buckley's goal to inspire controversy. The deluge of letters which poured in during his chairmanship were an index of his success. Patriotic sons of Eli resented his attacks on the Old Blue Team. Hackles and circulation rose at samples of the Buckley wit: "The greatest economic crisis the United States ever sustained was when Mr. Truman's haberdashery business failed."[3]

In 1951, shortly after his graduation, Buckley published *God and Man at Yale,* "a declaration of war against the present drift of American education." Buckley contended that it was the duty of a privately endowed university to promote the principles of religion and political economy which the alumni, the corporation, and the President professed to support. The vast majority of Yale graduates were Christians and individualists, yet the university's teachings tended to discredit both Christianity and free enterprise.

The basic sociology course was, according to Buckley, taught by an atheist. The largest religion course focused upon the Bible as a monument over Christianity's grave. The religion professors were of dubious orthodoxy—one admitting that he was "80% atheist and 20% agnostic." The department failed to teach Christianity as final truth. Students enrolled in the major religion course less from fervor than because of its reputation as a "gut."

In the Economics Department the basic course used four pro-Keynesian textbooks. The only course in comparative economics was taught by a collectivist. Buckley believed that the alumni should be polled on educational policy. "Reform" of the curriculum, in his opinion, would immediately follow. Research and teaching were to be separated. The professor who wrote a book on the virtues of socialism would be required to suppress the results of his research. It would be his duty henceforth to speak up for Christianity and free enterprise and to "deflate" wrong ideas.

Buckley's views did not find favor with the majority of Yale undergraduates. He had to modify a statement about the godlessness of one professor. It is questionable whether the poll would have gone quite as Buckley expected. An alumni report which made the front pages of the New York dailies absolved Yale on all counts. One intemperate alumnus compared Buckley to Torquemada. Another described him as a "twisted, ignorant young man whose ideas would have seemed reactionary to Mark Hanna."

His style was an open invitation to parodists such as Ira Wallach, who aped Buckley's passion for classification in *Hopalong-Freud Rides Again.*

> Mr. Hitchcock—Does not say his prayers.
> Mr. Babson—Does not say his prayers.
> Mr. Forrest—Says grace only when the bishop comes to dinner.
> The Bishop—Says grace whenever he eats with Mr. Forrest.
> Mr. Cheng Kee—Prays in a language unintelligible to God.[4]

Nonetheless, *God and Man at Yale* went into a gratifying number of printings. Soon Buckley and his brother-in-law, L. Brent Bozell, turned their nimble wits to the defense of Senator Joseph McCarthy of Wisconsin, *bête noir* of what they called contemptuously the "certified liberals."

During Buckley's senior year, Senator McCarthy made a

speech in Wheeling, West Virginia, stating that he had a list of State Department employees known to the Secretary of State as members of the Communist Party.

Later no one was sure just how many names he had mentioned—owing to bulit-in blaboff which protects the human race against political oratory. Estimates ranged from 205 down to McCarthy's subsequent figure—57.

The Tydings Committee was formed to investigate Communism in the State Department. A number of citizens were hauled up before Congress to answer questions about left-wing affiliations. A purge of the civil service had, by 1955, separated 2,200 "security risks" from government jobs, many as far removed from the State Department as the Post Office and the Department of Health, Education, and Welfare.

Buckley and Bozell's *McCarthy and His Enemies*, published in 1954, is one of the few attempts to invest McCarthy's free-wheeling attacks on the press, the Communist Party, the "anti-anti-Communists" and the "A.D.A. liberals" with the dignity of an intellectual position. In this book more Buckleyan bombshells are dropped into the State Department suggestion box.

The authors of *McCarthy and His Enemies* voiced the hope that McCarthy would broaden out his attack on intellectual deviates and lead America into a new age of conformity. If McCarthy failed to do this, it was not for want of trying.

In a 1952 campaign speech McCarthy lashed out at Adlai Stevenson, Democratic presidential candidate. He struck out at the anti-McCarthy press. He implied that James Wechsler, the anti-Communist editor of the *New York Post*, was a tool of the Kremlin. He spoke of Drew Pearson as the "sugar-coated voice of Russia." The *Washington Post* became the "Washington edition of the *Daily Worker*," the *New York Post* as "the uptown edition." Advertisers in *Time* and the *Milwaukee Journal* were warned that their dollars were being used to flood American homes with Communist propaganda.

Somewhat to Buckley's embarrassment, McCarthy attacked the loyalty of George Marshall, author of the Marshall Plan and Secretary of State under Harry Truman. While both Buckley and Bozell considered that Marshall had served the Soviet cause, they conceded that Marshall's thinking had the backing of most military men of his day. The Marshall case is treated in a special section of their book—separated from McCarthy's more brilliant achievements.

Later developments in McCarthy's career were not covered in the Buckley-Bozell apologia. McCarthy turned his guns on the State Department's overseas information program. Two young McCarthy henchmen named Cohn and Schine traveled to Europe to enforce a directive removing from the shelves of American overseas libraries all "books, music, paintings . . . of any Communists, fellow travelers, et cetera."

The *et cetera* category included works by the *New York Herald Tribune's* Bert Andrews; Walter White, head of the National Association for the Advancement of Colored People; *Time's* Richard Lauterbach; Clarence Streit, proponent of a North Atlantic federation; Foster Rhea Dulles, cousin of the late Secretary of State. Some libraries, not content with removing the books, burned them, provoking even the mild-mannered President Eisenhower to protest, "How will we defeat Communism unless we know what it is? What it teaches?— Why does it have such an appeal for men?"

Buckley and Bozell do not cover the turning point in McCarthy's career—the attack on the United States Army. For the first time America's vast TV audience had an opportunity to see the great anti-Communist crusader at work. On March 11, 1954, Secretary of the Army Robert T. Stevens filed charges against McCarthy. The charge: McCarthy, as chairman of the Permanent Senate Subcommittee on Investigations, along with Roy Cohn and Francis Carr, had sought to gain preferential treatment for army private G. David Schine.

McCarthy responded with countercharges. He was currently carrying on an investigation of Fort Monmouth, and Secretary Stevens had pleaded for easy treatment, using Schine as a "hostage." From April 22 to June 17, 1954, the television cameras were focused on the Senate hearings.

Nobody emerged with his nose completely clean. In *The Crucial Decade*, Eric F. Goldman said, "Had the McCarthy group sought preferential treatment for Schine? Clearly they had. Had the Army tried to stop McCarthy's investigation of Fort Monmouth? Equally clearly it had."

At one point, to establish friendliness between Stevens and

Schine, the McCarthy forces produced a picture, said to have hung in Schine's office, showing Stevens in the company of Schine. Army counsel Joseph Welch brought out the fact that the picture had been cut down from a larger one in which other figures had been present, deleted from the photograph by a "pixie," which Welch defined as "a close relative of a fairy."[5]

The McCarthy forces introduced a 2½-page document described as one of a series of letters from the F.B.I. warning against certain persons handling top secret radar material and addressed to Major General Alexander R. Bolling. Hoover was quoted as saying the document differed materially from a 15-page memo sent to Bolling relating to the same subject.

It was pointed out that McCarthy had accepted a classified document from an army intelligence officer. McCarthy served notice on two million four hundred thousand federal employees that it was their duty "to impart to him information about graft, corruption, communism, treason, and that there is no loyalty which can tower above and beyond their loyalty to their country." This loyalty, it appeared, should lead them to ignore such words as "secret" and "classified" and should transcend any presidential directive.

On December 2, 1954, McCarthy was censured for contempt of the Senate stemming from his abuse of Brigadier General Zwicker. He had addressed Zwicker in his customarily temperate tone: "You are a disgrace to the uniform. You're shielding Communist conspirators. You are going to be put on public display next Tuesday. You're not fit to be an officer."

McCarthy retaliated to the censure proceedings by describing the committee as the "unwitting handmaiden" of the Communist Party. He apologized for having supported Eisenhower —who had been notably cool to him during the proceedings. "The President smiled," said Eric Goldman in *The Crucial Decade*, "and the nation yawned."[6]

In 1957 Joseph McCarthy died. Editorialists wrung out posthumous tributes to him, like confessions extracted on the rack. Most of them took the safe and noncommittal tack ("I didn't know the Senator very well." "It is too early in the game to appraise the over-all influence of such a controversial figure."). With McCarthy gone, the conduct of government turned slowly to the hands of those middle-of-the-roaders whom Buckley called "the grave-diggers of the Republic."

During the McCarthy era other Americans had been dissatisfied with the government security program. The loyalty of federal employees came under official scrutiny in an act passed in August 1950, strengthened by an Executive Order in April 1953. The latter turned the old Truman loyalty program into a "security risk" program. A "security risk" was defined as a drunkard, drug addict, mental case, or other type of untouchable.

Such critics as the Honorable Harry P. Cain felt that the program did not give a fair break to the suspect employee. He believed that persons should not be called to account for *associations* with people known to be, or suspected of being, Communists. He objected to the looseness with which the term "Communist front" was bandied about. He believed that ties between "front" organizations and the Kremlin should be established by "competent jurisdiction." He believed that those accused of disloyalty should be allowed to cross-examine witnesses against them. This was frequently denied on the theory that the F.B.I.should "protect its confidential sources." "Perjury," said Cain, "ought to be as applicable to the accuser as to the accused."[7]

Buckley and Bozell criticized the government's handling of security cases, but on very different grounds. They believed that the government had a deplorable tendency to bend over backward on the employee's behalf.

In *McCarthy and His Enemies,* they give suggestions for the conduct of an anti-Communist State Department, which for monolithic orthodoxy was to look like a graduate school of Christian Individualistic Yale. "Quasi-judicial procedures" were to be scrapped. Reasons for the employee's dismissal were not to be made public. The employee's reputation was to be "protected" by never making it clear whether he was fired for being a Communist or for simply showing up drunk for work.

The employee who failed to satisfy his security board as to his innocence was to be removed from his job without "reference to traditional jurisprudential safeguards." The employee was to have his "day in court"—"not because he stands to gain from it, but because the government needs the information he possesses."

"The presumption of innocence will long remain the major barrier in the way of an effective security program," in the opinion of Buckley and Bozell. Loyalty boards should be staffed by "Communist experts," presumably not as susceptible as laymen to nostalgia for Anglo-Saxon folkways. "The rationale for staffing the loyalty boards with laymen is directly traceable to the common law notion that the ends of justice are best served when an unbiased tribunal of average citizens decides whether an accused is guilty or innocent. *But justice, we are saying, is not the major objective here.*"[8]

Buckley and Bozell list McCarthy's chief targets in an appendix at the back of the book, each name followed by a sinister-sounding roster of Communist front affiliations. There was frequently a discrepancy between McCarthy's listing of Communist fronts and those in the Buckley-Bozell appendix. One woman was described by McCarthy as having participated in 28 Communist fronts. Buckley and Bozell say, "Close examination . . . reveals that McCarthy showed evidence of only 24 Communist front affiliations (rather than 28) . . . that only four of the 24 groups had been cited as subversive by the Attorney General; not, as McCarthy had stated, nine."[9]

Another was accused by McCarthy of launching the American Union for Concerted Peace Efforts. It turned out that he had confused it with The Union of Concerted Peace Efforts, with which the accused was *not* associated.

This same victim was also said to have been instrumental in committing one organization to the support of such communistic activities as the grade labeling of canned goods. The organization informed the committee that the alleged subversive had not been their executive secretary, and that she had at no time any connection with the association's consumer program. "Here, pretty clearly," Buckley and Bozell remark, "McCarthy hadn't a leg to stand on."[10]

One might also question Moscow's liaison with another impeccable group dedicated to telling American families about the merits of the Nash Rambler, buys in Dr. Posner's Shoes, and the relative protection given the sunbather by different brands of suntan oil.

McCarthy described a certain professor as a member of thirty-five front organizations. *McCarthy and His Enemies* lists twelve. McCarthy connected this pedagogue with the African Aid Committee. "There is no evidence," Buckley and Bozell wrote, "that this organization has been officially cited or identified as a Communist front."[11]

Another professor was connected by McCarthy with the Conference Against Anti-Communist Legislation, Citizens to Abolish the Wood-Rankin Committee, and the National Committee to Defeat the Mundt Bill. "There is no evidence," write Buckley and Bozell, "that these organizations have either been officially identified or cited as Communist fronts."[12]

One well-known public figure was described by McCarthy as a member of The American Council of the Institute of Pacific Relations. McCarthy's young apologists admit that this group got a clean bill of health in 1951. Senator McCarthy associated the same man with the Coordinating Committee to Lift the Spanish Embargo and the China Aid Council. The evidence, Buckley and Bozell admit, is insufficient to establish his connection with the C.A.C. The pamphlet used to establish his subversive connection with the Spanish embargo appears to have been "a catchall for public statements for anyone in favor of ending the embargo. It is difficult to see how McCarthy could have mistaken it for anything else."[13]

In the prologue to *McCarthy and His Enemies*, William S. Schlamm remarked that the right to be wrong was forgivable in an artist who could be forgiven "a playful hour of nihilism," but that it was not forgivable when one's errors affect the lives of others like "the atrocious misjudgment of the certified gentlemen who have dropped ('Oops, sorry!') half of the world into irretrievable perdition."[14]

McCarthy's achievements are developed in the body of the text, while his bloopers are relegated to appendixes. To the persevering reader, considering that the careers of his victims were being weighed in the balance, there was a sizable number of "Oops, sorry's" in the McCarthy record of errata.

For Buckley and Bozell this is not very important, for "when a man's loyalty is questioned, more often than not it makes little difference to him just *how* and in what terms it is questioned."[15]

At the height of the McCarthy agitation, a joke appeared in *The New Yorker* magazine. A dismissed civil servant was protesting to a prospective employer: "It's true, sir, the State Department let me go. But it was solely because of incompetence." This luckless man might possibly have fallen into yet another of Buckley and Bozell's categories of untouchables—that of the "policy misfit."

Among their other rigorous requirements for government servants they also demanded infallibility. Whereas in Yale truth was to be defined by the alumni and trustees, in the State Department the party in power was to be the arbiter of ideological purity. Foreign policy was to reflect the ideas of people acting through their elected representatives, and "all employees whose responsibilities touch upon the making of policy, but whose demonstrated views and attitudes on critical issues are athwart the Administration's should be summarily sent on their way."[16]

Buckley and Bozell never considered that one might take a chance on a civil servant at one level of government and not at another. The McCarthy era made little distinction between the "security risk" on the Atomic Energy Commission and the "security risk" in the fish hatcheries.

John Stewart Service, for example, was described by McCarthy as "one of the dozen top policy makers in the entire State Department Far Eastern Division," while the Tydings Committee alluded to him as a junior grade foreign officer.

Service, arrested in 1945 for passing classified documents to the leftist magazine *Amerasia,* was finally cleared of the stigma of treason. It would seem that the removal of classified documents would, if proven, be sufficient reason for an employee's dismissal. There is something slightly hollow about the Buckley-Bozell indignation over his acquittal in view of McCarthy's solemn instructions to civil servants to snap their fingers at presidential directives and to march in and help themselves to any document that captured their fancy.

George Marshall was absolved of the charge of Communism by the authors (he would probably have qualified as a "policy misfit" but for the deplorable support given him by

Presidents Roosevelt and Truman acting through their elected representatives). In their gracious acquittal of Marshall, absolution is granted on rather curious grounds. Marshall, the authors contended, was not in a class with John Service or John Carter Vincent, "whose duties and qualifications called for expert reporting and shrewd interpretation of facts on which policy makers like Marshall were to rely."[17]

Here there is a serious confusion of the differences between policy making and reportage. The essential virtue of a good reporter is exactly the same as the requirement for a history professor, an ability to confront evidence honestly, whatever one's personal opinions. If a reporter twists evidence he should be fired. If his conclusions turn out to be consistently wrong, he should not be promoted. His responsibility is not as great as that of the policy maker. A policy maker should compare the reports of observers on all sides of the political fence, bring his own opinions to bear on them, and take the final responsibility for the course of action he takes. He should not wish this responsibility off on a reporter. The Secretary of State cannot shrug his shoulders and deny all blame after dispatching an army on the suggestion of the office boy.

Buckley and Bozell do not permit McCarthy's targets the luxury of errors in judgment, yet McCarthy himself was never called to account for errors of fact. When he failed to prove that he held in his hand the names of fifty-seven Communists, Buckley and Bozell remarked that these are "difficult things to prove at best . . . and all but impossible to prove to the satisfaction of the liberals."[18]

When McCarthy described another public figure as the "*pioneer* of the smear campaign" against Chiang, or when the State Department was pictured as being "infested" with card-carrying Communists, Buckley chuckles indulgently, "McCarthy can be depended on not to understate his case."[19]

When he "impulsively, and absurdly" mistook Edmund Wilson's *Memoirs of Hecate County* for a Communist tract despite Wilson's long record of anti-communism, McCarthy's impulsiveness and absurdity are dismissed as one might dismiss the lovable crotchets of a picturesque and eccentric relative.

When McCarthy gives his paraphrase of an author's viewpoint and puts it into direct quotes, he should be judged, according to his apologists, not by the standards of a scholar, but rather by the standards of a politician.

All this is justified in Buckley and Bozell's opinion by the effectiveness with which McCarthy waged his holy war against the Enemy. In reading their book on McCarthy, one is impressed by the speed with which the face of the Enemy changed.

"In 38 cases," Buckley and Bozell claim, "he [McCarthy] was guilty of exaggeration. On some occasions 'fellow traveller' had turned into 'Communist'; on others 'alleged pro-Communist' had developed into 'pro-Communist.'[20] Soon others would find themselves beyond the pale. The liberals, it was hinted ominously, don't need to worry *yet*.

When it was argued that McCarthyism was frightening people away from government service, Buckley and Bozell replied that courtroom etiquette was out of place in the Holy War. "The burden of proof, once the loyalty question is raised, falls on the accused."[21] "We live in an unbrave new world," the authors say, "in which certain cherished habits of mind are not only inappropriate but suicidal."[22]

Among other things, McCarthy was credited with having saved America from any resemblance to Europe—that "weary and cynical community of pettifogging nations."[23] Had McCarthy lived to "harden the conformity" as Buckley hoped he would, the next suspect group might have been the pro-Europeans.

As long as America was the world's undisputed leader, it was fashionable to believe in her ability to "go it alone." After Sputnik, America's built-in invulnerability was no longer taken for granted. Statesmen hastened to make "declarations of interdependence" and to foist off intermediate-range missiles on the "weary and cynical community of pettifogging nations." In a world echoing with cries of "Yankee go home," it was doubtful if the Buckleys and McCarthys had won many converts to the American way of life by dumping overboard every assumption which had made life worth living for millions of Americans.

The mid-fifties saw an upsurge of nostalgia for those archaic Anglo-Saxon standards. In January 1958 the United States

Court of Appeals ruled that the government must produce material documents, including F.B.I. reports, in proceedings before federal boards. A long step was taken toward making the able American a little less nervous in the Civil Service. In 1958, too, the army revised its policy of issuing less than honorable discharges to soldiers charged with pre-induction left-wing activities. G.I.'s who had gone through youthful pink periods had been stigmatized since 1953, when McCarthy had mobilized America against an army dentist with the cry "Who promoted Major Peress?"[24]

The government must admittedly have some way of ridding itself of the dishonest reporter, the bungler, and the habitual drunk; but the McCarthy era ran the risk of throwing the baby out with the bath. A recent survey conducted by the Harvard Business School Club of Washington, D.C., revealed that since World War II there has been a growing distaste among businessmen for government service. The "best brains" went to Washington with increasing reluctance and for increasingly shorter periods of time. Prior to the advent of McCarthy, the civil servant enjoyed a greater degree of job security than the neophyte facing the hatchet men in a TV network or a Madison Avenue advertising agency. Forced to choose between the jungle code of office politics and the "faceless accusers" who supplied information to loyalty boards, anyone might be forgiven for gravitating to the hatchet men who paid the most.

Some have charged that the sciences withered during the McCarthy era, that scientific advance was stifled by the McCarthyite obsession with secrecy. Such generalizations are hard to prove. Researchers, however, were unlikely to be attracted to government projects by the bull-in-the-china-shop accusations of the Fort Monmouth investigation. Here McCarthy conducted a dramatic series of closed hearings, coming up for air from time to time with unsubstantiated rumors of sinister scientists, microfilm thefts, and reports of a ring which had communicated with the atom spy Julius Rosenberg.

In the wave of Monmouth suspensions many were relegated to a temporary limbo without being informed of the charges against them. Unable to rely on living witnesses, McCarthy at one point invoked testimony from beyond the grave.

A scientist with the power to blow up a city must expect far closer surveillance in a government job than, say, an official of UNESCO. In the McCarthy era the mere fact of being a scientist was sufficient to make one suspect in the public eye. A post-Sputnik study made in 1958 by Opinion Research Corporation for *Life* magazine disclosed that a third of the people polled still doubted that scientists could be trusted with the secrets of "important new discoveries"! According to *Life* staff writer Paul O'Neil, 10 percent "really think that every scientist has a spy at his elbow or is in direct communication with the Kremlin." Such popular mistrust might well drive the budding scientist into "nonsensitive" fields such as plastic raincoats and cellulose thread.

The McCarthyite suspicion of science extended to free inquiry in other fields.

Buckley's books raise important questions about the approach of a whole society to the problem of knowledge. Buckley's Yale and Buckley's State Department are the battlegrounds for an age-old war of ideas between two hereditary enemies, the disciple and the researcher.

The researcher approaches knowledge inductively, drawing his conclusions from observation and experiment. The disciple approaches knowledge deductively, using some preconception as a starting point. Buckley would commit Yale for all time to Christianity and individualism, and the State Department to the faith of anti-Communism. The independent researcher would be abolished from education and politics if his, Buckley's, New Improved Yale and his New Improved State Department were to become features of the New Improved America.

Some reviewers of *God and Man at Yale* pointed out that Buckley's suggestions would not be out of place at a sectarian college. The aims of such a college are different from those of Yale, which Buckley defines as a "nondenominational educational institution not exclusively interested in the propagation of Christianity."[25] In approaching certain subjects some sectarian colleges feel called upon to inculcate into the student a set of *opinions* about that subject. Yale must approach any field of knowledge by bringing every available *fact* about it to the students' attention.

There are sectarian colleges which insist on some degree of orthodoxy in the faculty. The nondenominational college must strive for an intellectually balanced aquarium. The sectarian college aims primarily at turning out well-educated people, who are good Catholics, good Protestants, or good Jews. Yale aims primarily at turning out students who approach Christianity, communism and Judaism with the disciplines of good researchers. In fields such as philosophy, religion, and occasionally history and science, a teacher in a sectarian college tries to make his students accept his point of view. A Yale professor encourages his students to contradict him, provided that they can find evidence to support their arguments. "Here are the facts, kids," such a professor must say in effect, "go to it." The sectarian college urges young people to sing hymns and say prayers. Yale urges them to study the Dead Sea scrolls. Most fundamental of all is the yardstick which is taken as the measure of truth. Yale teaches its undergraduates to come to tentative conclusions on the basis of past experience. The sectarian college hopes they will accept certain final conclusions on the basis of a guess about the future.

Buckley's detractors did not give him credit for hitting on one of the basic flaws of such liberal arts colleges as Yale. Yale does not, like the sectarian college, attempt to furnish its graduates with an "ultimate standard on which human beings must base their behavior."[26] It does not, because, Buckley notwithstanding, it cannot. The Yales of the educational scene aim at criticizing basic principles. Buckley's new improved Yale would aim at defining them.

If *God and Man at Yale* became a best seller it was partly because the book revived interest in the unfashionable practice of "value inculcation." The Victorian inculcated values with such a heavy hand that the process had been in bad odor ever since. Since the twenties, parents had considered it bad form to tell their children to take their toys out of the living room, to enforce a few simple principles on them with an occasional spanking, or to send them to Sunday School to learn the tenets of one of the great religions. There were parents in mid-century America who seriously argued that their children's psyches would be irreparably harmed if they were forced to learn to say "thank you."

Suddenly faced with the fanaticism of Soviet Communism, more and more Americans were called upon to defend a set of beliefs without being quite sure just what those beliefs were.

It might be that the frankly religious school would henceforth perform an invaluable service in defining them. There was an enormous need in America for a more mature type of religious education—for schools, colleges, and courses of instruction which helped the pupil to face the objections which the nonbeliever might level against him. Such education furnished exactly the kind of intellectual yardstick that Buckley desired. There was a growing realization that to be a good Catholic, a good Protestant, or a good Jew is not, after all, such a mean goal in life; that every young researcher might do well to serve a part of his educational apprenticeship as a disciple.

A university such as Yale cannot, however, commit itself to a preconception, because preconceptions are hostile to the spirit of research. On the basis of experience alone it is impossible to confirm with certainty the views of the Christian, the Moslem, the Jew, the atheist, or the agnostic. Five students can write five papers on the same subject, all get the same mark, and arrive at five different sets of conclusions— all of them tenable at the time. The fact that will prove which one is right may not emerge until five years or five millennia after the five graduate.

Buckley has put his finger on the Achilles' heel of the inductive method, the fragmentary nature of experience. If all the facts about the universe were available at once, one could confirm the truth of an idea as decisively as we say 2 plus 2 equals 4. Since the evidence is dug up piecemeal one can reach wrong conclusions, because the fact that proves them to be wrong has yet to become a part of history. The world was no less round, as Buckley shrewdly points out, when the majority believed it to be flat.

Inductive reasoning has grave pitfalls, and those who deny it ignore the brilliance and penetration of Buckley's argument. Experience can be as misleading as a jigsaw puzzle which promises at one minute to be a Spanish galleon, at another to be the Empire State Building. Not, perhaps, till the history of the human race is completed will we see the unmistakable outlines of Anne Hathaway's cottage.

Why not, then, commit *all* education to some widely accepted view of reality? Why not fire professors who don't agree with it, "deflate" ideas that are hostile to it, mark the papers of students who refuse to accept it with an *F?* Those who would follow such a course forget that the deductive method has its drawbacks too. When opinions are taken as the yardstick of truth, even if they are correct opinions, there is a temptation to monkey with the evidence, which does not exist for the professor whose only allegiance is to the facts.

Reasoning from a preconception offers serious pitfalls. There is the danger of making opinions more important than the means of arriving at them; of seeing one's own cause in terms of white and the opposition's in terms of black. There is the danger that suppression will take the place of criticism, that inconvenient evidence will disappear; that painting a picture in the proper blacks and whites will become more important than telling the truth. The student, instead of learning to analyze facts, may be taught to memorize predetermined conclusions, and may graduate having developed little more than a talent for giving back what teacher wants to hear. Why bother to work the puzzle when you know that it's going to be Anne Hathaway's cottage? Inductive educational institutions may reward the pupil who, on insufficient evidence, concludes that 2 plus 2 equals 5. They are unlikely to fall into the opposite error of rewarding the student who concludes that 2 plus 2 equals 4 with as little conception of the issues involved as the child who peeks at the answer book.

The perils of deductive reasoning became painfully evident in the McCarthy period. The very conception of a "security risk" depends on someone's *opinion* of someone else rather than on proven *facts.* McCarthy's peccadilloes, which Buckley smiles on so tolerantly, could not be excused for a moment in a newspaper reporter. They are the faults which the devout overlook in a militant defender of a faith. Who cares, the anti-Communist faithful argue, if McCarthy quoted out of context? He was, as Buckley claims, an *interpreter* of the facts. Who cares if the F.B.I. document wasn't quite what McCarthy said it was? It added up to the same thing, didn't it? Who cares if a figure was cut out of the picture, as long as one is on the side of the angels? Who cares if the *New York Post* editorials were demonstrably at odds with the party line? The really clever Commies are the ones who throw in some crack against Russia to confuse you. Who cares if the accused can prove she didn't really belong to that organization? It certainly sounded awful and where there's smoke there's fire. What does it matter if the facts get twisted, as long as the faith is preserved?

Buckley was but one of many during the McCarthy era who would impose a viewpoint on the educator. The viewpoint happened to be one to which 99 percent of the American people subscribed—the view that life in America is better than life in the Soviet Union. The nightmare of the McCarthy era was the fear that the uncommitted researcher might discover some naughty fact that would upset this axiom. Educators were subjected to popular pressures to sign loyalty oaths and avoid "controversial" issues. "Follow the facts wherever they lead," society said, "but promise that this is what they'll prove."

A random glance at the *New York Times* education section in 1951 reveals the following events at a large state university: The board of trustees adopted a resolution stating that before a speaker could appear on campus he must be "screened" for loyalty and background. The request of a campus Quaker group to hear a Quaker pacifist was turned down. On the same day the trustees also ruled that all questionnaires prepared by an individual employed at the university should be submitted to the president before they could be issued. Because of the "screening" rule, plans for a Religion-in-Life week which would have brought some sixty suspect speakers to the campus were virtually dismantled. A political science professor suggested that the ruling meant that to speak on university grounds a person must express ideas palatable to the board of trustees. Would screening of books come next? How could one prohibit Harold Rugg of Teachers College from addressing the students and permit his books in the college library?

The issues raised here were raised elsewhere. The "loyalty oath" at the University of California became a national *cause célèbre.* As Dr. Theodore M. Greene of Yale testified before a Senate subcommittee in 1951, there was a "growing suspicion of anyone who, as a loyal and intelligent citizen, has taken the trouble to learn something about communism."[27]

The Americans who sympathized with McCarthy were not interested in digging out every available fact about the Soviet system. They were interested in learning only the facts about Russia which would prove the superiority of the United States.

These were the Americans who investigated a textbook for saying that America and Russia had certain products in common. They banned the story of Robin Hood because Robin Hood was a foe of capitalism. They confiscated the contents of a gum machine because the wrappers around the gum contained the unsettling information that Russia was the largest country in the world. In stifling evidence, the McCarthy era overlooked the threat to American institutions from another quarter. There are serious weaknesses in American society which would have been instantly apparent to anyone with the humility to set up an organization for the translation of Soviet scientific journals. Any professor who suggested such a thing in 1951 would have been in serious jeopardy of losing his job.

In the wave of *mea culpas* which followed the launching of Sputnik, liberals and conservatives alike had reason to beat their breasts. Those of every political coloration had contributed either to the flaccid permissiveness of American education, to the stagnation of government leadership, or to the worship of Chanel 5 and Channel 2.

Even among those with intimations of infallibility, accidents will happen. James Burnham, who accused the liberals of misreading history, made the following statement a few weeks before the launching of Sputnik. It appeared in the *National Review*, a magazine edited by William Buckley, presumably with the Buckley imprimatur.

> The Soviet "atomic explosion" announced by President Truman in 1949, was probably not even an atomic bomb, and certainly no sign that Soviet production of nuclear weapons had started. But

from that moment on the gullible opinion in the West granted Moscow an "atomic stalemate." The Communists gained the political and strategic advantage of a complete nuclear arsenal years before they had it—if indeed they have it even today.[28]

The dangerous Myth of the Dumb Slav did as much for the Russian cause as a dozen Alger Hisses. Even those patriots on the side of the angels did their bit in perpetrating the greatest "oops sorry" of them all.

After the death of McCarthy, the researcher was slowly let out of his chains. There was a realization that by giving him his head, the disciple had something to gain. The researcher may unearth inconvenient evidence. History may discredit the dissenter. But together they point out chinks in the armor of the righteous, which the supporters of the righteous fondly overlook.

America is big enough for both the disciple and the researcher, as it is big enough for more than one kind of school.

The botanist Edmund Ware Sinnott said, on retiring from the Yale faculty, that there are two roads to truth and their disciplines are not the same.

> The way of science, confident in reason, and the way of faith, depending on their insights of the spirit, do not follow the same course. [Yet we should not] regret these differences but rather rejoice in them. They are the two halves that make the whole; from tension between them, character is born.[29]

Everyone's actions are governed by some unprovable preconception. The Christian, the Communist, the atheist, and the Jew stake their lives on a guess about the future. Buckley and McCarthy would have silenced everyone who guessed differently from themselves. They would guarantee the triumph of their views with a shillelagh. The liberal believes that the shillelagh breeds a hostility to an idea that a fair fight between truth and error does not, that by being generous he may one day win the dissenter to his side. The liberal relies on the facts to support his case. The evidence may be sketchy and often susceptible to misinterpretation. Yet the person who reads the future correctly is the only one who can *afford* to be generous. History is on the side of the one who guesses right.

The true idea, the great work of art, alone can stand the test of experience. Buckley accused Yale of subscribing to a tacit "value orthodoxy" when it discredited the racial philosophy of Houston Chamberlain and the poetry of Joyce Kilmer. He does not consider that both Kilmer and Chamberlain have weathered the test of experience badly.

No one can predict with certainty the scientific discoveries or the literary tastes of the future. One cannot dismiss the possibility of a vindication of Chamberlain or a Kilmer renaissance. One can say with confidence that, *at the moment*, Chamberlain's racial theories are at odds with the biological evidence; that *in the past* the qualities of the poem *Trees* have not recommended it as a work of art to the ages.

If the disciple kicked the researcher around during the McCarthy period, during the twenties and thirties the researcher had often condescended to the disciple. The stir caused by *God and Man at Yale* showed that America had never found a middle ground between worship of diversity and worship of conformity, between reason and faith, between innovation and tradition, between reverence for experiment and reverence for authority.

Buckley's later career as an aging *enfant terrible* suggests that he has something to gain from preserving those "cherished" but "suicidal" habits of thought. Along with Senators Tower, Goldwater and Thurmond, he is the darling of the young intellectual right wing. He has appeared at Radical rightist rallies sponsored by the Conservative Party[30] and Young Americans for Freedom, Inc. This latter organization in 1961 gave Buckley the Conservative Award for Journalism.[31] He appeared at the Christian Anti-Communism Crusade in the somewhat improbable company of Dr. Fred C. Schwarz, Herbert A. Philbrick, Cardinal Spellman's representative, Colonel McGee, and Pat Boone.[32]

His views on foreign policy are as decided as his views on education. He took up the cause of Moise Tshombe and the Katanga Freedom Fighters.[33] Tshombe, too, was a favorite of Young Americans for Freedom, Inc. and was invited to their 1962 rally[34] on March 7 in Madison Square Garden. Because of his defiance of the UN, the Katanga secession movement, until its collapse, was something of a right-wing *cause célèbre.*

Others have felt less empathy for Buckley's viewpoint on Congolese affairs. At the annual convention of the National Student Association at Madison, Wisconsin, Buckley again lived up to his reputation as a creator of controversy. A tape-recorded version of a Buckley speech declared that it was impossible to equate the deliberations of Washington, Franklin and Jefferson with those of Patrice Lumumba, Joseph Mobutu and "other semisavages in the Congo." Returning to his favorite target, Buckley described liberalism as a "calcified ideology." Four foreign students launched a protest. One Negro with a rhetorical gift almost equal to Mr. Buckley's criticized "the base and debased, colonial, repressive slave-owning kind of mentality that can exist in a hard fascist-type regime."[35]

Fidel Castro is another Buckley *bête noire.* Buckley accuses the Kennedy Administration of pursuing a policy of "diplomatic nothingness" with regard to Cuba. "Survival," according to Buckley, depends on "bravely" facing the possibility of war.[36]

As with many of the radical right, nothing short of a bomb on Havana will do. At a rally in Madison Square Garden, where Buckley appeared, more than 8,000 vociferous Conservatives booed the Cuban blockade, accused the Kennedy Administration of doing "too little too late," clamored for the rescue of the Bay of Pigs prisoners, and roared their determination to invade Cuba.[37] This at a time when news of the President's action was causing runs on ammunition in Florida, sellouts of canned tomatoes in Los Angeles, and panic among holders of real estate in such tropical paradises as Nassau and Eleuthra.

Buckley continues as something of a firebrand in the world of letters. In 1954, he published *Up From Liberalism.* He has debated with novelist Norman Mailer on the nature of the right wing. He is editor of the *National Review*—a far-right magazine. This magazine lost $100,000 a year at its outset, but by the second half of 1962 it had 70,000 subscribers, and after seven lean years may have reached the break-even point. In time, the *National Review* may become the right-wing equivalent of *The Nation* or *The New Republic*.

The *New York Times* describes the helter-skelter atmosphere of the editorial offices:

> At deadline time, any or all of its editors may be addressing political meetings in Indiana or skiing in Switzerland. The magazine's offices are awash with solemn, cerebral young men who hope to start conservative magazines at their respective colleges.

Biweekly editorial lunches are held in Mr. Buckley's town house in New York's East Thirties. Guests at these meetings are colorful and varied. One recent session described in the *Times* brought together a professor who demanded that the magazine take a firmer stand on Serbian independence; a Mexican politician who urged an article on Communist gains south of the border; a young South American student who praised a military *coup d'état* in Peru. (As the *Times* remarked in one of its cattier editorial asides, it turned out that his father was a general.)

The *National Review* shows no monolithic orthodoxy of opinion. Its contributors often take diametrically opposed positions. If the *National Review* has come out against Albert Schweitzer and the United States Supreme Court, it has also charged that Robert Welch of the John Birch Society was damaging the cause of anti-communism.[38]

Buckley himself has accused the far-right hero Major General Edwin Walker of political ignorance.[39] With his blessing, the *National Review* has commented unfavorably on Pope John XXIII's encyclical *Mater et Magistra*, dealing with world social problems. The Pope had lapsed into heresy against Adam Smith by praising measures of the welfare state that did not impinge on individual freedom. The *National*

Review's stand precipitated a broadside from the Jesuit magazine *America*. The *National Review* ticked off *America* as "impudent." *America* commented tartly: "It takes an appalling amount of self-assurance for a Catholic writer to brush off a papal encyclical."[40]

Buckley notably exempts himself from the standards he sets for others. In *McCarthy and His Enemies,* he recommended depriving "security risks" of the most fundamental civil liberties. Yet on Jack Paar's television program he defended his own right to staff the *National Review* with ex-Communists, who were evidently cleansed of their guilt through exposure to him.

Perhaps his double standard became most evident in his battle against Hunter College. Late in 1961 Buckley ran afoul of the Higher Education Board of New York City. For several years *National Review* forums had been held from October to May in the Hunter College auditorium. In 1961 college authorities refused to renew the lease.[41]

The Board refused to let the *National Review* use the hall for symposia on the grounds that the magazine "did not fit the revised criteria for outside rental."[42] When this dictum was challenged, the authorities backed and filled. New York City Corporation Counsel Leo Larkin said that Buckley's programs were not "debates or forums educational in nature, but rather one-sided presentations of a distinct point of view . . . in opposition to those of other groups or movements and thus in clear violation of the criteria for the use of Hunter College facilities."[43] Hunter's Auditorium Chairman Rosenberg claimed that the tenant-landlord relationship was the issue,[44] a tie that is usually strained when the heat is off rather than when it is on.

Early in 1962, Buckley's suit against Hunter was dismissed by the New York State Supreme Court on a technicality;[45] but in June he won his point. Judge Jacob Markowitz ruled that regulations governing the use of facilities for political forums and lectures were "unconstitutionally vague or else embody an unconstitutional principle of selection." He urged the *National Review* to reapply when the college revised its rules.[46]

In self-defense, the McCarthyite had reverted to the language of Voltaire. Buckley claimed that the policy violated constitutional guarantees of freedom of speech and permitted precensorship. When he presented his arguments for diversity of opinion, his cause was championed by devotees of the "calcified ideology." His brief was submitted to the court by the New York Civil Liberties Union.[47]

His role as a dissenter made him no more tolerant of intellectual crotchets in others. In October 1962, the Yale Political Union withdrew its invitation to the Communist leader Gus Hall. At the urging of Buckley, the undergraduate forum had made this decision by a vote of 86 to 83.[48]

The McCarthy era was over. The limits of "tolerable opinion" were still narrowly drawn, though Buckley was quick to cry "sanctuary" against those whose definition of "correct" ideas did not include his own.

Buckley's disregard for Queensberry rules was repudiated by a society which did not share his assumptions but which had always given him the floor. He had done America a service by pointing to some motes in the liberal eye. The first half of the twentieth century had glorified the dissenter out of all proportion to his worth. It had often been enough to be *against* something even if the something was as necessary an evil as motherhood.

The avant-garde of the twenties and thirties had had a field day of smashing the icons. It was to be hoped that the 1960's would not follow Buckley into the more ancient error of smashing the test tubes.

13

The Defector

CLAUDE BATCHELOR

Texarkana is an oil-army-and-cow town with Tennessee Williams overtones. One half of it is in Texas, the other half in Arkansas. What they speak of as the "famous State Line Avenue" is the dividing line. On the Texas side, Texarkana is dry; on the Arkansas side—wet. Neon signs blink invitingly across the street, advertising liquor to the thirsty patrons of a hotel aptly called the Grim. Strolling about the streets, the visitor is very conscious of being a stranger. Curious eyes stare at the alien face from knots of soft-spoken Negroes, from groups of sombreroed kids, and white-shod ladies wearing jerseys marked "Optimists' International" or "Soroptimists." The proliferation of Baptist churches, the papers from Shreveport, the plane passengers headed for Little Rock, the smell of rancid grease, the fly-specked bologna and cheese, serve notice on the traveler that this is regional America with a vengeance. Yet to a boy from Kermit, Texas, who had spent most of his adult life in prison, Texarkana was a terrifying link with the outside world.

Out beyond the Negro shacks at the edge of town, Texarkana's Federal Correctional Institute is set among pleasant rolling lawns. It is a federal prison with a progressive reputation, worlds apart from the tough state institution on the Arkansas side. Its degree of freedom was alarming to a recent alumnus of a closely supervised army prison like Leavenworth.

"Dear Joel," Claude Batchelor wrote to his lawyer in January 1958, "I was informed this morning of my impending transfer. . . . I will therefore take advantage of the permission granted previously to use two sheets of stationery and discourse on my opinions regarding that subject." There followed several paragraphs of soul-searching as to whether Batchelor could withstand the "assault on my morals by 'older, wiser, more incorrigible minds.'" Was Texarkana, he asked his lawyer, "conducive to a healthy adjustment? . . . My time has ran out. The final analysis rests with you."[1]

Batchelor had, in his heart, decided to accept the transfer but apparently could not get out of the habit of clearing every decision with GHQ. He was accustomed to looking to someone higher up for everything from second sheets of paper to a life plan.

From the age of nineteen until his parole in 1959, Batchelor had been confined behind bars of either iron or bamboo. He was born in Texas on December 14, 1931. He was remembered in Kermit as a rather nondescript character whose one distinction was his playing the trumpet in the school band. His mother was a devoutly religious Baptist who sent young Claude to Sunday school. He went through the tenth grade at the local school. In July 1948 he lied about his age and went into the army.

On December 1, 1948, he arrived at Yokohama. While in Japan he met a dance-hall hostess named Kyoko Araki. A letter which he wrote to his mother after he had been going with Kyoko for a year showed this latter-day Pinkerton and Butterfly caught in a clash of cultures.

Dearest Mom [he wrote, in an unformed school-boy hand],

I am grown up now. You know. When I went to Hamlin a few years ago I started to find out what life is really like. I think I had a pretty good idea of it before. Yet when I started making life on my own I began to see what it was a little better. . . .

I realize fully the responsibilities of marriage and as far as her being Japanese doesn't make hardly any difference except for what some other people might think. . . .

She believes the Christian way now. She was formally [sic] of the Shinto religion which is also of God.

I have also went out with two American girls over here just to see if I had forgotten anything about the States. Kyoko is by far tops with me.

He explains that their marriage under Japanese law will not be recognized by American authorities but that pressure is being brought to bear to have the law changed.

I have a good friend that works with Scap [sic] over here. He says they are going to conference on it very soon and it seems to be very much in our favor. I have heard the thing all over from many people. Scap, by the way just about runs this country right now. They are about like our congress while MacArthur is more or less like Truman.

[He discusses the low cost of living and the new house he and his wife are having built.] Please I beg of you, send me a notarized paper stating that we have your permission to marry. Remember I have a brain of my own. Don't forget my age in the army as that could mess me up.

Good bye and *Please*
With all my love
Claude

P.S. Am sending pictures of us on our wedding day.[2]

Claude and "Kay" were married in a Shinto ceremony. A few months later, Batchelor was sent to Korea and late in 1950 he fell into Chinese Communist hands. When he was captured, his unit had no idea that China had come into the war. In preparation for his experience he had little more than the worldly wisdom he had picked up in Hamlin. His political awareness might be gauged by his statement about MacArthur and Truman. In the light of certain well-publicized differences between them the comparison would hardly have been welcomed by either.

When Batchelor was taken prisoner, the Chinese impressed their lovable qualities upon him in an absolutely unforgettable way. Newly captured prisoners were lined up facing a ditch. Behind them they could hear an enemy officer ominously clicking a pistol. As the prisoners trembled with fear, the Chinese passed up and down the line, turning each G.I. around and shaking his hand. The feeling of relief made the boys look upon their captors almost as deliverers.[3] The first step in the decline and fall of Claude Batchelor came when the enemy induced in him the first of many Pavlovian reactions: "Thank you, pal, for not putting a bullet in my back."

Batchelor was sent to Camp #5 at Pytok-tong—which was a pilot for the whole P.O.W. indoctrination program. It was to P.O.W. education what Teachers College is to Deweyism.

Camp #5 was dedicated to one of the most unpleasant educational experiments in history. Modern psychology teaches us that everyone has hidden hatreds and hidden guilts. It was the purpose of the Chinese to channel guilt feelings into breast-beating confession and public recantation, to tap the wellsprings of hatred and turn them against something offensive to the Politbureau; and to use endless repetition and suppression of facts to bring about conversion to a Marxist-Leninist view. The Chinese posed as the prisoners' friends. Their quarrel, they said, was not with the boys but with America's imperialists and militarists.

Intensive indoctrination was accompanied by subtle physical suasion. Those accused of offenses were forced to stand on the ice as punishment. The diet of millet was meager enough to make a man submissive but not meager enough to kill him. Wormy food and dirty water made for a very high death rate. Casualties were abandoned on the road. The strong stole food from the weak, and men with dysentery were thrown out in the cold to die. Many retreated into a womblike trance, taking no interest in providing themselves with food and shelter, in keeping their quarters or clothes clean, in delousing themselves.

Prisoners slept in thatched huts on floor space about half as wide as a Pullman berth. The heating was inadequate, and there was only one electric light bulb, although there was, in winter, only about three hours of sunlight. There was an epidemic of "give-up-itis"—in which one man after another would simply turn his face to the wall and die.[4] There was a flourishing black market, and as Batchelor said in his 30,000-word reminiscence of his prison experiences, morale was very poor. Yankee know-how seemed to have gone with the flush toilet.

Wretched conditions in the camp, it was explained, were the result of "merciless" U.N. bombings. The boys' mail was cleverly edited. There was no snipping out of passages. If a letter contained something the Communists didn't want the recipient to see he never got it at all. Letters containing gripes about the Korean War got through in toto. This served a threefold purpose. It gave the impression that the Korean War was indeed the work of "war-mongering imperialists" in Washington. It made the boys think that the folks had deserted them. The lack of obvious deletions made the unwary believe that their mail wasn't censored at all.

At the beginning of his prison term, Batchelor and his group made the mistake of thinking that they could roll with the punches. Batchelor was appointed a monitor. He was to attend indoctrination lectures and to act as moderator of the evening discussion period. The boys were supposed to write their opinions of the talks. They got together and drew up non-incriminating views. They attached various names to them. Each man's "opinion" was first submitted to him for approval. By playing it cool, they felt, they could augment their meager rations of tobacco and food.

Tobacco and food, however, were not forthcoming, and at one point Batchelor rebelled. He went to the Chinese instructor and said that he didn't believe what he was being taught, that he was not going to pass on any more misinformation to his fellows. It was then that the Chinese struck. The class was immediately dismissed. The instructor took Batchelor aside. He was polite and all ears. Did Batchelor have any suggestions as to how food and studies might be improved? Batchelor was taken off guard, and spoke more freely about his problems than he ever had before.

The early indoctrination lectures had dealt with the sins of the American government. Batchelor's criticism of this approach is revealing. "We were getting pretty fed up at having to listen to all this stuff about our government which we didn't know anything about anyway."[5] The Chinese tactfully shifted the terrain to China—an area about which the young scholars knew even less. It was then that the voyages to Damascus began.

Using their opinions about China as a basis, the boys were divided into three groups: the pros, the antis and the neutrals. The pros and antis would compete to see who could convert the most fence sitters. When all the B (neutral) group had joined one side or the other, the A's and the C's went to work on each other. When the objections of the last two anti-Communist mavericks were overcome, the Communists turned next to the appealing subject of peace.

Batchelor was put on a Peace Committee. He was selected for this honor by an elaborate electoral process devised by the Communists. By perpetuating the illusion of the democratic process, the Reds were able to single out natural leaders among their enemies and to give everyone a cozy feeling of audience participation. The boys were urged to write their pacifist sentiments home to their parents. They were told repeatedly, and with some justice, that the Korean War was unpopular at home. They were exposed to pictures of Americans staging peace rallies, signing petitions. Taking a stand against peace is rather like being against Mother and for leukemia. In the service of this impeccable cause, Batchelor found himself beginning to believe his captors.

Along with isolation, and unending exposure to books extolling the cause, the Communists had other ways of bringing

their quarry to heel. Most valuable was the information
gained through "self-criticism." Autobiographical essays were
assigned as penances for various infractions. Group criticism
forced the individual to do an intellectual strip tease in public.
In these merciless examinations of conscience the submerged
man revealed himself. All the boys' secret hopes and dreams,
fears and frustrations, were brought to light; from a Nazi
victim's lack of knowledge about America to an ex-delin-
quent's highjacked car. The underprivileged childhood, the
alcoholic mother, the faithless wife, the classmates' cruel
sobriquet, the rivalry with a stepfather, the brother in prison
—all were grist for the brainwasher's mill.

In Batchelor's case the Achilles heel seemed to be overblown
idealism and overblown self-esteem. He was flattered out of
all proportion by his appointment as monitor. His captors
praised him for his "mass line." They referred to him as a
"young Lenin." Batchelor would have been better off if someone had read to him the fable of the fox and the crow.

Batchelor's happiest moments in prison camp were those
when he was most completely divorced from reality. At an
age when many boys are Big Men on Campus, he was Big
Man in the Compound.

He was chairman of the Living Affairs Committee, dedicated to improving food, sanitation, and discipline. He was
a writer for the Chinese Communist publication *Toward
Truth and Peace*. Within the camp the Chinese were organiz-
ing a secret subversive organization which was to maintain
contact with the Communist Party after the war. Batchelor
was to be its future head. An amateur theatrical group was
organized among the prisoners, and Batchelor appeared in
various camp productions, sometimes going on tour with the
basketball team. The works of Clifford Odets were popular
with his captors, and Batchelor went onward and upward in
the arts in the role of Tom Moody in *Golden Boy*.

Meanwhile he was kept busy as a beaver writing letters
home and getting signatures on petitions. Within the limits
of his growing delusion he clung to some shred of integrity.
He was horrified to see that one boy's "voluntary" signature
to a peace petition was obtained after a three-hour detention

at Communist GHQ. He was so disillusioned that he burned the petition, only to start in afresh the next day collecting sixty authentic new names.

One of the charges leveled against him when he emerged from prison camp was his signing of a document charging America with the use of germ warfare. The propaganda pitch in P.O.W. camp was designed to convince maturer minds than his.

In prison camp Batchelor met a young lieutenant, one of thirty-six captured American aviators who were hounded into confessing that they had dropped germ bombs. This Communist dupe toured the prison camps lecturing to study groups and broadcasting to captive audiences over loudspeakers. He seems to have been so thoroughly indoctrinated that he himself finally believed what he was saying. G.I.'s more skeptical than Batchelor looked him over in vain for marks of the truncheon. "He looked perfectly healthy," one is reported to have said, "and there weren't any Chinese around to make him say anything he didn't want to say." Many returned progressives who, when they came home, repudiated all the works of the party still believed the germ-warfare story, a tribute to his impact as an exhibit.

This meeting inspired Batchelor to write an open letter in *Toward Truth and Peace* complimenting the lieutenant on his confession. His letter to the *Winkler County News,* his home-town newspaper, was written shortly thereafter.

> I beg, plead and implore you [he wrote] that you will publish this letter. . . .
>
> Undoubtedly you have heard of the controversial arguments concerning the American use of bacteriological warfare against the Korean and Chinese people. The hideousness of such a bestial crime does not have to be stressed, but I would like to remind you that once such a weapon is in use it endangers the lives of everyone. . . . Germ warfare is no longer a question, it is an established horrible reality. The profit-seekers in Washington are endangering our lives. The C.P.V. has given us various inoculations

against many types of diseases for our safety. Isn't it indeed humiliating that our so-called enemy has to protect us from our own misanthropic authorities?[6]

Batchelor suggests elsewhere in the letter that his father will surely volunteer to pay for publication of a message of such importance to humanity. As in the case of his comparison of Truman and MacArthur, one cannot say that he had his finger on the pulse of public opinion in America!

The way of the convert was not an easy one, and Batchelor underwent periods of great mental agony. Anyone tempted to dismiss this boy as a slick opportunist has only to read his prison-camp reminiscences. The guilt is here, all right; but it is not the guilt of one who has betrayed his buddy for thirty pieces of silver. This is the guilt of one who has seen the vision of the City of Man and wants with all his heart to be a part of it. The feeling of betrayal was always a feeling of betrayal of the *Communists*. He was a man who cried out in despair, "I believe, O Lord, please help my unbelief."

The first dark night of the soul came sometime after the "voluntary" signatures on the peace petition. The Chinese reluctance to send sick men to the hospital seemed to Batchelor at odds with their humanitarian sentiments. Occasionally he had doubts about inconsistencies in Communist books. Sometimes he even sensed that the preoccupation with "peace" might be just chimerical, another carrot dangled to lure converts into the fold.

Whenever illusion was threatened, the misery would descend. He was unable to concentrate, even in casual conversation. He had to keep asking people to repeat things. His mind wandered. He feared that he was going crazy. He contemplated suicide, took up marijuana, and at last wrote a letter withdrawing from the study group. He urged his superior to keep his withdrawal a secret so that the power of his example would not ruin the show for others. He was by this time supremely confident of his powers as a leader of public opinion.

He sent in his resignation by mail because he was afraid

his superiors would talk him into staying on. Whenever he strayed, Comrades Lim and Chang brought him smilingly back and made him toe the party line. These two apparently combined the eloquence of Demosthenes with the telepathic powers of J. B. Rhine. One could make strong men cry when he brought up incidents in their past. Batchelor remembered how he tried to keep this man from learning what he was thinking because "that would have given him something to work on."[7]

His captors retaliated to his resignation by isolating him from the rest of the camp. He was lectured endlessly about the Communists' nobility. One anecdote was told him about four "People's Fighters," one of whom got "berry berry" [sic] and had his "penice" [sic] bloat up from an infection while marooned behind enemy lines. An idealistic nurse sucked the poison from the inflamed member, by way of showing that no sacrifice was too great for the cause.

The Chinese were only partially successful in relieving his misery. Their technique was to snatch him out of the Valley of Despair by enlisting his aid in a new project. The doldrums about the study group were followed by the exciting meeting with the lieutenant who lectured on the germ bombs. It was his defections from the *Communists* that Batchelor regarded as lapses from grace. "After a month up there [in isolation]," he wrote, "I began to get in the sane way again."[8]

His first fall from grace was punished by an assignment of a 25-page "self criticism." It was read aloud and applause greeted his description of himself as "despicable, big-headed and a coward." "I didn't mean a word of it," he wrote later on. "My moral [sic] was still low."[9] Later he was offered a job in an area where the dedicated convert should not tread—interpretation of the news.

Batchelor was offered a job of editing broadcasts from Radio Moscow. He was forced to rely even for sports news on two-month-old *Daily Workers*. Once more doubt obscured the City of Man.

> I asked them why I could not listen to Radio Tokyo. Was there something the Communists were afraid I would find out about them? I said that they

claim that radio Tokyo is all lies and propaganda
so why should they be afraid for me to listen to
Radio Tokyo to see for myself?[10]

Batchelor and an A.P. correspondent began to lay plans to
escape. News of the prisoner exchange "Operation Little
Switch" convinced them that they would do better if they
stayed behind. It was at this point that the Communists dangled the leadership of the postwar P.O.W. organization. This
hit Batchelor in a vulnerable place—the ego. He was chosen,
he felt, "because I had the highest prestige among the men."
He discusses the qualifications of another candidate who had a
"mass line" of almost equal potency. Of another who was considered as his successor he remarked that he was the best
qualified "to take my place on this special project. However I
am not certain that he got the job."[11] He sounded like an
executive choosing a dynamic district manager to beef up a
branch office of General Motors. One blinks at the curious
way he combines Communist catchwords with the sales-team
terminology of the organization man.

As the larger-scale prisoner exchange, "Operation Big
Switch," approached, pressure was brought on the progressives
to remain in Red China. Again Batchelor wavered. He thought
he might continue his life work as a non-Communist Peace
Fighter. (Paul Robeson was cited as an example.) He was
offered an education and trips to Asia and Europe in return
for his aid in the cause of peace. He was given an intensive
working over. It was pointed out that he would not get along
for very long in America with a Japanese wife. He elected to
go to China.

All around him there was a great deal of doubt and soul-
searching. Debate about who was worthy of the privilege of
non-repatriation was carried on with the deadly intensity that
heralds a tap for Skull and Bones. Batchelor attempted to talk
one "non-repat" out of going because he felt him unequal to
the honor. A second was undecided, and another P.O.W. was
said to have asked Batchelor for permission to kill him. Still
another did not wish to go because he was afraid he would
miss his mother too much. This indomitable woman got as far

as Tokyo in an effort to dissuade him. Others were in one way or another feeling the tug of the umbilicus. A splinter group was secretly planning to go to North Korea, a project which had to be carefully concealed from the Chinese, who had very little time for the "individual heroist."

Batchelor moved through this babel outwardly wise and all-seeing. He took upon himself the role of the just and kindly moderator. When pressure was brought to bear on the doubter, Batchelor was horrified at the suggestion that he be killed. "I told him that we were not that kind of people."[12]

Batchelor describes how he hoped to save a mental inferior from Chang, the silver-tongued interrogator. The boy, in his opinion, didn't have the intellect to have any real political ideas and I felt for the kid for getting into such a mess and perhaps ruining his entire life."[13] Batchelor's own susceptibility to Chang's insidious persuasions might have been considerably lower if he hadn't been so busy playing God.

But the worm of doubt continued to nibble away. When the P.O.W.'s were transferred to the neutral zone, the Communists were no longer able to confiscate the prisoners' mail. But so great was their hold over their charges that they were able to persuade them to pile it under their beds unopened.

Batchelor began to wonder what was in the letters. He read an issue of his old favorite, the *Reader's Digest,* and came across an article on Communism by Whittaker Chambers. "Everything he said in this article seemed to be just about what I knew although I had not thought of it in that light before."[14] He was also shaken by Eisenhower's plan for control of atomic energy. Formerly such plans had always been represented as Communist firsts, to which America had contributed nothing but road blocks.

Curiosity at last got the better of him, and he took the letters into the latrine. He had always considered that his mother shared his views on the war, but on seeing her unbowdlerized opinions, he was appalled to discover that she was staunchly anti-Communist. He reread Marx and Lenin on religion and discovered that what in 1951 had appeared to be a plan for peaceful coexistence with the godly was actually a blueprint for doing away with them altogether.

Letters from his wife were widely credited with having been the straw that broke the camel's back. The Associated Press made a great point of Kyoko's letters—even, some sources say, to the point of having forged some of them from Tokyo. Batchelor himself claims that the only letter which he saw from Kyoko "even looked as if I could still get her to come to China."[15]

Toying with the idea of repatriation, Batchelor was assailed by doubts. On New Year's Eve 1953, he made his decision. He pleaded sick and went to the medical inspection room. Then he announced "I'm all right. I want to be repatriated." Of the twenty-three who initially decided to go to Red China, one had already reneged. Batchelor was the second to want out.

Kyoko was overjoyed. "I am a very happy New Year's girl," she said when she heard the news.[16] Great, too, was the rejoicing in Kermit. High school kids carried banners through the streets: "Claude B. is coming home, yay!"

Elsewhere Batchelor was not quite so cordially received on his return. His manner was offensive to the Americans. He spoke glowingly of the high esteem he had inspired in the Chinese. For some strange reason the first thing that he repudiated was his germ warfare statement. He was still proud of his role as a peace fighter and explained to *Time* reporters that he "just wanted to help the Communists advance some of their ideas such as that America was an aggressive nation and the Soviet Union was peaceful."[17]

Ugly tales were cited in the press about Batchelor's prison activities. One colleague claimed that Batchelor was a member of a "progressives' court" that had tried him in prison camp and recommended that he be shot. John J. Megeyesi and First Lieutenant Walter Mayor testified later at his trial that they had had a movie camera with which they were photographing Chinese atrocities, and that they had been thrown into solitary because an allied prisoner had informed on them to a prison official affectionately known as "the Screaming Skull." Megeyesi and Mayor did not identify the squealer. Staff Sergeant Bernard Buli claimed that it was Batchelor.

The Luce publications had it in for Batchelor. *Time* magazine compared him to a conscienceless seal, who flipped from democracy to Communism, and who, when it suited his convenience, flopped with ease right back again. *Life* published a photograph of some of Batchelor's fellow G.I.'s—a grim-jawed, snub-nosed bunch of virile young Americans with accusing stares and clenched fists, laying for the boy who had ratted.

In September 1954, at Fort Sam Houston, Claude Batchelor began his day in court. The charges against him fell into two categories. One involved his collaboration with the enemy, which the defense made no effort to dispute. The second concerned the "additional charges" of informing. Batchelor was represented by a San Antonio lawyer named Joel Westbrook, an intelligent and humane man who saw in the boy's case something of a personal cause.

The prosecution charged that because of Batchelor's informing, two G.I.'s who had thrown a brick through the progressive club window had been subjected to long and painful interrogation. The charges were all at odds with Batchelor's idealized self-portrait. "I have always played the game straight," he said, "and never committed acts against any of my fellow prisoners."[18] He aspired to a reputation as "a progressive that didn't squeal."[19]

The defense contended that Batchelor was insane at the time of his collaboration with the enemy. However, two army psychiatrists, Major Henry A. Segal and Colonel Albert J. Glass, examined Batchelor and pronounced that he was sane enough to know right from wrong. Col. Donald L. Manes, Jr., the court-martial law officer, pronounced Batchelor sane enough to be tried though he would not go out on a limb as to the boy's sanity when he collaborated. He threw out Westbrook's plea that Claude had been brainwashed. Brainwashing, he ruled, could be introduced for the purpose of showing character traits, not as a defense against the basic charges. The word "menticide" had not yet joined "megadeath" and "fallout" as commonplaces in the twentieth-century vocabulary of horrors.

Batchelor's guilt in the rock-throwing incident was never clearly established. The defense challenged the credibility of two prosecution witnesses, Corporal Robert H. Ghyers and

Sergeant Buli. Westbrook cited the opinion of a psychiatrist named Dr. Bloesma that Buli was suffering from a "fence complex syndrome," a mental illness common among P.O.W.'s which expressed itself in tales of fantasy.

Batchelor's syndrome seemed to be operating to protect him from unpleasant reality. After repatriation he wrote to G-2 offering his services to Army Intelligence and was startled when the letter turned up later amid the evidence against him. One searches his 30,000-word memoir of his prison experiences in vain for the names of Buli, Megeyesi, or Mayor. His record of walkaway triumphs in one election after another is devoid of any suggestion that he had his detractors. Syndrome or no syndrome, the faces of those boys in *Life* did not suggest that they had come to hand out first prize in a popularity contest.

While Batchelor was on trial the Defense Department was backing and filling on a vital question—whether psychological suasion had been used on P.O.W.'s, and to what extent individuals were responsible for their derelictions. Before this was settled, the army cheerily went ahead prosecuting collaborators. Colonel Frank Schwable, who signed a germ-warfare affidavit, was declared blameless by the Marine Corps, which then turned around and barred him from all positions of leadership. Corporal Dickenson, who threw in his lot with the West just before Batchelor, was dishonorably discharged and given ten years. The twenty-one remaining defectors to Red China were dishonorably discharged *in absentia*. In October 1954 Batchelor drew the stiffest penalty of all—life. Senator McCarthy was currently putting the heat on Fort Monmouth and Secretary Stevens. The severity of the sentence may have been the army's way of showing that it was not "soft on Communism."

Almost immediately voices were raised against the decision. A member of the draft board at Big Spring, Texas, resigned his job as a result of the decision. Major Segal, who testified as to Batchelor's sanity, had addressed the American Psychiatric Association a few months before. He had said then that the Communists were using psychiatric knowledge to produce drastic changes in men's fundamental beliefs. The man in the psychiatrist's hat was not in full agreement with the man in the soldier's helmet.

Other brainwashing authorities, Dr. Leon Freedom, Dr. David Keedy, and the author Edward Hunter, claimed that Batchelor had been deluded into thinking that he was doing the right thing. Dr. Joost A. Meerloo, a psychiatrist who had some firsthand experience with inquisitorial techniques under the Nazis, issued a warning in a book called *The Rape of the Mind*. Everyone has a breaking point. When the Communists discover it, you too, dear reader, will confess. Dr. Meerloo believed that behind the Iron Curtain whole nations of Claude Batchelors were suffering from "induced political psychosis."

One psychiatrist who disagreed with the army verdict saw in Batchelor evidence of megalomania, a Messianic complex, and delusions of grandeur. He cites the language of the letter to the *Winkler County News* as having been composed with "the deadly earnestness of the psychotic who tries to convince his neighbors and friends that St. Jude is putting sassafras in his tea."[20]

The techniques used on Batchelor were extraordinarily ingenious: first the conditioning phase, which involved a subtle torture of body, mind and emotion; next the indoctrination phase, which sent him off on Cloud Nine into the never-never land of political unreality. Some of the persuasions of Communist torturers sound straight out of Fu Manchu. However, Batchelor's torture chamber had no dripping water or Malay boot. Yet it softened him up for the library cards, study groups, bull sessions, peace petitions and basketball matches which, divorced from Pavlov, might have served him as instruments of intellectual growth.

There was another, more poignant side to the young Lenin. In P.O.W. camp the Communists tapped a region of Batchelor's mind never reached by the Winkler County public school system. After his repatriation his lawyer asked him to make out a reading list of books that had impressed him before, during and after captivity. The literary landmarks of his youth reveal a mind blissfully untouched by education.

At the age of twelve or fourteen, he was fascinated by a series of books about a boy called Tod Moran. Claude felt great sympathy for Tod, who shipped out on tramp steamers and always got the worst jobs to do because of his tender years, but who always ended by "gaining the respect and friendship of other responsible members on the boat." At fourteen or fifteen, he stayed up till four reading *Knock on Any Door.* Again, he felt empathy, this time for the twenty-one-year-old hero who was electrocuted for killing a cop. "Blame," he said, "did not seem to rest on any one person but on those conditions of life in which he lived." This work also had the effect of increasing his love for his mother and dramatizing the justice of her warnings about the dangers of getting in with the wrong set.

Next Claude tried *Night and the City,* an English novel which he didn't enjoy. "I couldn't understand many of the English terms and the book was involving prostitution in England—something I knew nothing about."

Then came the heady delights of Rosamond Marshall. "I remember very well a book that I read that I cannot remember the title of. It was either *Kitty* or *Duchess Hotspur* or at any rate, the same author who wrote *Kitty* wrote this book. Whether this book was *Kitty* and the same author wrote another book, I cannot recall. This book is, I beleive [sic] considered to be something of a semi-classical love story." The "semi-classical love story" filled him with a feeling that "life seemed to be strange" and with a disappointment that the sex scenes were never quite "to the point."

Other reading was confined to the comic books, the works of Erle Stanley Gardner and the *Reader's Digest.* One *Digest* piece inexplicably made a lasting impression on him. It was called "Can Coyotes Smell Guns?" The reading of his boyhood was sketchy, his reactions to it hardly profound. He had the vagueness about titles and authors common among nice old ladies who unwittingly shatter the sanity of bookstore personnel.

During Batchelor's thirty-eight months in prison camp, he read probably twenty or thirty times as much as he had read in his entire life. Fresh from the coyotes and *Duchess Hotspur* (or *Kitty,* as the case might be), he was plummeted into the works of Lenin, into *Socialism and the Individual.* He struggled to understand meaningless phrases. "The emancipation of the masses is the main condition for the emancipation of the individual." He moved his lips over unfamiliar words, "metaphysical," "proletariat," "oligarchy," "collectivization." Sometimes he lugged the heavy tomes back to the library in despair.

He particularly remembers *High Treason,* by Albert E. Kahn; *Peekskill, U.S.A.,* by Howard Fast; *The Great Conspiracy,* by Albert Kahn and Michael Sayers; *The Twilight of World Capitalism,* by William Z. Foster. Sometimes the classics of literature gave him a brief respite from politics. He read Tolstoy, Gorki, Hemingway, Steinbeck, and Twain. But after resting briefly on his oars he was always plummeted back into one of the two warring camps. On one hand there was the inferno of war-mongering capitalists, oppressed Negroes, and black-marketeering American diplomats. On the other was paradise—the People's Democracy in China, the newly "liberated" satellites, with their power stations, rest homes for workers, communal farms, and fringe benefits for working mothers. (Maternity care, for some strange reason, was a subject close to Batchelor's heart.)

In his reactions to what he read he revealed what his two years of high school had failed to do. The liquidation of the kulaks, the Moscow trials, are events he had obviously never heard of. He learned of the theory of Warren Gamaliel Harding's abrupt removal from the national scene in a book called *High Treason.* The events following the Teapot Dome scandal were covered here along with other mysterious deaths and suicides as the result of some monstrous capitalist plot to strip the Communists of their rights. He was unfamiliar with figures known to any cover-to-cover reader of *Life.* He refers to *Soviet Power* by the Dean of Canterbury: "I forget his name—something like Johnson." Stalin's *Problems of Leninism* confused him with its constant harping on the theme of revolution. "All I'd heard about revolutions before were the one in 1776 in America and some other ridiculous fantasies in the comic strip 'Li'l Abner.'"

He desperately wanted to believe every word of what he read. He turned to the writings of the great Communist masters in the hope that they would help him lick "this trouble of mine." As he battled his "trouble" he experienced the first feeble flutterings of curiosity and doubt.

For a youth so susceptible to flattery he was curiously unsophomoric. "The more I learned," he wrote, "the more I found that I was ignorant." In the old days his most usual reaction to a book was to want to see the movie. Now *For Whom the Bell Tolls* whetted his interest in the Spanish Civil War as well as in Ingrid Bergman.

He had always had a childish reverence for anything and everything he read. If you found it in a book, it must be true. At a considerable price in mental agony he began to develop skepticism toward the printed word.

There were puzzling and disturbing experiences. In the back of one history of the U.S.S.R. he came across an article by Joseph Stalin entitled *Dizzy from Success*. This contained some statements about the liquidation of the peasants, which Batchelor was too naïve to recognize as rationalizations. He modestly assumed that the lack was in him. He tried so conscientiously and unsuccessfully to understand the author's viewpoint that he eventually came back to the book to have another crack at it. Lo and behold, *Dizzy from Success* had disappeared!

> I looked around for *Problems of Leninism* to find this article and never found the book. I don't know what happened to it but the only copy of *Problems of Leninism* I found was a different edition without the articles of Stalin in the back.

Fancy that!

When he read about the satellites, his doubts about Cardinal Mindszenty were laid to rest by a book called *People's Democracies*. Others lingered on. "It seems as though there was something disagreeable about some election that was held. I cannot remember very much of it now, but I do remember that I couldn't read very much after that."

There were moments of outright rebellion. Of *The Berlin Question* he remarks, "Like much of the other stuff I read, it didn't seem to contain the key point. Seems like they tried to hide the key point under a lot of hooey about 'rights of the people' and denunciation of America."

The measure of Claude's critical growth could be seen from

the re-evaluation of an article on religion which he had read in 1951. Now, too, he began to notice the authors and titles of the books he read. A giant step toward evaluating the ideas in any given book is taken when one has some notion of who wrote it.

He began to consider the sources of statements he saw in print. He was impressed at the beginning by some glowing tributes quoted from the capitalist press about the achievements of the Five-Year Plan. Later he came to realize that such statements had little more meaning than the carefully edited raves from unknown reviewers which appear in ads for struggling books, plays, and movies.

He began to advance in self-expression and to write creditable English prose. His malapropisms and misspellings became more ambitious than the "berry berry" and "penice." "The government of Finland," he wrote, "seemed to be in cohesion with the Nazis."

Reading the memoirs of this lonely young scholar, one is touched by his struggles toward the light as he floundered amid suicidal capitalists, black-marketeering diplomats, and problems of Leninism. How different it would have been had he had the College Outline Series or a sympathetic teacher to guide him through the treacherous currents of opinion back to the bedrock of fact. Perverted as the aims of his teachers were, clever as they were at the game of rearranging history, there is a gloomy moral to be learned from his autobiography. He discovered more in the long run about democracy from his stay in Camp #5 than he would ever have learned in Kermit.

If the Communists won his mind for a short time, their long-range program of indoctrination was a miserable failure.

"What sounded good in P.O.W. camp don't sound good any more over here." Thus more than one G.I. has commented on the persuasions of the enemy. On their release most prisoners experienced something of the feeling of a returned city vacationer who has spent two weeks on a diet of nothing but village journalism. Even in a free society there is a sense of getting back to the "real" world that comes with the morning copy of the *New York Times*.

Batchelor's P.O.W. experiences colored everything he read

on his return. No one who has avoided prison camp could be as disturbed as he was by Orwell's *Nineteen Eighty-Four*. A book called *Japan and America* gave him an insight into the edited version of experience he had been getting from the Communists. This book admitted that the American Army of Occupation had scattered its seed prodigally about Japan. For the first time he learned that the callous imperialists had set up an agency to care for illegitimate Japanese babies.

His political views have taken on a new independence. *Uncle Tom's Cabin* failed to inflame him because he had observed a dwindling of anti-Negro prejudice in the American Army. He watched the Army-McCarthy hearings, and said of McCarthy, "I believe that it is men like him that tend to make more Communists than destroy them."

His reactions to Carl Van Doren's *The Great Rehearsal* show a simple understanding of what he read which augurs well for the future. He writes of the framers of the Constitution: "The men who through debates, compromises, etc., made up our constitution all had each his own specific interest in mind. The interests of some were the best for the people at large. The interests of others were for their own particular state and others had their own selfish interests at heart. It was for the interests of all to come to a common agreement for the protection of each of these interests, without which it was probable that all might fail.

"I do not have to explain further why this book was so interesting to me."

Elsewhere he expresses his feeling of guilt for his activities in prison camp even though they were "not much and not very effective." This phrase alone speaks volumes. The young Lenin had at last come back to earth.

As with Harold Russell, war had given him an education that was truly liberal. His background occasionally betrayed him, as when he confused Secretary of State George Marshall with the author of *Mr. Jones, Meet the Master*, an unexpected laurel for the author of the Marshall Plan. But he was reading and thinking for himself.

As a final footnote to his reading list he remarks that he

has trouble with the prose of James Gould Cozzens. This is true of a good many other Americans who have come upon *By Love Possessed* without toughening up their attention spans on *Socialism and the Individual.*

Batchelor's life sentence was commuted to twenty years, then to ten years, and finally to seven, and in May 1958 he was transferred to civilian custody. Early in 1959 he was paroled. In the years following his sentence the realization had slowly spread that he was a political innocent who had been more sinned against than sinning.

The realization also spread that in the twentieth century, such a degree of political innocence was nothing short of suicidal. Books and articles were written on the subject of his twenty-one fellow "non-repats," exploring the motives of anyone who would choose Communism over the best of all possible worlds.

Certain patterns emerge in the life stories of these twenty-one renegades from democracy. Three were Negroes, the rest were white. Sixteen were Protestant, four Roman Catholic, one Greek Orthodox. None were Jewish. Twenty had never heard of Communism except as a dirty word. Twenty had no idea what they were fighting for in Korea. Eighteen had grown up in poverty. Sixteen came from small towns or rural communities. Seventeen never finished high school. Sixteen came from broken homes. Nineteen felt unloved or unwanted by fathers or stepfathers. Only one was ever chosen by his classmates for anything. Fifteen were under twenty-one when they were captured. Nineteen were considered undereducated by teachers—no matter what grade they had attained in school. Five were veterans of the Second World War. Prior to dishonorable discharge following Korea, two had won the Bronze Star for heroism.[21]

"Communism is the faith of the cities," said Whittaker Chambers. Yet the urban intellectual is hardly represented among the twenty-one. The closest any of these boys got to the concrete jungle was Akron or Detroit. The real sitting duck for the Communists was the boy who had little reason to remember his country kindly—starved for affection, underedu-

cated, and a nonentity to his classmates. He was less likely to
be a gum-chewing subway rider than a small-town lone wolf.

Batchelor came from a relatively stable home and a relatively prosperous family. He certainly suffered from acute
undereducation. He and the "non-repats" were extreme cases.
But in Batchelor's narrative one can read between the lines
ugly evidence of general moral softness among the G.I.'s—in
the shirking of details, the avoidance of exercise (those who
did an occasional push-up usually lived longer), in the condition of the compound, which repelled even the Chinese, who
had not had our advantages in the field of plumbing. Dysentery was widespread, and many of the boys didn't make it to
the latrines. The Chinese, according to Batchelor, suggested
a disciplinary patrol for those "who was dropped their waist
[sic] all over the area and didn't clean it up."[22]

The very standard of living for which the boys were fighting
was often their worst enemy. The far lower death rate of the
Turks may have been partly due to the fact that the wretched
prison camp food wasn't too different from what they had
been used to at home.

The Defense Department did not dismiss its Batchelors
lightly. The *New York Herald Tribune* told of an advanced
training course designed to teach the Air Force how to survive
under primitive conditions. Pilots were dropped in the middle
of the Sierra Nevada Mountains, imprisoned in a mock P.O.W.
camp, interrogated by mock brainwashers, ratted on by mock
informers, and told to escape and get themselves back to the
pick-up point as best they could. They were provided with
helpful hints: how to make a tent or a snare out of a parachute;
how to make a deer trap out of a flattened ration can; how to
make a nutritious meal out of a cockroach or a porcupine.
Boys who were perfectly at home in the air at seven hundred
miles an hour became hungry, helpless, and mad when confronted by the tests of the frontier. The civilized viewpoint
was the greatest obstacle to survival. Overcome your prejudices, boys, they were told in effect, let's see everyone tuck
into that rattlesnake!

Collaboration with the enemy was a polio of the spirit which had its greatest ravages among those accustomed to chlorine, hot tubs, and Anahist. A great deal depended too upon the intangible known as morale. The army attempted an indoctrination program to inspire the boys with the virtue of their cause. They were subjected to lengthy lectures on the evils of communism, the Declaration of Independence, the Bill of Rights, the Constitution, and the responsibility of citizenship. Yet there was a feeling that something more was needed than a rehash of high school civics.

Other substitutes were suggested—a more rigorous military training with more emphasis on spit, polish, and pride in the unit. Some military authorities wished to play the Communists' own game by capsulizing American freedoms and Communist evils in simple arresting phrases, to keep firing word-bullets at trainees, until they slavered like good Pavlovian dogs at the sight of the flag and snarled at the hammer and sickle.

The P.O.W. experience brought discussion back to William Buckley's problem of "value inculcation." It became increasingly obvious that it was unfair to educate a boy to the level of Claude Batchelor, snatch him out of the classroom, induct him into the army, force him to spend his most impressionable years in the Far East, wave a flag in front of him, and expect him to behave like Joan of Arc in the equivalent of the Sierra Nevada exercises, when the game went on for thirty-eight months and was played for keeps.

For many years "indoctrination" had been a dirty word, but many succumbed to Red blandishments because they didn't know what they were fighting for. It was evident that the G.I. had to be strongly dedicated to something to make the enormous sacrifices demanded of him seem worth while.

More educated youths than Batchelor boggled at life in Korea. A Princeton senior who wrote under the cloak of anonymity in *The Un-Silent Generation,* described Korea as a prison for the "fifty thousand loneliest men in the world." He got off some highly articulate opinions on Korea's freezing tents, knee-high mud, remote shower points, and malodorous natives. Most of the G.I.'s who fought in Korea, he said, had no idea of what they were doing there. Short of outright war it would take "a court order and an armed platoon" to get this Ivy Leaguer back into the army again. This was an intelligent youth who had never experienced the horrors of prison camp. Small wonder that Claude Batchelor bit, when he was told that the Korean War was unpopular.

Several of Batchelor's fellow "non-repats" got as far as Red China and decided to come home. A few were freshly aware of the rights of the individual; but many were prompted by a nostalgia for TV and morning coffee. This raises the unpleasant possibility that more boys will defect from the Paradise of Creature Comforts the minute the Reds can offer them Chase and Sanborn and *I Love Lucy*.

When one is not quite sure of one's total commitment, the teachings of childhood sometimes come to the rescue. Batchelor repudiated the fundamentalist Protestantism of his youth; but a feeling of good will toward religion made him see through the sophistries of Russia's so-called supporters of the Deity. As a point of departure one has to take something on faith. The open mind is not to be confused with the *tabula rasa*.

Perhaps a combination of intelligently instilled religious principles and rigorous habits of scholarly skepticism offer the best hope for the future. The experiences of the prison camps should be revealing to those followers of William Buckley who would protect the young by shutting up the Socialist professor and "screening" the visiting speaker. Those who chose Red China were more susceptible to Communist arguments *because* they had never heard of Communism except as a dirty word. Their Pavlovian snarls at the sound of the word "Commie" subsided when they saw that their captors did not really eat their own young.

Among those many patriotic Americans who kept their equilibrium in the brainwashing chambers were, surprisingly enough, a large percentage of Negroes. A whole company of Negroes, drawn from all the prison camps, were put into an enclosure to be worked over *en masse*. The plan backfired. They were annoyed at being segregated. Furthermore, as one of them said, "a lot of our boys had been worked over by the Communists at home. They knew the answers and they gave the rest of us the benefit of their experience."[23] With little formal education and with less reason than most to love their country, their hard-won political sophistication stood them in good stead. It is a great mistake of the patriot to believe that ignorance is strength.

Today Claude Batchelor lives in San Antonio, Texas. He divorced his Japanese wife, remarried in 1961, and is now the father of a baby girl.

Before moving to San Antonio, he lived in Andrews, Texas, a small town near Kermit. He worked for an accountant for six months and later did odd jobs. He still finds much in common with his childhood friends. He currently works for a manufacturing firm which makes hospital casework and laboratory furniture. He has progressed from the duties of a common laborer to the mysteries of cost accounting and price estimating. When his parole situation was being reviewed, the Executive Vice-President of his company described him as a "career employee" and gave him an efficiency rating of "outstanding." Prison camp seems like a place he lived in a long time ago.

Batchelor was away from Texas between 1948 and 1959. He found on his return that nothing was the same. Wandering in and ordering a cup of coffee was a strange new experience. Going down the street for a walk was an activity which branded him as an eccentric. During his years in prison, automated America had lost the use of its feet.

Other things too had changed in America.

Gone was the day when the young could shrug off the rest of the world with a peace parade—when the Pentagon's plans were of interest to nobody but the readers of Foreign Affairs. As the shrinking world encroached on Kermit, parents and teachers were in the front lines. The older generation was endlessly cautioned about its power to create "syndromes," "performance factors," "Oedipus complexes," "insecurity" and "neurotic guilt." It wasn't enough for a boy to learn to shoot a gun in this day of "induced political neuroses." The infant science of psychology had become a Frankenstein monster. Freud and Krafft-Ebing had invaded the domain of Major George Fielding Eliot.

The sight of Claude Batchelor, uneasy in the mantle of

Lenin, might have given pause to Edna Millay, as she and the free spirits at the Hell Hole fought the good fight against repression. F. Scott Fitzgerald, sipping apéritifs on the Riviera, would have been stunned to see his successors counting the calories in cockroaches. Lindbergh with the future spreading gloriously before him, as he came down Broadway in a blizzard of paper, would have denied the bitter knowledge of later life—that the child of the jet age stands perilously close to the cave.

Batchelor might have given a few hints at those indoctrination sessions for the Air Force. Compared with the mistresses of the French kings, American history isn't very interesting. But when one comes to Philadelphia out of the backwash of the October Revolution, the old clichés take on a new meaning. The scorched plains, the army camps, the bright new skyscrapers of Texas appear in a fresh perspective when one has been relegated, fairly or unfairly, to the special hell of the rice Christian.

'The Hemingway time was a good time to be young."
After the Lost Generation, by John W. Aldridge

"Somewhere along the way tomorrow had been lost."
After the Lost Generation

14

The Disillusioned Rebel

JOHN W. ALDRIDGE

The jacket of one of John Aldridge's books describes him as "a conscious seeker after the stimulus of heresy." In the conformist 1950's this puts him in a class with Diogenes in search of an honest man. Unlike the Harold Russells and the Haywood Pattersons, he came through a war and a depression without any visible scars. Unlike Charles Lindbergh and Whittaker Chambers, he was never moved to change the course of events in the cockpit of a monoplane or the last car of a subway train. Yet more than many of those in the middle of the fray, he was aware of what his era was doing to him; for he was born with an acute period sense and a talent for sitting on the sidelines of history and making intelligent notes.

He was born with a sense that he was living in the tail end of the twenties. Like many of the Lost Generation writers whom he admired, he was a young man from the provinces.

He was born in Sioux City, Iowa, on September 26, 1922. Between 1934 and 1940 he lived on a farm outside of Chattanooga, Tennessee. He had the intellectual's sense of isolation from his schoolmates, but learned early to hide it. He read science fiction and wrote poetry surreptitiously, while chewing tobacco and rolling cigarettes in public. "It was the old story of doubleness and mask," he recalls. In 1940 he won a scholarship to the University of Chattanooga. Here, amid classmates of alarming precocity, he was at last able to come out in the open and admit that he had a mind.

His campus experiences belong to a bygone age of the college maverick. He became editor of the school paper and lost out on a student loan because of a scathing review of a history book written by the college president. "I was living at the time in an office building as a caretaker and working as an elevator operator at the Y.M.C.A.," he recalls, "and sitting alone in a dark building writing frenzied poetry and reading. I was also trying to have love affairs and discover who I was besides Eugene Gant."[1]

Like many of his generation he turned to Hemingway and Wolfe to learn of life with a capital L. He and his friends could quote backwards and forwards from the writers of the Lost Generation. They deluged their English instructors with slice-of-life stories in the Hemingway manner, featuring prostitutes, pimps, and prizefighters, men cooly sipping Anis del Toro and women confessing to unrealized Lesbianism. They drank black coffee, reminisced about Château-Thierry and the Battle of the Marne (which none of them was old enough to remember). They were on intimate terms with a vast gallery of literary characters. Their seductions as well as their stories were inspired by Papa's clipped dialogue and pugilistic morals, and by girls who got drunk and tried to emulate the defiant nymphomania of Lady Brett.

Aldridge later went overseas with the Third Army. He eventually got his degree from the University of California at Berkeley. He has taught English at the University of Vermont, at Sarah Lawrence, the New School for Social Research, Queens College, and N.Y.U. He has been connected with a formidable variety of erudite projects—seminars, writers' conferences, editing Wodehouse stories for the Modern Library, contributing to literary magazines from *Harper's* to *Mandrake* —and has rubbed elbows with the high muck-a-mucks of literary criticism.

In working on his current novel, he has had ample opportunity to observe the decline of revolt among the young and the domestication of the avant-garde in the senior common room. These topics form the subject of *After the Lost Generation* and *In Search of Heresy*—his two penetrating, book-length "think pieces."

After the Lost Generation, published in 1951, describes the death of the little world of Ernest Hemingway. The heroine of Aldridge's college days was Lady Brett Ashley. Her frenetic amours and the sexual inadequacies of her would-be lover, Jake Barnes, furnished the plot of Hemingway's great Lost Generation novel *The Sun Also Rises*. In the fifties, this star-crossed pair suffered a Hollywood reincarnation in the comely, wooden shapes of Ava Gardner and Tyrone Power. "When I was in college in the Forties," Mr. Aldridge wrote in the *Sarah Lawrence Alumnae Bulletin*, "Hemingway's Brett Ashley . . . glamorized sexual promiscuity for all those who had not yet had the opportunity for it as well as for those who wanted to enjoy the thrill of it without going into the expense of it. . . . She made the extremes of sensation appear to be the mean, and allowed us to imagine for a while that we too could live life at the extremes of grace."

On coming back from the war, however, Aldridge discovered that Lady Brett was an anachronism, that Papa's magic had lost its spell. Young women who a few years before, fired by Brett's example, were intent on losing their virtue, now took refuge in a "fatigued virginity." Their fatigue was mirrored in an equally weary literature.

The stimulus to revolt was gone. There was nothing brave about defying convention when there were no conventions left to defy. Aldridge had lived in expectation of a Brave New Postwar World of transition, adventure, and revolt. When he returned from the war he saw little evidence that the golden age was at hand. After corresponding exhaustively with several similarly disenchanted friends, he concluded that he had "been keeping alive and making love to an illusion."

Sherwood Anderson and Hemingway could report on a

sexual revolution in the days when one could still shut one's
eyes to back-seat dalliance and wife-swapping at the local
country club. The Victorian novel, as he continued in the
Sarah Lawrence *Bulletin,* had been concerned "with the de-
piction of manners in a more or less fixed class of society." In
the twenties the modern novel could still shock Mrs. Grundy
with the "exposure of truth, no matter how harsh, of the
human predicament." The Victorian novel "had seemed to
walk on tip toe around the facts; the new novel blundered
heavy-footed through them." By the mid-century, however,
the bloom had worn off two of the favorite themes of the Lost
Generation: the changing social scene and the horrors of
modern warfare. In *After the Lost Generation* Mr. Aldridge
demolishes some of the heavy-footed blunderings of his mid-
century writing contemporaries.

He tucks into the "effete and tremulous" outpourings of
Truman Capote; the contrived copulations, the rigged suicides,
devised by Merle Miller, "journalist of sham"; the sterility
masked by Frederick Buechner, behind the elaborate trappings of the legend of the Fisher King. Robert Lowry and
Alfred Hayes are dismissed as "neo-Hemingways," who ape
the Master's mannerisms without his genius. John Horne
Burns, Irwin Shaw, Gore Vidal, Paul Bowles, and others are
doomed to a literary limbo where they dish up a stale diet of
warmed-over naturalism and rewrite *A Farewell to Arms.*

> They have seen pedantry, obscurantism and snob-
> bery sprout like anemic flowers from the dead
> health of Stein and Joyce. They have learned that
> after the innovators come the specialists and after
> the specialists the imitators, and that after a move-
> ment has spent itself there can only come the in-
> cestuous, the archaeologists and the ghouls.[2]

Aldridge's second book, *In Search of Heresy,* describes the
new conformism which has replaced the old literary values
of disaffiliation and dissent. In the twenties any novelist had
but to find out what the mass of people were for and to protest against it. In the fifties the indignant intellectual had been

absorbed into the universities, where his output had been infected with the paralyzing pedagogical touch. The university has spawned the incestuous campus exposé: Mary McCarthy's *The Groves of Academe*, Randall Jarrell's *Pictures from an Institution*, whose scope is limited to the after-class backbiting of the in-group on Faculty Row. The novelist crass enough to try to reach a mass audience through the pages of *Mademoiselle* forfeits his membership in what Aldridge calls "the Kenyon-Sewanee hierarchy of distinguished young writers."

The mixed press which greeted Mr. Aldridge's first novel *Party at Cranton* in 1960, suggests that he, too, may have strolled the Quadrangle too long. Comments ranged from the Chicago *Tribune's* "devoid of life or interest" to the *Commonweal's* "heady and accomplished piece of writing."

The party at Cranton was a faculty party at a small university. The talk to the uninitiate was a little bit special. The *New Yorker* was annoyed by references to "persons, places, situations, circumstances, habits and jokes not known to the ordinary reader." Virginia Kirkus advised the book trade that it "might have been written by one of the Cranton set."[3]

The creative John Aldridge seems to have a membership card in that coterie of survivors of the "brave little magazines that died to make verse free." The critic John Aldridge yearns for the vigor of *transition* and *Broom*. The Double-crostic is a shoddy substitute, as are Norman Cousins' platitudes about the brotherhood of man and the columns for the fanciers of woofers and tweeters.

Outside the ivory tower the picture is even gloomier. The novelist is forced to dramatize the undramatic values of conformity, tolerance, and security. In the *Sarah Lawrence Alumnae Bulletin*, Aldridge describes the campus type which has arisen since the "Hemingway time."

> The average American college student . . . is a contented, wholesome, well rounded, healthy, emotionally sluggish individual who, if female, seems to be complacently heading for a babies and Bendix split-level paradise. And if male, a safe and permanent nest in a benevolent corporation, guaranteeing the maximum of fringe benefits.

The novelist who attempts to dramatize the conflicts of this emotional vegetable ends up with something like Herman Wouk's *Marjorie Morningstar* or Sloan Wilson's *The Man in the Gray Flannel Suit,* which, according to Aldridge, "confirm the prejudices of the mass of people, and . . . make them like what they're stuck with." Conflict, in these paeans to the commuter-hero, is reduced to a tense session with the first-of-the-month bills; a showdown with a vicious boss; a roll in the hay with an unscrupulous Bohemian—after which the protagonists end up happy in the local P.T.A. and in a life of nirvana and mulching.

The feeling of empathy between the mid-century college student and the man in the gray flannel suit is shown in a letter to the *New York Herald Tribune.* A Columbia student explains the goal of what has sometimes been called the "non generation."

> Briefly stated, it is directed at the solution of the following problem: how to infuse into the gray flannel suit an enduring vitality of life so as to preserve a heritage of freedom in an ever increasing complexity of the Behemoth state without, at the same time, undermining its authority.[4]

Life was certainly more complicated than in Mr. Aldridge's day, when all a fellow had to worry about was "who he was besides Eugene Gant."

In Search of Heresy shows the influence of two more sociological views of mid-century conformism: *The Organization Man,* by William Whyte, and *The Lonely Crowd,* by David Riesman. Both of them "portray a culture whose very essence is undramatic and passive." *The Lonely Crowd* in particular is recommended by Mr. Aldridge as "a book which no novelist at the present time can safely ignore . . . for it may be read as a record of the disappearance from our culture of the social forms which have traditionally afforded the novel its dramatic materials."[5]

David Riesman is one of the most provocative and widely quoted thinkers of twentieth-century America. His ideas are discussed on the slick pages of *Look* magazine and on the scratchier surfaces of more rarefied publications. Riesman has set business girls to talking about "peer groups" and has put such sociological terms as "inner-directed" and "other-directed" on a par with the "inferiority complex" and the "defense mechanism" in the glossary of the newsstand sciences.

To the cyclical population theories of Toynbee and Spengler Riesman has now added the S-curve. The demographic history of the human race has, according to Riesman, in the past, gone in three stages. The bottom line of the S represents the "tradition-directed society" of, say, Europe in the Middle Ages, where the number of births equals roughly the number of deaths and where both are very high. The vertical bar represents the "inner-directed society" where improved sanitation has brought about a vast increase of births over deaths, causing a "population explosion." This is what has happened in the West beginning with the seventeenth century. The top bar of the S represents the societies where the birth rate slows down and population growth is again small, this time because birth and deaths are both low. At this point "the other-directed" man makes his appearance.

At all stages of the S-curve, society produces the kind of person the economy needs. Primitive civilizations at the bottom are slavishly guided by what has happened in the past. Societies in the "transitional" stages of population growth are conditioned by the teachings of their parents and dedicated toward certain clearly defined goals such as money, possessions, power, knowledge, goodness, fame. Finally, as the birth rate begins to follow the death rate downward, man finds himself "in a centralized, and bureaucratized society and a world shrunken and agitated by the contact—accelerated by industrialization—of races, nations and cultures."[6]

The economy now requires consumers of goods rather than producers. At this point, the "other-directed" type emerges— the man whose goals are set by his contemporaries, by friends and acquaintances, whose opinions are, in turn, influenced by the mass media. Subjugation to one's parents is replaced by subjugation to the "peer group." It is Dr. Spock rather than Mother who "knows best." Life becomes an endless popularity contest, with the child competing for the acclaim of his classmates in playschool; the man competing for the admiration of the others on the "sales team"; the boss seeking to appear lovable to his secretary. Mr. Riesman's "other-directed man" or the "organization man" (to use Mr. Whyte's label) is forced to handle his contemporaries "as customers who are always right."[7]

It is in the other-directed world of the lonely crowd that the mid-century novelist is forced to function. The young people in this book who grew up in the twenties, thirties, and forties were pilgrims en route to Riesman's gray new world. The plight of the sick men of letters reflects the plight of the sick men of life. They were manipulated by the same social forces which turned Lady Brett Ashley into Marjorie Morningstar.

Riesman as a sociologist and Aldridge as a literary critic have both noted youth's drift in the direction of "pleasureless respectability." Both of them have ignored two great forces at work on the American personality which have done their share toward making young people old before their time. One is the influence of modern science and the other is the influence of American foreign policy. Aldridge concedes that scientific discoveries in the twenties had their effect on the behavior of Jake and Brett. He writes in the *Sarah Lawrence Alumnae Bulletin:*

> . . . the rise of modern science and particularly modern psychological techniques helped to create an atmosphere of realism and truth which seemed to clear the air of the reticence, politeness and evasiveness of the Victorian novel and to promote the outhouse realism of the modern novel.

It was modern science which had put sex into the realm of things to be discussed and explored. It was science that replaced the Ten Commandments with the analyst's couch and the caseworker's notebook. It was science that turned "Thou shalt not covet thy neighbor's wife" into a vocabulary of jawbreaking Riesmanisms—and that made sex an activity to be studied and tabulated for its varying degrees of "interpersonal emotion." It was science that produced the best-selling *Kinsey Report*, where the statistical method was applied to such hitherto tabu subject matter as the amours of farm boys and goats. It was science that permitted Brett to horrify the Victorians with her forthright discussions of Jake's problem; for it was science that put Jake's impotence into the public domain.

It is Mr. Aldridge's belief that the idea of scientific progress died at the end of the nineteenth century. Perhaps among philosophers it did; yet it lingered on at the *Saturday Evening Post* level, providing a vision of a hopeful future that paradoxically banked the fires of protest. As Margaret Marshall wrote on Fitzgerald's death, the vision took one form in the twenties.

> The post-war intellectuals . . . were destroying the past to make way for the future. The outlines of that future were obscured by the blazing light of the October Revolution, but its portent was certainly socialism, freedom, the good life, art, music, love and it was not far off.[8]

In the thirties the idea of the "perfectibility of history" spread its radiance over the figures of the noble sandhog, and for this we have no less an authority than Mr. Aldridge himself. He describes those novels of the depression that featured

> the prescribed stereotype capitalists who were always bad, and the crowds of decent, clean-cut workers who were always depicted at the end, marching triumphantly, their picks on their shoulders, the Internationale on their singing lips, up out of the valley of oppression into the ruddy dawn of the new proletarian tomorrow.[9]

In both the twenties and the thirties, "tomorrow" was the operative word. The protest movement was a romanticization of despair; and literary despair becomes considerably less romantic when "tomorrow" is something that only the strong of stomach dare to contemplate.

"What a rotten time we've all had," says Jake to Lady Brett in the course of one of their discussions of his problem. The scene is an army hospital during the first World War. Brett has just told of having lost a fiancé in the war. She is dressed in the inevitable Hemingway uniform of a Red Cross nurse. As played by a becomingly lighted Ava Gardner, the whole scene might be taken from a recruiting poster for Woman's Most Rewarding Career.

It was the scientist who brought down the curtain on this romantic scene by deglamorizing modern warfare. What is Jake's problem as compared with the prospect of ICBM's and unborn generations of two-headed children? What horror can a protest novelist dream up in the 1950's to rival the horrors in a family newspaper? The scientists who made it possible to discuss Jake's difficulties at all have also robbed them of their poignancy. The atomic age has dated Hemingway's noble prostitutes and disemboweled mules, his *castrati* and his brave nurses with the quivering lips. Papa has become as dead as a W.P.A. post-office mural, and what really killed him was the Bomb. The wave of scientific skepticism has receded. The tides of fashion are ebbing away from the rebellious, the experimental, and the "futuristic"—from the protest novel, the lower-case sentence, the double profile, and the progressive school.

With the rise of modern science a new loop has been added to Riesman's S-curve. Never before in history has the human race had so much power to change the balance of nature. The civilizations of Greece and Rome were Riesman's models for the period of population decline. But the ancients were not equipped with antibiotics and atomic rockets. Their control over their environment was limited to what they could accomplish by means of infanticide and drains.

The development of the Soviet satellite has presented man with some staggering possibilities. The provincial writer is dead, says Mr. Aldridge, and the age of the heroes is over. Yet the day may not be far off when the earth itself will become a province of the solar system, when adventurous young men will take off into space in pursuit of knowledge and fame, with their eyes on the distant stars. And their names may be Igor or Dimitri rather than Charles Augustus.

Science has certainly contributed to the demise of the carefree youth. For there is also another possibility that will put an end once and for all to Mr. Aldridge's speculations about the future of the novel. The Harold Russells of the Third World War will be lucky if their hands are *all* they lose. The next postwar generation will not be, like Scott and Zelda, fleeing the booboisie amid the ruins of Chartres. They will have been superseded by figures in bearskins carrying hatchets rather than Baedekers.

The hope of our civilization, says Mr. Riesman, is the "autonomous personality." Autonomous types are capable at any given time of transcending the culture in which they live. "The autonomous person's acceptance of social and political authority is always conditional: he can cooperate with others in action while maintaining the right of private judgment." Modern totalitarianism, says Mr. Riesman, "must wage total war on autonomy—with what ultimate effectiveness we do not know."[10]

The political history of the atomic age was the story of a total war waged ruthlessly against anyone who could take authority or leave it. It was a struggle in which no American could afford to remain a neutral. This realization had certainly had its effect upon the "structure of personality." If society produces the type the economy needs, it is also sensitive to the demands of the State Department.

In *After the Lost Generation* Mr. Aldridge devotes considerable space to what he calls the "spectatorial attitude" of the First World War generation. Frederick Henry, hero of Hemingway's *A Farewell to Arms*, expresses the spectatorial attitude when he says, "This war did not have anything to do with me. It seemed no more dangerous to me than war in the movies."[11]

For Malcolm Cowley, "war was in a class with the display of Moroccan horsemen given for our benefit on the Fourth of July before we all sat down at a long table to toast *la France héroique* and *nos amis Americains* in warm champagne."[12]

With America's rise to the position of a leading world power, the spectatorial attitude became passé. No longer did America produce romantic innocents to blush at the Paris *spectacle*, and to weep over death among the poppies as at mutilation in a soap opera. The postwar era, gloomily preoccupied with the time-consuming mechanics of survival, produced instead a generation of middle-aged bill payers. The personalities of young Americans were formed, more than they realized, by the ambassadors abroad who had led them from spectatorship to involvement in foreign affairs—by Wilson, the innocent among the riverboaters, by Roosevelt the practical idealist; by Dulles, the testy international prefect passing out gold stars and raps on the knuckles, to the naughty nations of Europe for maltreating Algeria, withdrawing from NATO, defeating Poujade, or tripling the production of Volkswagens. A whole generation was unconsciously aged by the knowledge that they could not, like Mr. Wilson, pick up their marbles and go home when the bad boys of Europe brought out the marked deck and the dirty pictures.

Politically and scientifically postwar youth had its troubles in Riesman's Gray New World. The young people in this book were also affected by two trends of which Aldridge and Riesman have written exhaustively. The first is Riesman's switch from the age of "inner-direction" to the age of "other-direction," or what Whyte calls the switch from the "Protestant ethic" to the "social ethic." The second great trend is what Aldridge has described as the decline of protest.

The "inner-directed man" of letters, as described in *The Lonely Crowd,* was primarily concerned with shake-ups of class. As people poured into the cities "the novel begins to concern itself with subtle class differences between individuals: rises, falls, and collisions of status."[13]

F. Scott Fitzgerald lived in just such an age of shifting possibilities, for the early Fitzgerald was among the last of the inner-directed men. Fitzgerald's early novels describe collisions of class, because there were still classes left to collide. Fitzgerald's snobbism may offend the reader who subscribes to what Aldridge calls the "egalitarian frenzy," but "collisions of status" furnish him with subject matter denied to the modern novelist who is deprived of the turn-at-the-roast dinner-table ethic of Emily Post's Mrs. Oldname.

Fitzgerald's youth was spent in a bygone age of inner-direction which was noteworthy, among other things, for its

Spartan schooling. School in the age of inner-direction was a little torture-chamber-away-from-home.

> Home, school, and way-stations between may be places for hazing, persecution, misundertanding,

says Riesman of those dear old Golden Rule days.

> No adult intervenes on behalf of the lonely or hazed child . . . No sociometrically inclined teacher will try to break up friendship cliques in school to see that no one is left out . . . Often the children, unaware that they have rights to friendship, understanding or agreeable play . . . suffer in silence and submit to the intolerable.[14]

Now listen to old schoolmaster Fitzgerald admonishing the unhappy Andrew Turnbull:

> The mouth tight and the teeth and lips together is a hard thing, perhaps one of the hardest stunts in the world, but not a waste of time because most of the great things you learn in life are in periods of enforced silence. . . . Remember to think straight. The crowd at camp is probably right *socially* and you are probably wrong.[15]

The problems of *The Great Gatsby* belong to the age of inner-direction.

The inner-directed man, says Riesman, pursues the bluebird in the form of money, possessions, power, knowledge, goodness, and fame. In his quest he is aided by the "internalized pocket watch that he has substituted for the chimes of the Middle Ages."[16]

After the death of the Great Gatsby, Mr. Gatz shows Nick Carraway the schedule Gatsby made out for himself as a boy.

It was dated September 12, 1906, and presented the following time table:

Rise from bed 6.00 A.M.
Dumbbell exercise and wall-scaling 6.15–6.30
Study electricity, etc. 7.18–8.15
Work 8.30–4.30 P.M.
Baseball and sports 4.30–5.00
Practice elocution, poise and how to attain it
5.00–6.00
Study needed inventions 7.00–9.00

GENERAL RESOLVES

No wasting time at Shafters or (a name, inde-
cipherable)
No more smoking or chewing
Bath every other day
Read one improving book or magazine per week
Save $5.00 (crossed out) $3.00 per week
Be better to parents[17]

Clocking himself by this "internalized watch," Gatsby rose
to fame, to fortune, and to final annihilation at the edge of
the swimming pool. His career illuminates the "collisions of
status" of a whole society. The old morality clashes with the
new sophistication. The respectable wealth of the coupon
clipper vies with the suspect riches of the bootlegger. The
country cousin tries to emulate the city slicker. The clashes
between Gatsby and the citizens of West Egg are as real as
any of Jane Austen's, though they take place over the Bronx
cocktails instead of the afternoon teacups.

By the time Fitzgerald wrote *The Last Tycoon*, the ruling
classes of the earlier novels were abdicating their authority
to what Riesman calls the conflicting "veto groups." Adam
Patch had been reincarnated as Monroe Stahr. The modern
novelist as painted by Mr. Aldridge became suspicious of any
genteel definitions of what is and is not done, sensing behind
Fitzgerald's gentleman's code "some odious political doctrine
threatening to the constitution of the United States."[18]

In *The Last Tycoon*, Fitzgerald himself succumbed to the
"egalitarian frenzy," preoccupying himself rather unsuccess-

fully with Communist organizers, gangsters, and other unfamiliar representatives of the great unwashed.

Like Fitzgerald's Great Gatsby, Charles Lindbergh was a survivor of the age of inner-direction. Mid-century "popular culture," says David Riesman, "stresses the dangers of aloneness and, by contrast, the virtues of group-mindedness.[19] As the emphasis shifted to teamwork instead of solitary endeavor, it was unlikely that America would worship at the shrine of another Lone Eagle.

Like Lindbergh and Fitzgerald, Barbara Hutton had one foot in the inner-directed age. Her grandfather was one of the most successful exponents of the old individualistic Protestant ethic. David Riesman describes the inner-directed man as follows:

> Perhaps he lavishes money and energy on a house to the point where it comes to resemble a department store . . . Perhaps he gathers the treasures of Europe, including titled sons-in-law. Perhaps he goes in for steam yachts or diamonds or libraries or, united with rich cronies in civic spirit, for theaters, planetariums, and zoos.[20]

Read "Woolworth Building" for "steam yachts," "pipe organs" for "diamonds," "grandsons-in-law" for "sons-in-law," and the passage could be a description of Frank Woolworth. The only difference was that he never lived to see his Mdivani, his Von Cramm and his Haugwitz-Reventlow.

As the Protestant ethic gives way to the social ethic, Barbara Hutton is the girl in the middle. Her yachts, her castles, and her husbands are left over from the bygone era. Her clashes with the revenooers belong to the decade when income leveling and "pump priming" were being tried out as a means of getting people to consume more.

Though Brenda and Cobina came along a scant eight years after Babs, the switch from a production economy to a consumption economy was a *fait accompli*. The Lords of Creation had been dethroned and had become putty in the hands of the "veto groups." When Brenda led off at the Velvet Ball, when

Cobina was nominated as the best-dressed woman in the night clubs, both were playing the game of organized commerce, the jewelry industry, the velvet industry, the lace industry, the trees-for-Fifth-Avenue movement, the National Doughnut Association, and all the other pressure groups that camouflaged their aims beneath a façade of sweet charity. The courier between was the "publicity gal." It is significant that to a press agent, publicizing a member of the sacrosanct "Four Hundred" is now referred to as "handling flesh."

The bobbing curls of little Shirley Temple are symbols of a consumption economy—for a vast amount of purchasing power is concentrated in the hands of America's little folk. A child who pulled down a salary of $75,000 a year would have been unthinkable in the "tradition-directed" society of the Inca Indian or in the early days of the industrial revolution. David Riesman discusses a peculiarly American phenomenon—"the child consumer trainee"—who manipulates his elders and is in turn manipulated by them. Any parent who has dragged a "child consumer trainee" through a supermarket is appalled by the ingenuity with which the ad men deflect the trainee's tiny footsteps from the straight and narrow path to the checkout counter. Adults who have never bought anything from an advertisement in their lives before they became parents know how true it is that "a little child shall lead them." "You can turn off the commercial, but you can't turn off your child," runs the deadly reasoning of the Madison Avenue manipulators. Little Shirley, with her dimples and her merchandise tie-ins, stood as a monument to the death of inner-direction. For "spare the rod and spoil the child" gave way once and for all in the thirties to the newer, unspoken motto, "woo the consumer of Wheaties."

Scott, Charles Augustus, Babs, Brenda, Cobina, and Shirley were all caught in the social revolution whose end products were the Raths, protagonists of *The Man in the Gray Flannel Suit*—and literary characters for whom John Aldridge has very little time. The Raths are plodding suburbanites. Tom Rath, the hero, is emotionally torn because his highly paying job leaves him no time for the front lawn, the wife and kiddies, and the local P.T.A. In the end he takes a less taxing job and sacrifices the paycheck for the home.

The vast reading public were apparently wrestling with some similar domestic dilemma. Judging by the book's sales, mid-century man found in Tom Rath a mirror of his innermost struggles. *The Man in the Gray Flannel Suit* is a monument over the grave of inner-direction. The emasculation of the tycoon which began with Monroe Stahr is completed in the person of Tom Rath's boss, a monster named Hopkins. He is given to bits of social philosophizing which would do credit to Fitzgerald's old Adam Patch. "You killed seventeen men in the war," he says to Tom, "but in the world of big business you're not tough enough." In the age of "other-direction" this philosophy no longer brings him solace. His loved ones detest him. The all-important meaning of life has eluded him. He has committed the cardinal sin against the new normality. He has flunked his course in life adjustment.

If the inner-directed man has gone the way of the dinosaur and the great auk, so too have the old-style political "indignants." "Our democracy in its current form gives them neither a dogma which might provide a basis for heretical action nor an opportunity to discover and choose a politics or faith or way of life which would represent a heresy of democracy," laments Mr. Aldridge.[21]

The careers of Whittaker Chambers and Haywood Patterson have shown why Americans have become disenchanted with the great political heresy of the thirties. The shattered remnants of the Left have joined Harold Russell in rallying about the figure of the American Negro. But the revolutionary fervor is gone. The militant Marxist, the suffragette who set mailboxes on fire have been replaced by the genial cynic, the influence peddler and the five-percenter.

The same fate has overtaken the moral indignant or Bohemian. Edna St. Vincent Millay has become the godmother of the lost sex. Her descendants are the ghouls that dance on the grave of Jimmy Dean. The Brandos and the Deans may inspire admiration, but nobody seems to care much about joining them in whipping the tired horse of nihilism. For, like the buildings in Kansas City, the moral revolution has gone about as far as it can go.

There is little in the way of "outhouse realism" that the mid-century writer cannot put between the covers of a book. Little girls in celluloid cuffs hardly bat an eye at the amours of the most esoteric literary bedfellows; brothers and sisters whose relationship reaches a hasty and clandestine fulfillment in an upstairs closet between courses at a Thanksgiving dinner; father and daughter who consummate same in an outhouse; masseur and client whose sado-masochistic flirtation runs its Krafft-Ebing course with a promise of a grand finale of cannibalism.

An occasional publisher would say that there was a point beyond which no fine old house could be pushed; but on the whole, the literary protest against bourgeois morality had ended up under the counter.

Mr. Aldridge is fond of telling a story about a girl who was cautioned by a friend that it might be wise to take it easy in her erotic ventures with her boy friend. "Oh, *that!*" said the girl offhandedly. "We decided we ought to try it, but it wasn't much fun, so we never did it again." Her sisters may well be responsible for the success of Marjorie Morningstar. The revolutionary of 1950 was the literary heroine who *didn't* lose her virginity. Marjorie's endless pages of hemming and hawing before she submitted to her lover reflected the doubts of a generation which had tried it and found that it wasn't much fun. The reticences of Fitzgerald's "speeds" concealed an excitement all but forgotten by young ladies earnestly debating the future of their hymens, with all the clichés of modern psychiatry. Mother's furtive kisses might well inspire them with the nostalgia of an old Bolshevik for his days on the barricades.

The moral revolution had led from the ambulances of Hemingway and Dos Passos to James Dean's Porsche. The social revolution had taken the upper classes out of Barbara Hutton's palazzo and set them down with their market baskets in front of the frozen-food counter at the A&P. The revolution of the twentieth century had ruthlessly eliminated the two classes of society that ever got any fun out of life. The aristocrat, imbued with Grotonian prejudices, was now forced to maintain these prejudices on a C.P.A.'s salary. The one-time slum dweller had to eschew the Saturday night drunk for fear of reprisals from his Republican peer group in some development called Sagamore Hill or Whispering Woods. The Bohemian had produced a society almost without tabu. The social reformer had produced a society almost without class.

The result satisfied practically no one. The bright young New Dealers would have been appalled to see that the "Russia with money" which the Roosevelt tax policies brought into existence voted Republican and was dedicated to the small safe goals of the despised bourgeoisie. The Bohemian who had worked for a world where anything goes had, like Mr. Aldridge, ended by losing the "stimulus of heresy." The marijuana party, the free-love colony, the Dadaist convention, and the candlelight reading of Joyce are exciting when the cops may come bursting in at any moment. They lose their spice when one's respectable neighbors merely ask politely that you turn down the volume.

For if the "indignant" has disappeared from the forum, he has disappeared also from the garret. The position of the Bohemian in America was reflected in the works of Herman Wouk—another of Aldridge's *bêtes noires*.

Bohemians in the Woukian cosmos are generally unsympathetic figures. Tom Keefer in Wouk's *The Caine Mutiny,* Noel Airman in *Marjorie Morningstar,* appear like vices in a medieval morality play to obstruct the virtuous characters in their Pilgrim's Progress to Suburbia. The struggles which stir the sympathies in Riesman's Gray New World are the perils of Babbitt rather than the amours of Lady Brett. The religion of art which prevailed in the twenties has been scaled to the vision of Marjorie Morningstar, whose responses to the esthetic are roughly what one might encounter in a change-of-life painting class.

The Gray New World was a product of the revolutions of the twenties and thirties. Morally it is a world which has kicked over the traces and has lost its faith in scientific skepticism. Socially it is a world where everybody struggles to look like everybody else, where the nightmare of the young is the fear of being called a "square." Scientifically it is a world where man for the first time has the power to end his stay on earth. Politically it is a world where the "autonomous man" has his back to the wall, and where the Soviet satellite serves notice that the war against him may be going into a critical phase.

Betsy Rath of *The Man in the Gray Flannel Suit* speaks of the world beyond her native Greentree Avenue when she says:

> If this were just a dull place, I wouldn't mind it
> so much. . . . The trouble is, it's not dull enough—
> it's tense and it's frantic. Or, to be honest, Tom and
> I are tense and frantic, and I wish to heaven I knew
> why.[22]

Mr. Aldridge's irritation at the petty struggles of the Raths should not blind us to the fact that their tense and frantic world has one or two advantages. The social revolution has brought about an economic system which should, theoretically at least, be less susceptible than the old laissez-faire capitalism to the vagaries of the business cycle. The Bohemian's revolt against Mrs. Grundy has had a few happy results as well.

The revolution of the twenties did away with Victorian hypocrisy about sex. It made possible a greater camaraderie between boys and girls than has existed at any time in history. It gave women a chance to know something of life besides *Kirche, Küche,* and *Kinder.* It ushered in a pleasant, easygoing social order, built on the realization that a lot of buttons do not automatically make a girl good.

The upheavals of the twentieth century, however, did one unfortunate thing. They did away with what Mr. Aldridge speaks of as "values." Or, as he says in *In Search of Heresy,* the kind of over-all philosophy "which, because it is backed by morals, religious principles and social codes of manners, helps to make possible the delineation of scene and character in fiction."[23]

The search for such values is reflected in the last three biographies of the uneasy denizens of the postwar world. It is behind Claude Batchelor's *mea culpas* to the brainwashers, behind William Buckley's attempts to truncheon his professors into the worship of an ancient God. It is behind Mr. Aldridge's own nostalgia for the long-lost "stimulus of heresy."

Protest becomes outmoded when it has accomplished its purpose. Society now is in the position of an eighteen-year-old on his own for the first time. The big family scene is over. Father has pulled out all the stops. He has been over his early struggles and the better life he wanted for his children. Mother has staged her heart palpitations to no avail. Baby has moved away from home.

Now he sees his parents for the first time in a new perspective. With the Victorians he has been through the childish phase of believing that Mother knows everything. In the twenties and thirties he went through the adolescent phase of believing that Mother knows nothing. He has been through the reflex action of contradicting Mother on every subject. He has the suspicion of one on the brink of maturity that there may have been a few subjects on which Mother was right.

Mr. Aldridge's perceptive notes point to mid-century man's most crying need—values to replace the tyranny of the "peer group" and the driving faith of unbelief. Neither the "chickie run" nor the Dale Carnegie handshake really constitutes a philosophy of life when one has not only one's own latchkey but one's own apartment.

"I can show my shoulders
I can show my knees
I'm a free born American
And can show what I please."

Rhymed ultimatum of a group of flappers who broke
up a PTA meeting in Somerset, Pa., quoted in the *New
York Times,* August 25, 1923

"I reject the idea of the perfectibility of man"—Statement of a campus orator at the University of Wisconsin,
quoted in *The New York Times,* May 17, 1962, p. 34

15
Go Forth to What?

"Dear Class of 1963: "I am here today to bid you farewell
as you leave these ivied halls forever. More years ago than I
care to remember (heh, heh), I sat as you are sitting, listening
to some old windbag dispatch me on life's great adventure.
He said many of the same things I am going to say to you.
The world is your oyster. Here it is on a silver platter. Do
better with it than we did.

"In wishing you bon voyage I shall try to be brief. Miss
Smallsbach has urged me to keep my envoy down to half an
hour. But first a word about why we call this solemn occasion
commencement. It is known as commencement because it is,
in a sense, a beginning. And that reminds me of a story. . . ."

In tens of thousands of assembly halls, these words will
shortly be intoned, as chairs scrape, as the clock ticks on from
weary hour to weary hour, Miss Smallsbach notwithstanding.
And the child of the mid-century who preserves even a

semblance of respectful attention will find little to help him in the commencement orator's formidable arsenal of platitudes.

What has the class of '10, '20, '30, or '40 to say to the hard-eyed realists of '63? In the first half of the century every child was a hopeful spectator at a Futurama which promised as its happy ending a World Safe for Democracy, a Century of Progress, a Century of the Common Stock or the Common Man. The class of '63 has wisely abandoned the belief that youth has only to grab the football of progress and run with it.

The life plans of the fourteen young people in this book run the gamut from the sublime to the ridiculous: to see the Flatiron Building or the Eiffel Tower, to be a bigwig in the People's Republic, to discover the secret of eternal youth, to popularize the Camay complexion, to get a seven-year contract or a bid to Ivy, to find a tenant for a dream castle, or simply to get out of the clink. One of youth's favorite fantasies recurs in various settings, as Edna Millay, Scott Fitzgerald, James Dean, and William Buckley, Jr., plot in their various ways to preside over the Massacre of the Elders.

On the Princeton campus and the air circus, on Sunset Strip and the Ritz ballroom, these fourteen dreamed the dreams for all of us. They saw the hopeful vision fade at Le Bourget airport, on the floor of the Stock Exchange, at Winfield House, and at Panmunjom.

As each successive rainbow disappeared, the rest of us went on as if nothing had happened. The older generation vowed solemnly that the young would never be used as cannon fodder. A few years later, they turned around and handed out guns. Those who had been inspired by Adam Smith and Karl Marx settled at last for Eisenhower's undisturbing People's Capitalism. One year the old bombarded the young with loyalty oaths—the next year with "crash programs" for catching up with Russia. We bemoaned the veterans' distaste for revolution. We sent an SOS to the sociology department when their younger brothers obliged us with a ducktail haircut, a bent spoon, and a switchblade knife. In self-defense we can only say this: from the millpond to Miltown it's been quite a trip.

Who can blame the class of '63 if they take everything they are told with a grain of salt?

Some years ago, eleven anonymous Princeton seniors published, in a book called *The Unsilent Generation,* their provocative views on life and love. The book caused outraged cries of "O tempora, O mores," in many quarters. (There is always a segment of the public that is stunned by the news that thoughtful college boys are occasionally assailed by religious doubts, and that sex is a popular preoccupation among healthy twenty-two-year-old males.)

What *was* outstanding about the eleven was their extraordinary flat-footedness and the extent to which they were the products of history. Of every big solution that their parents had pinned their hopes on, the eleven said wearily "Oh, we've *had* that bit."

They rejected both cynical conformism and self-conscious Bohemianism—the gray flannel suit and the Dharma bum's goatee. While moral relativism and pragmatism had been as much a part of the intellectual climate as the air they breathed, there were signs that they were turning on John Dewey and Oliver Wendell Holmes.

One expressed reservations about the Holmesian belief that to doubt one's first principles was the be-all and end-all of civilized man. A self-styled "liberal" described his impatience with the "flaccid permissiveness" of modern education and the caseworker's approach to larceny and rape. "We are often so busy understanding why a crime has been committed that we forget that an evil attack has been made upon civilized society, an attack that should be severely punished."[1]

When the first Greenwich Villageites began "spading about" in each other's unconsciouses, it would have been unheard-of for a liberal to revert to the idiom of the avenging Jehovah.

To the non-silent ones the once-controversial F.D.R. had achieved the mellow status of an elder statesman. To the mid-century bull session he was the unsung Messiah of free enterprise. With the bourgeois leanings of That Man exposed to all, "the fervor of social responsibility of the Thirties dies a quiet death on today's college campus."[2] Long forgotten were those famous Roosevelt breakfasts of capitalist on toast.

The eleven regarded the older generation with the amused tolerance that one might extend to a benign and slightly senescent Mr. Chips.

One boy pointed to the wars, depressions, technological innovations, shifts in public opinion that have made understanding between young and old all but impossible. Another spoke with nostalgia of the freedom of the twenties and thirties to give all for a glorious flop. "A Federal Reserve System of the Imagination," he ruefully remarked, prevented him from attending cell meetings or Dada conventions in public toilets.

This same thoughtful senior claimed to have no desire for rebellion because his elders had done the rebelling for him. "Their present point of view, created in their own old age, coincides so nicely with *our* present point of view, created in our youth, that the myth of the son's rebellion against the father seems to have exhausted itself."[3]

Now, a few years after the *Unsilent Generation*, the pendulum has taken another swing. The political extremist has once again come into his own. After the semislumber of the Eisenhower era, the campus has become politically aware. Multilettered organizations have suddenly burgeoned: SPAD—Students for Peace and Disarmament; SNCC ("Snick") Student Nonviolent Coordinating Committee of southern integration groups; SAAT—Students Associated Against Totalitarianism; SCANR—Students Committed to Accurate National Representation; SCCP ("Skip") Southern Camp Construction Projects; BASCA HUAC—Bay Area Student Committee to Abolish the House Unamerican Activities Committee; around Berkeley, California ACTAKFF—American Committee to Aid Katanga Freedom Fighters; and the Intercollegiate Society of Individualists.

Youthful liberals have become inflamed by A-tests and Jim Crow. In the 1930's college students renounced lunch to aid the Spanish Loyalists. Today there have been peace fasts, marches on Washington and three-day water-only diets. There is always someone around with a sense of humor. In the thirties the Veterans of Future Wars dedicated themselves to collecting a soldier's bonus for a conflict that had not yet taken place. In the Sixties there is SOAN—The Scrutinizers of Over-bearing and Antiquated Necessities.[4]

The placard bearers of the sixties, unlike those of the thirties, number members of the far right in their ranks. At Wisconsin, Young Socialists throw eggs at Young Conservatives and vice versa. The Young Republican Club has drifted way to the right of Richard Nixon; and the road to political suicide is open to all who call themselves moderates.[5]

In the chorus of dissent against nuclear testing, Young Americans for Freedom ominously rattle their rockets: "I like Nike"; "Test, *Sí*—Disarm, No."[6]

The dialogue between youth and age has been recast in a different form. The old protest seems outmoded, because it has accomplished its purpose. To those of us who grew up in dun-colored rooms still cluttered with Victoriana, rebellion seemed a natural thing. Within our lifetime *An American Tragedy* was considered a dirty book. We couldn't date on a school night; and furtive little thrills ran up our spines when someone was described as a "first-night necker."

In our lifetime a British prime minister assured us that nobody need lose any sleep over a faraway country like Czechoslovakia. What nuggets of wisdom can we pass on to sophisticates from the age of interplanetary law? What can we offer to replace the fun of rebellion, now that Edna and Scott belong to the ages?

The young today, like young people throughout history, refuse to play the game on our terms. When the G.I.'s returned to their campus "Vetsvilles," their docility seemed to us alarming. Having spent our youth chasing rainbows, we were equally appalled a few years later. For the hard-eyed men of the *Unsilent Generation,* the rainbow had obviously never existed. We were amazed that a college senior could write: "If I have to die in a war, it will probably be the war which marks the end of our way of life."[7]

To today's young Conservatives we want to cry: "Mother may have been right about a lot of things, but for God's sake, she wasn't right about *everything!*" We're amazed to read editorials by people under thirty *in favor of* the Regents' Prayer, Fraternity rush week, and right-to-work laws; *against* federal subsidies to baby sitters and expatriate Americans in Mexico. If this is the way you talk now, we think, we'd hate to meet you at fifty. Next you'll be trying to revive the chastity belt!

The search for values led Claude Batchelor into writing tirades against bacteriological warfare. It led James Dean down the Dead End Street of Protest. William Buckley, Jr. has charged off in the opposite direction on the Inquisitor's High Road to Paradise. We can only ask you, aren't there any other alternatives?

Most of the young people in this book were raised on illusions. They may never have caught up with the rainbow, but in the chase they displayed an enviable gusto. With many of their illusions went a vitality which we seem to have lost.

The vignettes that their names conjure up are varied: Edna Millay's peaceful Maine village, the type-crowded pages of *St. Nicholas;* ads of children in Buster Brown bobs; the *Goblin Market;* the white frame houses of Whittaker Chambers' boyhood; young Lindbergh dropping Roman candles from a plane with a dragon on the fuselage, owned by the Mil-Hi Airways and Flying Circus; Haywood Patterson making hops between hobo jungles, getting his first exciting glimpses of a world beyond Opelika and Paint Rock.

We were not around when Staten Island was desolate enough for Edna and her cronies to frolic in the buff. But we can remember when the rivalries of armies and the intrigues of the conference table were blotted out for a golden moment by Lindbergh's charming smile.

We have met reformed revolutionaries at cocktail parties who free-lanced for the *New Masses,* experimented with recipes attributed to Mother Bloor, and carried banners in the May Day parade, proclaiming that "the Scottsboro boys shall go free."

We remember going *out* to see Shirley Temple as a bobby soxer, Claudette Colbert as the noble wartime mother, or Joseph Cotten with battle fatigue. Many of our contemporaries have shown Harold Russell's magnificent fortitude when betrayed by the fiction of a war to end war.

Shirley's infancy may have seemed a trifle prolonged to us

but we have nothing but admiration for her disciples in khaki. She was a symbol of something to those G.I.'s who crowded around the entrance of her hotel; to those reverent fans who named an army transport after her; who removed her photograph from the Jap sniper's body and shielded it from the unsavory company of Der Führer. A praiseworthy brotherhood was sustained on lonely atolls by the memory of her bobbing curls.

Mid-century youth may have learned the facts of life at too high a price. The *joie de vivre* has gone. Fitzgerald and Millay came to loathe New York, but we can envy them their first rapture at the sight of the skyline. The class of '63 has seen the pigeon droppings, smelled the subways, and lived through too many February cold snaps.

It is more typically American to be against something than for something. Now that Dada, the flying machine, and the *Daily Worker* have failed, are we doomed too?

The hour is very late, but we still dare to ask, "Does it have to be a lost paradise?" From the rainbow chasers' ironic inheritance we remember too much that is worth saving.

To the class of 1963 let us wish a revival of the excitement generated by yesterday's fiascoes. Let them feel the fervor they might once have put into hating us. Let the class of '63 recapture the verve of a simpler age when tomorrow was shining with promise and the voice of youth was clear. "Kick off your stays! Down with Mrs. Grundy! Long live free thought! Get rid of the old fogies, kids, and we have it made!" Somewhere out of the richness of the American past, there must still be some ideological Geritol to serve as an antidote for our tired blood.

"And now Miss Smallsbach, on with the show. 'Pomp and Circumstance,' please."

NOTES

CHAPTER TWO

1 *The Far Side of Paradise,* by Arthur Mizener, Houghton Mifflin Company, Boston, 1951, p. 121.
2 *Ibid.,* p. 117.
3 *Ibid.,* pp. 152–153.
4 *F. Scott Fitzgerald: The Man and His Work,* edited by Alfred Kazin, World Publishing Company, 1951, p. 16.
5 *Ibid.,* p. 125.
6 *Time,* January 29, 1951.
7 *F. Scott Fitzgerald,* by Kazin, p. 44.
8 *This Side of Paradise,* by F. Scott Fitzgerald, Charles Scribner's Sons, New York, 1920, p. 8.
9 *Ibid.,* p. 86
10 *The Far Side of Paradise,* p. 67.
11 *The Beautiful and Damned,* by F. Scott Fitzgerald, Charles Scribner's Sons, New York, 1921, p. 232.
12 *The Crackup,* by F. Scott Fitzgerald, edited by Edmund Wilson, New Directions, 1945, p. 20.
13 *Ibid.,* pp. 43–49.
14 *Ibid.,* pp. 32–33.
15 *The Last Tycoon,* by F. Scott Fitzgerald, Modern Standard Authors Edition, Charles Scribner's Sons, New York, 1953, p. 5.
16 *The Beautiful and Damned,* pp. 14–15.
17 Quoted in *F. Scott Fitzgerald,* by Kazin, p. 107.
18 *Taps at Reveille,* by F. Scott Fitzgerald, Charles Scribner's Sons, New York, 1935, p. 406.
19 *The Crackup,* p. 22.
20 *This Side of Paradise,* pp. 160–161.
21 *Tender Is the Night,* by F. Scott Fitzgerald, Modern Standard Authors Edition, Charles Scribner's Sons, New York, 1953, pp. 117–118.
22 *The Beautiful and Damned,* pp. 23–24.
23 *This Side of Paradise,* p. 245.
24 *Ibid.,* p. 255.
25 *The Beautiful and Damned,* pp. 254–255.
26 *The Crackup,* pp. 16–17.
27 *This Side of Paradise,* p. 65.
28 *Ibid.,* p. 198.
29 *Ibid.,* p. 68.
30 *The Beautiful and Damned,* p. 235.
31 "Scott Fitzgerald at La Paix," by Andrew Turnbull, *The New Yorker,* April 7, 1956, pp. 98–110.
32 "Further Notes on Fitzgerald at La Paix," by Andrew Turnbull, *The New Yorker,* November 17, 1956, p. 162.
33 *The Great Gatsby,* by F. Scott Fitzgerald, Modern Standard Authors Edition, Charles Scribner's Sons, 1953, p. 137.

CHAPTER THREE

1 *The Spirit of St. Louis,* by Charles A. Lindbergh, Charles Scribner's Sons, 1953, pp. 391–392.
2 *Ibid.,* p. 482.
3 *Literary Digest,* June 25, 1927, p. 52.
4 *Ibid.,* October 1, 1927, pp. 26 and 41.
5 *Ibid.,* June 11, 1927, p. 35.

6   *Ibid.*, June 18, 1927, p. 29.
7   *Ibid.*, June 25, 1927, p. 5.
8   *Ibid.*, May 18, 1929, pp. 56–58.
9   *Ibid.*, May 9, 1931, p. 19.
10 *Ibid.*, February 16, 1929, p. 25.
11 *Ibid.*, January 28, 1928, p. 18.
12 *Ibid.*, June 25, 1927, p. 6.
13 *Ibid.*, June 4, 1927, p. 8.
14 *Ibid.*, pp. 5–6.
15 *Arrow in the Blue*, by Arthur Koestler, The Macmillan Company, 1950.
16 *Literary Digest*, January 19, 1935, p. 11.
17 *Newsweek*, February 23, 1935, p. 18.
18 *Life*, August 11, 1941, p. 65.
19 "Aviation, Geography and Race," by Col. Charles Lindbergh, *Reader's Digest*, May 1940, p. 44.
20 *Ibid.*, p. 64.
21 "What Substitute for War?" by Col. Charles A. Lindbergh, *Reader's Digest*, May 1940, p. 19.
22 *Time*, September 22, 1941, p. 19.
23 "Why Lindbergh Is Wrong," by Major Alexander de Seversky, *American Mercury*, May 1941, p. 521.
24 *Of Flight and Life*, by Col. Charles Lindbergh, Charles Scribner's Sons, 1948, p. 28.
25 *Ibid.*, p. 29.
26 *Ibid.*, p. 28.
27 *Newsweek*, December 26, 1949, p. 2.
28 *New York Times*, June 13, 1962, p. 39:2.
29 *New York Times*, June 28, 1961, p. 32:5.
30 *New York Times*, December 11, 1961, p. 37:2.
31 *The Spirit of St. Louis*, p. 469.
32 *Of Flight and Life*, p. 50.

CHAPTER FOUR

1   *Distressing Dialogues*, by Nancy Boyd (pseud. for Edna St. Vincent Millay), Harper & Brothers, 1924, p. 263.
2   *Letters of Edna St. Vincent Millay*, edited by Allan Ross Macdougall, Harper & Brothers, 1952, pp. 118–119.
3   *Ibid.*, p. 18.
4   *Ibid.*, p. 20.
5   *Edna St. Vincent Millay and Her Times*, by Elizabeth Atkins, University of Chicago Press, 1936, p. 31.
6   *Collected Poems*, by Edna St. Vincent Millay, Harper & Brothers, 1956, p. 127.
7   *Ibid.*, p. 128.
8   *Edna St. Vincent Millay and Her Times*, pp. 65–68.
9   *Distressing Dialogues*, pp. 273–274.
10 *Collected Poems*, p. 160.
11 *Ibid.*, p. 625.
12 *Ibid.*, p. 235.
13 *Edna St. Vincent Millay and Her Times*, pp. 81–89.
14 *The King's Henchman*, by Edna St. Vincent Millay, Harper & Brothers, 1927, p. 123.
15 *Collected Poems*, p. 130.
16 *Letters*, pp. 99–100.
17 *Homecoming*, by Floyd Dell, Farrar and Rinehart, 1933, pp. 246–251.
18 *Distressing Dialogues*, pp. 97–108.
19 "Edna St. Vincent Millay, A Memoir," by Edmund Wilson, *The Nation*, April 19, 1952, p. 376.
20 *Letters*, p. 135.
21 *Ibid.*, p. 142.
22 *Ibid.*, p. 144.

23 *Edna St. Vincent Millay and Her Times*, p. 200.
24 *Collected Poems*, p. 715.
25 *Conversation at Midnight*, by Edna St. Vincent Millay, Harper & Brothers, 1937, p. 95.
26 *Ibid.*, p. 37.
27 *Ibid.*, p. 71.
28 *Ibid.*, p. 60.
29 *Ibid.*, p. 61.
30 *Ibid.*, p. 69.
31 *Ibid.*, p. 76.
32 *Ibid.*, p. 59.
33 *Make Bright the Arrows*, by Edna St. Vincent Millay, Harper & Brothers, 1940, p. 3.
34 *Ibid.*, p. 21.
35 *The Indigo Bunting*, by Vincent Sheean, Harper & Brothers, 1951, p. 37.

36 *Ibid.*, p. 51.
37 *Ibid.*, p. 35.
38 *Homecoming*, p. 303.
39 *Letters*, p. 292.
40 *Ibid.*, p. 323.
41 *Collected Poems*, p. 586.
42 *Edna St. Vincent Millay, America's Best Loved Poet*, by Toby Shafter, Julian Messner, Inc., 1957, p. 184.
43 *Letters*, p. 348.
44 *Ibid.*, p. 94.
45 *Ibid.*, p. 120.
46 *Ibid.*, p. 94.
47 *Ibid.*, p. 217.
48 *Distressing Dialogues*, p. 289.
49 *Letters*, p. 376.
50 *Women as World Builders*, by Floyd Dell, Forbes & Co., 1913, p. 104.

CHAPTER FIVE

1 "The College of the Few," by Mark Van Doren, *New Republic*, April 16, 1924.
2 "The Damn Fool," by John Kelly (pseud. for Whittaker Chambers), *Columbia Morningside*, March 1922.
3 *Witness*, by Whittaker Chambers, Random House, 1952, pp. 91–193.
4 *Ibid.*, p. 406.
5 *Ibid.*, p. 466.
6 *Ibid.*, p. 470.
7 *Current Biography*, 1947.
8 *Witness*, p. 674.
9 *Ibid.*, p. 373.
10 *In the Court of Public Opinion*, by Alger Hiss, Alfred A. Knopf, Inc., 1957, p. 42.
11 *Witness*, p. 380.
12 *In the Court of Public Opinion*, p. 217.
13 *Witness*, p. 431.
14 *Ibid.*, pp. 307–308.
15 *Ibid.*, p. 346.
16 *In the Court of Public Opinion*, pp. 75–76.

17 *The Unfinished Story of Alger Hiss*, by Fred J. Cook, William Morrow & Company, 1958, p. 29.
18 *In the Court of Public Opinion*, p. 121.
19 *Ibid.*, p. 122.
20 *Ibid.*, p. 125.
21 *The Unfinished Story of Alger Hiss*, p. 49.
22 *In the Court of Public Opinion*, p. 227.
23 *Witness*, p. 508.
24 *Ibid.*, p. 546.
25 *The Unfinished Story of Alger Hiss*, p. 155.
26 *Witness*, p. 695.
27 *The Autobiography of Mark Van Doren*, by Mark Van Doren, Harcourt, Brace & Company, 1958, p. 307.
28 *Witness*, p. 473.
29 *New York Times*, July 12, 1961, p. 1.
30 *New York Times*, July 12, 1961, p. 32.
31 *Witness*, p. 123.

CHAPTER SIX

1 *Scottsboro Boy*, by Haywood Patterson and Earl Conrad, Doubleday & Company, Inc., 1950, p. 6.
2 *The American Earthquake*, by Edmund Wilson, Doubleday Anchor Books, 1958, p. 334.
3 *The American Earthquake*, p. 337.
4 *Ibid.*, pp. 343–344.
5 *Ibid.*, p. 345.
6 "The Negro and the Communists," by Walter White, *Har-per's Magazine*, December 1931, p. 68.
7 *Scottsboro Boy*, p. 258–259.
8 *Trial by Prejudice*, p. 114.
9 *Ibid.*, p. 114.
10 *Scottsboro Boy*, p. 49.
11 *Ibid.*, p. 111.
12 *Ibid.*, p. 156.
13 *Ibid.*, p. 246.
14 *Ibid.*, p. 245.
15 Quoted in "Cause Célèbre and Cause C.P." by Hodding Carter, *Saturday Review*, June 10, 1950, p. 12.

CHAPTER SEVEN

1 *Time*, July 4, 1938, p. 27.
2 *Fortune*, November 1936, p. 202.
3 *Time*, January 11, 1954, p. 17.
4 "Dime Store," by John Winkler and Boyden Sparkes, *Saturday Evening Post*, March 9, 1940, p. 80.
5 *Ibid.*, p. 78.
6 *Ibid.*, February 24, 1940, p. 82.
7 *Ibid.*, p. 82.
8 "The Sad Story of Barbara Hutton," by Eleanor Harris, *Look*, July 27, 1954, p. 86.
9 "Dime Store," March 16, 1940, p. 55.
10 *New York Daily News*, December 23, 1930, p. 12.
11 *Time*, July 4, 1938, p. 27.
12 *Ibid.*, p. 27.
13 *New York Times*, June 6, 1935, p. 23:2.
14 *Ibid.*, March 17, 1936, p. 23:6.
15 *Ibid.*, June 25, 1938, p. 17:2.
16 *Ibid.*, July 6, 1938, p. 2:3.
17 *Christian Century*, July 20, 1938, p. 888.
18 *Time*, July 4, 1938, p. 27.
19 Quoted in *Literary Digest*, January 1, 1938, p. 8.
20 *New York Times*, March 15, 1937, p. 1:7.
21 *Ibid.*, October 22, 1939, p. 37:4.
22 *Look*, July 27, 1954, p. 89.
23 *New York Times*, October 22, 1939, p. 37:4.
24 "Dime Store," February 24, 1940, p. 82.
25 *Look*, July 27, 1954, p. 88.
26 "Dime Store," March 9, 1940, p. 77.
27 *Time*, July 4, 1938, p. 27.
28 "Dime Store," March 16, 1940, p. 50.
29 *New York Times*, August 31, 1945, p. 19:5.
30 *Time*, October 16, 1950, p. 42.
31 *New York Times*, September 13, 1949, p. 31:7.
32 *Time*, January 11, 1954, p. 16.
33 "Rubi's Back and Zsa Zsa's Got Him," by Irene Corbally Kuhn, *American Mercury*, August 1954, p. 8.
34 *Life*, January 11, 1954, p. 25.
35 *Newsweek*, January 11, 1954, p. 28.

36 *Life,* January 11, 1954, p. 25.

37 *Time,* January 11, 1954, p. 17.

38 "Rubi's Back and Zsa Zsa's Got Him," p. 11.

39 *Time,* June 4, 1956, p. 46.

40 *Look,* July 27, 1954, p. 91.

CHAPTER EIGHT

1 *New York Journal-American,* December 28, 1938, p. 11:2.

2 *Time,* January 9, 1939, p. 18.

3 *I Never Grew Up,* by Cobina Wright, Sr., Prentice-Hall, 1952, p. 103A.

4 *New York Journal-American,* December 27, 1938, p. 8:1.

5 *Ibid.,* December 28, 1938, p. 1:2.

6 "Profile of Brenda Frazier," by E. J. Kahn, Jr., *The New Yorker,* June 10, 1939, p. 26.

7 *Ibid.,* p. 24.

8 *Ibid.,* p. 24.

9 *Scribner's Magazine,* February 1939, p. 63.

10 *The New Yorker,* June 10, 1939, p. 25.

11 *I Never Grew Up,* p. 64.

12 *Ibid.,* p. 152.

13 *Ibid.,* p. 30.

14 *Ibid.,* p. 186.

15 *Ibid.,* p. 172.

16 *Ibid.,* p. 188.

17 *Ibid.,* p. 30.

18 "The Corporal Sees His Duty," by Kyle Crichton, *Collier's,* March 21, 1942, p. 57.

19 *I Never Grew Up,* p. 210.

20 *Ibid.,* p. 211.

21 *Ibid.,* p. 247.

22 *Ibid.,* p. 265.

23 *Ibid.,* p. 32.

24 *New York Journal-American,* October 25, 1938, p. 8:2.

25 *Ibid.,* November 14, 1938, p. 10:1.

26 *Ibid.,* October 19, 1938, p. 18:7.

27 *Ibid.,* October 2, 1938, p. 2.

28 *Ibid.,* p. 3.

29 *The New Yorker,* June 10, 1939, p. 25.

30 *Life,* November 14, 1938.

31 *Ibid.,* p. 28.

32 *New York World-Telegram,* February 3, 1939, p. 17:1.

33 *Ibid.,* February 6, 1939, p. 11:1.

34 *Ibid.,* February 1, 1939, p. 25:4.

35 *Ibid.,* February 6, 1939, p. 11:1.

36 *Ibid.,* February 14, 1939, p. 21:1.

37 *Ibid.,* February 9, 1939, p. 12:6.

38 *New York Journal-American,* November 18, 1938, p. 12:1.

39 *Ibid.,* November 20, 1938, p. 2:4.

40 *New York World-Telegram,* May 9, 1939, p. 13:4.

41 *New York Times,* November 9, 1941, IV, 2:6.

42 "The Corporal Sees His Duty," p. 15.

43 *New York Journal-American,* June 19, 1941, p. 6:4.

44 *I Never Grew Up,* p. 277.

45 "The Corporal Sees His Duty," p. 59.

46 *New York Times,* June 10, 1942, p. 23:6.

47 *Time,* April 14, 1952, p. 40.

48 *I Never Grew Up,* p. 286.

49 *Ibid.,* p. 268.

50 *Ibid.,* p. 118.

51 *Ibid.,* p. 128.

52 *Ibid.,* p. 141.

53 *Ibid.,* p. 128.

54 *New York Journal-American,* November 16, 1938, p. 1:1.

CHAPTER NINE

Most of the material is taken from *Victory in My Hands* (Creative Age Press, 1949) and from a release supplied by Russell's publicity agent. The MacKinley Kantor quote is from *Glory for Me*, by MacKinley Kantor (Coward McCann, 1945), pp. 13–14.

CHAPTER TEN

1 *American Magazine*, February 1935, p. 94.
2 *Photoplay*, November 1934, p. 35.
3 *Motion Picture*, August 1934, p. 30.
4 *Ibid.*, p. 31.
5 *My Young Life*, by Shirley Temple and the editors of *Look*, Garden City Publishing Company, 1945, p. 31.
6 *Pictorial Review*, August 1935, p. 40.
7 *New York Times Magazine*, February 11, 1945, p. 18.
8 *Motion Picture*, August 1934, p. 31.
9 *Modern Screen*, April 1949, p. 96.
10 *Pictorial Review*, August 1935, p. 41.
11 *Ibid.*, September 1935, p. 45.
12 *American Magazine*, February 1935, p. 94.
13 *My Young Life*, p. 231.
14 *Ibid.*, p. 177.
15 *New York Times Magazine*, November 2, 1941, p. 8.
16 *Time*, January 27, 1958, p. 62.
17 *Modern Screen*, April 1949, p. 45.
18 *American Magazine*, February 1935, p. 93.
19 *Pictorial Review*, May 1936, p. 9.
20 *Ibid.*, p. 81.
21 *Ibid.*, September 1935, p. 52.
22 *American Magazine*, February 1935.
23 *Ibid.*, p. 92.
24 *Pictorial Review*, December 1936, p. 25.
25 *New York Times Magazine*, November 2, 1941, pp. 8–9.
26 *Current Biography*, 1945.
27 *Pictorial Review*, September 1935, p. 54.
28 *Photoplay Research Society Pamphlet*, 1922.
29 *Modern Screen*, April 1949, pp. 40–43.
30 *My Young Life*, p. 235.
31 *Modern Screen*, April 1949, pp. 40–43.
32 *Life*, October 4, 1943, p. 40.
33 *New York Times Magazine*, February 11, 1945, p. 18.
34 *American Home*, April 1945, p. 91.
35 *My Young Life*, p. 180.
36 *Good Housekeeping*, November 1957, p. 131.
37 *Modern Screen*, February 1949, pp. 111–112.
38 *Life*, October 1, 1945, p. 45.
39 *Modern Screen*, April 1949, pp. 97–99.
40 *Woman's Home Companion*, February 1948, p. 4.
41 *Modern Screen*, February 1949, p. 11.
42 *Photoplay*, July 1949, p. 64.

43 *Modern Screen*, January 1950.
44 *Photoplay*, February 1950.
45 *Modern Screen*, April 1949, pp. 47–51.

46 *New York Herald Tribune*, April 13, 1958, section 4, p. 3.
47 *New York Times Magazine*, November 2, 1941, pp. 8–9.

CHAPTER ELEVEN

1 *James Dean Album*, Ideal Publishing Co., 1956, p. 7.
2 *James Dean Official Anniversary Book*, Dell Publishing Co., 1956, p. 68.
3 "Delirium Over a Dead Star," by Ezra Goodman, *Life*, September 24, 1956, p. 88.
4 "The Strange James Dean Death Cult," *Coronet*, November 1956, p. 112.
5 "James Dean," by George Scullin, *Look*, October 16, 1956, p. 126.
6 *James Dean* by William Bast, Ballantine Books, 1956, p. 67.
7 *Ibid.*, p. 93.
8 *Ibid.*, p. 101.
9 *Look*, October 16, 1956, p. 128.
10 *Life*, September 24, 1956, p. 76.
11 *James Dean Album*, p. 57.
12 "The Real James Dean Story," by Aljean Meltsir, *Motion Picture Magazine*, September 1956, pp. 25–27.
13 *James Dean Official Anniversary Book*, p. 68.
14 Letter received by Warner Brothers.
15 Letter received by Warner Brothers.
16 Letter received by Warner Brothers.
17 Letter received by Warner Brothers.
18 *Photoplay*, November 1956, p. 112.

19 *James Dean*, by Bast, p. 146.
20 *Photoplay*, November 1956, p. 112.
21 *Jimmy Dean Returns*, Rave Publishing Corp., p. 45.
22 *Life*, September 24, 1956, p. 85.
23 *Whisper Magazine*, February 1956, p. 13.
24 *Ibid.*, pp. 13–16.
25 *Coronet*, November 1956, p. 113.
26 Quoted in *The Real James Dean Story*, p. 55.
27 *James Dean*, by Bast, pp. 110–111.
28 *James Dean Album*, p. 29.
29 *Ibid.*, p. 62.
30 *James Dean*, by Bast, p. 95.
31 *Ibid.*, p. 122.
32 *Ibid.*
33 *Ibid.*, p. 134.
34 *James Dean Official Anniversary Book*, p. 58.
35 *James Dean*, by Bast, p. 143.
36 *Ibid.*, p. 41.
37 *Ibid.*, p. 148.
38 *Look*, October 16, 1956, p. 123.
39 *Hollywood Love and Tragedy*, November 1956, pp. 37–38.
40 *James Dean*, by Bast, p. 42.
41 *Coronet*, November 1956, pp. 113–114.
42 *Look*, October 16, 1956, p. 122.
43 "Why the 'Rebel' Craze Is Here to Stay," *Photoplay*, November 1956, p. 121.

44 *Ibid.*, p. 60.
45 *Ibid.*, pp. 121–122.
46 *James Dean Official Anniversary Book*, p. 6.
47 *Ibid.*

48 *Life*, September 24, 1956, p. 88.
49 *James Dean Official Anniversary Book*, pp. 8–9.
50 *James Dean*, by Bast, p. 13.

CHAPTER TWELVE

1 Quoted in *Saturday Review*, December 15, 1951, p. 45.
2 From an advertisement for *God and Man at Yale*.
3 *Yale Daily News*, May 14, 1949, p. 2.
4 *Hopalong Freud Rides Again*, by Ira Wallach, Henry Schuman, 1952, p. 99.
5 *The Crucial Decade, America, 1945–1955*, by Eric F. Goldman, Alfred A. Knopf, Inc., 1956, p. 274.
6 *Ibid.*, p. 289.
7 "Strong in Their Pride and Free," speech by the Honorable Harry P. Cain, 1955.
8 *McCarthy and His Enemies*, by William F. Buckley, Jr., and L. Brent Bozell, Henry Regnery Company, 1954, pp. 247–250.
9 *Ibid.*, p. 81.
10 *Ibid.*, p. 127.
11 *Ibid.*, p. 350.
12 *Ibid.*, p. 349.
13 *Ibid.*, p. 346.
14 *Ibid.*, introduction.
15 *Ibid.*, p. 277.
16 *Ibid.*, p. 253.
17 *Ibid.*, appendix on Marshall case, p. 390.
18 *Ibid.*, p. 52.
19 *Ibid.*, p. 302.
20 *Ibid.*, p. 60.
21 *Ibid.*, p. 150.
22 *Ibid.*, p. 281.
23 *Ibid.*, p. 340.
24 *Bulletin of the American Civil Liberties Union*, February 1958.

25 *God and Man at Yale*, by William F. Buckley, Jr., Henry Regnery Company, 1951, p. 4.
26 William Buckley on "Night Beat," March 21, 1957.
27 *New York Times*, June 21, 1951, p. 29.
28 *National Review*, October 5, 1957, p. 300.
29 *Time*, July 16, 1956, pp. 62–65.
30 *New York Times*, October 23, 1962, p. 28:4.
31 *New York Times*, March 4, 1961, p. 1:1.
32 *New York Times*, June 29, 1962, p. 1:7.
33 *New York Times*, October 12, 1962, p. 4:5.
34 *New York Times*, December 17, 1961, p. 3:3.
35 *New York Times*, August 23, 1961, p. 30:6.
36 *New York Times*, September 30, 1962, p. 45:6.
37 *New York Times*, October 23, 1962, p. 28.
38 *New York Times*, August 23, 1962, p. 45.
39 *New York Times*, April 7, 1962, p. 12:4.
40 *New York Times*, August 14, 1961, p. 12:5
41 *New York Times*, January 4, 1962, 31:1.
42 *New York Times*, October 15, 1961, p. 52:1.
43 *New York Times*, December 23, 1961, p. 24:8.
44 *New York Times*, November 22, 1961, p. 29:4.

45 *New York Times,* January 4, 1962, p. 31:1.
46 *New York Times,* June 26, 1962, p. 35:8.
47 *New York Times,* December 23, 1961, p. 24:8.
48 *New York Times,* October 26, 1962, p. 28:1.

CHAPTER THIRTEEN

1 Letter from Claude Batchelor to his lawyer, Joel Westbrook.
2 Letter from Claude Batchelor to his mother, read by the defense at his court-martial.
3 *Brainwashing* by Edward Hunter, Farrar, Straus and Cudahy, 1956, p. 217.
4 "A Study of Something New in History," by Eugene Kinkead, *New Yorker,* October 26, 1957.
5 From Claude Batchelor's reminiscences of his stay in Camp #5, p. 5.
6 Letter read at Batchelor's court-martial.
7 P.O.W. Reminiscences, pp. 48–49.
8 *Ibid.,* p. 53.
9 *Ibid.,* pp. 54–55.
10 *Ibid.,* Continuation A4.
11 *New York Times,* September 17, 1954, p. 8:1.
12 P.O.W. Reminiscences, p. 6b.
13 *Ibid,* p. 119.
14 *Ibid.,* p. 115.
15 *Ibid.,* p. 8b.
16 *New York Times,* January 1, 1954, p. 1:1.
17 *Time,* January 11, 1954, p. 11.
18 *New York Times,* September 4, 1954, p. 5:2.
19 *Ibid.,* January 2, 1954, p. 2:2.
20 From the transcript of Batchelor's court-martial.
21 *21 Stayed,* by Virginia Pasley, Farrar, Straus & Cudahy, Inc., 1955, pp. 245–246.
22 P.O.W. Reminiscences, p. 10.
23 *21 Stayed,* p. 21.

CHAPTER FOURTEEN

1 Biographical material supplied by Mr. Aldridge.
2 *After the Lost Generation,* by John W. Aldridge, McGraw-Hill Book Company, Inc., 1951, pp. 243–244.
3 *Book Review Digest,* 1960.
4 *New York Herald Tribune,* November 9, 1957, p. 14:6.
5 *In Search of Heresy,* by John W. Aldridge, McGraw-Hill Book Company, Inc., 1956, p. 113.
6 *The Lonely Crowd,* by David Riesman, Doubleday Anchor Books, 1953, pp. 33–34.
7 *Ibid.,* p. 165.
8 F. Scott Fitzgerald, *The Man and His Work,* edited by Alfred Kazin, World Publishing Company, 1951, p. 115.
9 *In Search of Heresy,* pp. 169–170.
10 *The Lonely Crowd,* p. 288.
11 From *A Farewell to Arms,* by Ernest Hemingway, quoted in *After the Lost Generation,* p. 7.
12 From *Exile's Return,* by Malcolm Cowley, quoted in *After the Lost Generation,* p. 5.
13 *The Lonely Crowd,* p. 116.

14 *Ibid.*, p. 90.
15 *The New Yorker*, April 7, 1956, p. 106.
16 *The Lonely Crowd*, p. 144.
17 *The Great Gatsby*, by F. Scott Fitzgerald, Modern Standard Authors Edition, Charles Scribner's Sons, 1953.

18 *In Search of Heresy*, p. 81.
19 *The Lonely Crowd*, p. 183.
20 *Ibid.*, p. 142.
21 *In Search of Heresy*, p. 4.
22 *The Man in the Gray Flannel Suit*, by Sloan Wilson, Pocket Books, 1956, p. 113.
23 *In Search of Heresy*, p. 7.

CHAPTER FIFTEEN

1 *The Unsilent Generation*, edited by Otto Butz, Rinehart and Company, 1958, p. 170.
2 *Ibid.*, p. 185.
3 *Ibid.*, p. 184.
4 *New York Times*, May 14, 1962, p. 32.

5 *New York Times*, May 17, 1962, p. 34.
6. *New York Times*, May 16, 1962, p. 20.
7 *The Unsilent Generation*, p. 90.